THE EMERGENCE OF THE THEORY OF THE FIRM

From Adam Smith to Alfred Marshall

THE EMERGENCE OF
THE THEORY OF
THE FIRM

From Adam Smith to Alfred Marshall

PHILIP L. WILLIAMS

ST. MARTIN'S PRESS NEW YORK

© Philip L. Williams 1978

Printed in Great Britain
First published in the United States of America in 1979
ISBN 0-312-24387-1

Library of Congress Cataloging in Publication Data

Williams, Philip L   1949–
    The emergence of the theory of the firm.

    Bibliography: p.
    Includes index.
    1. Microeconomics–History.   I.   Title.
HB75.W6   1978   338.5   78–13349
ISBN 0-312-24387-1

Contents

Acknowledgements   vii

1 METHOD AND ORGANISATION   1

2 ADAM SMITH   11
  1. The Motivation of the Firm   12
  2. Costs and Cost Functions   19
  3. Equilibrium and Stability under Competition   24
  4. Monopoly   35

3 J. S. MILL   40
  1. The Motivation of the Firm   41
  2. Costs and Cost Functions   48
  3. Value and Equilibrium   54

4 ALFRED MARSHALL   70
  1. The Influence of Cournot   70
  2. The Motivation of the Firm   76
  3. Costs and Rents   81
  4. Cost Functions and Supply Functions   87
  5. Free Competition   102
  6. Equilibrium and Stability under Competition   108
  7. Monopoly   121
  8. Bilateral Monopoly   130
  9. Duopoly   136

5 MARSHALL AND AFTER   144
  1. The Motivation of the Firm   145
  2. Cost Functions and Supply Functions   151

Contents

3. Competition and the Size of Firms   155

4. Equilibrium and Stability under Monopoly   159

6 SOME REFLECTIONS   166

Endnotes   171

Index   202

Acknowledgements

The present study was originally prepared for submission to the University of London as a PhD thesis. Throughout the period in which it was written, I received assistance from two supervisors both of whom were extraordinarily accessible and helpful. Professor Basil Yamey of the London School of Economics welcomed me to the School and has been my constant adviser, critic and friend. Professor Mark Blaug of The University of London Institute of Education suggested the subject matter of the thesis and then agreed to help with supervision. He has tried desperately to give some shape to my indulgent musings. Later, Professor Terence Hutchison, acting as external examiner, offered many thoughtful suggestions.

While Professor Maureen Brunt and Mr. Courtney Wright of Monash University first stimulated my interest in the theory of the firm, it was not until I attended lectures by Lord Robbins at the LSE that I began to understand how fascinating and valuable pre-Samuelsonian economics can be. The seeds sown at Monash were fed by Lord Robbins. Professors Blaug and Yamey acted as gardeners – sometimes tending and encouraging, sometimes trying to discipline a wild and unruly bush.

While these people deserve my lasting gratitude, my warmest thanks are to my wife, Elizabeth, who has supported me in body and soul these past three happy years.

Philip L. Williams

1 Method and Organisation

This study analyses the way in which the theory of the firm's production and selling decisions emerges from the eighteenth century until the death of Marshall in 1924. By the time of Marshall's death the broad outlines of present debates in the field had been drawn. The penultimate chapter substantiates this proposition and reviews the evidence to determine whether we can distinguish good theory from bad.

This introductory chapter aims to outline the methodological approach which has been adopted in the studies proper. It explains the basis of the value judgments taken; and it gives reasons why alternative methodologies have not been followed. Those readers who are interested in the studies, but less interested in methodological issues, may prefer to begin reading at Chapter 2.

The study focusses on the choices firms make within the enironment of a market system. Adam Smith produced one of the most lucid explanations of how individual decisions mesh together in that pattern of unconscious co-ordination which we call the market system. Operating within that system, firms can be defined as units for the conscious co-ordination of resources.[1] Or, using D. H. Robertson's metaphors, they are ' . . . islands of conscious power in this ocean of unconscious co-operation, like lumps of butter coagulating in a pail of buttermilk.'[2]

The determinants of the decisions of firms constitute the theory of the firm. Such determinants may include the past decisions made by firms, their internal structure, the personalities influencing policy within the firm, the policies of close competitors and the framework of law provided by government.

A study of the historical development of the complete theory of the firm would be redundant. It would be redundant because there already exist standard historical treatments of the firm's decisions in factor markets.[3] So the present study relates only to the literature of those decisions of the firm which relate directly to product markets – the pricing and production decisions.

Because the firm is one of the least aggregated units recognised in economic theory, hypotheses as to firm behaviour are embedded in that

1

economic theory which moves on higher levels of aggregation. Indeed, von Hayek suggests that practitioners of the social sciences reason from their experiences of how individuals operate (methodological individualism). For this reason he characterises the method of the social sciences as compositive (from Menger) or synthetic.[4]

Keynes appears to be one leading economist who eschewed the path of methodological individualism.[5] Although he may have derived his macro-economic propositions from observations of the behaviour of disaggregated units, he did not argue for his propositions from an analysis of disaggregated behaviour. But social science concerns the interactions among the behaviour of individuals. So hidden behind Keynes' functions of consumption and of the demand for money there are propositions as to the behaviour of individuals. The inadequacy of the *General Theory* in synthesising individual behaviour has necessitated much effort in the post-Keynesian period devoted to elaborating the micro-foundations of macro-theory.[6]

Because social science concerns the interactions among the behaviour of individuals, the theory of the firm is (along with consumption theory) one of the basic building blocks of the theory of markets. The primacy of this theory makes it imperative for economists to understand the precise nature of the debates between theoreticians and to try to assess the relative merits of the various hypotheses.

Problem Shifts

Lakatos has pleaded for an 'internal' retelling of the history of science. In arguing for the importance of internal history as compared with external history he argues two propositions. In the first place, he argues that the selection of topics for research is determined primarily by the nature of the research programme (that is, the selection is internally determined). Any research programme will consist of a hard core (propositions which are not tested directly), a protective belt of auxiliary hypotheses (which bear the brunt of testing and are adjusted or replaced so as to defend the hard core), and a positive heuristic. ' . . . the positive heuristic consists of a partially articulated set of suggestions or limits on how to change, develop the "refutable variants" of the research-programme, how to modify, sophisticate, the "refutable" protective belt.'[7]

One issue discussed in this study is the extent to which the history of the theory of the firm is internally directed in this sense: the extent to which the work of J. S. Mill, Senior and Marshall was suggested by the model of Adam Smith, and the extent to which it was directed by factors external to that model.

Chief among the external influences is public concern with the problems of economic policy. This stimulus presents to economists problems which may not be suggested directly by their current research programme.[8] Adam Smith's outrage at government grants of monopoly marked the culmination of a long line of earlier public debate which led to a developing analysis. The re-kindling of this moral fire (particularly in the United States) towards the end of the nineteenth century led to the production of valuable case studies and to the improved analysis of price discrimination and of joint costs.

The study gives some support to von Hayek's generalisation: 'It is probably true that economic analysis has never been the product of detached intellectual curiosity about the *why* of social phenomena, but of an intense urge to reconstruct a world which gives rise to profound dissatisfaction.'[9] Not only does political debate suggest problems for economists to solve, but also political debate imposes on scientists standards of clarity and of truthlikeness. If an economist suggests that political decisions should be based on predictions which turn out to be wrong, the adviser will then be confronted (often in public) with the wrongness of the predictions.[10] An illustration of the salutary effect of political debate can be found in those economists who have undertaken industry studies or given government specific advice on monopoly policy. These have been much less ready to accept the doubtful proposition that the number of firms is the most significant determinant of monopoly power, than have the pure theorists.

Rational reconstruction

In the previous section it was noted that Lakatos argues for the primacy of internally-directed problem selection. The second meaning he gives to his plea for an internal account of history is that the historian should tell the logical development of a story with the benefit of hindsight. Important developments in the story will be those developments which, with hindsight, can be seen to have been good. Developments in the story which were bad, but of contemporary influence, should be treated much more cursorily. Lakatos terms this approach the rational reconstruction of history. He suggests: 'One way to indicate discrepancies between history and its rational reconstruction is to relate the internal history *in the text*, and indicate *in the footnotes* how actual history "misbehaved" in the light of its rational reconstruction.'[11]

Lakatos argues that history '. . . without some theoretical "bias" is impossible.'[12] The present writer accepts this dictum and will proceed to a rational reconstruction. Because this study was undertaken so as to learn about the behaviour of firms, the results of the study will be presented so as to show that which has been learned. The material selected will be that which teaches us something about firms; and the material will be rationally reconstructed in the sense that it will be interpreted in the light of what it can teach us. This positive approach to rational reconstruction may be contrasted with the approach of Cannan and of Stigler, in their books on production and distribution theories mentioned above, who have reconstructed history so as to illustrate the mistakes and the confusions of earlier writings.

This study's approach to the literature is not that of linguistic analysis: it does not pretend to report the 'true' meaning of Adam Smith or Alfred Marshall; that would be both dishonest and unhelpful. The approach will be to see whether we can learn anything from the writings as to regularities in social behaviour.

The methodology of scientific research programmes

To engage in the rational reconstruction of history one requires a clear indication as to what one regards as rational – as to what one regards as good and bad science.

Popper has always argued that the goodness of a conjecture must be assessed by comparison with observations. But he has always been aware that, when confronted by an apparent refutation, a 'conventionalist' can always make his theory fit the facts by changing an hypothesis.[13] Such adjustments (by means of auxiliary hypotheses) may lead to improvements in the theoretical structure – they may bring us closer to the truth; but, they may be a conventionalist ploy to save bad conjectures.

To sort acceptable from unacceptable adjustments Popper proposed the following criterion: 'As regards *auxiliary hypotheses* we propose to lay down the rule that only those are acceptable whose introduction does not diminish the degree of falsifiability or testability of the system in question, but, on the contrary increases it.'[14]

This criterion for the demarcation of auxiliary hypotheses provides Lakatos with an important launching pad for a new set of normative standards. By permitting certain auxiliary hypotheses, Popper has admitted that a 'direct hit' by confronting a conjecture with an observation is very difficult to achieve. If bodies of hypotheses are allowed to adjust in response to anomalies, then we must assess the direction in which the theory is moving.

Lakatos rejects Popper's standards for assessment because, in the first place, Popper's approach does not admit anomalies to be acknowledged temporarily as exceptions to be clarified by later developments in the theory (a process which Lakatos regards as both normal and healthy); and, secondly, Popper's demarcation criterion permits the grafting of a previously unrelated theory on to an existing structure. [15]

Lakatos' first objection is more a matter of the relative eagerness of a researcher to dispose of an anomaly than of a clear criterion of demarcation. However, his second objection is worth further consideration as it reflects many basic disagreements between Lakatos and Popper. Lakatos wants a dynamic appraisal of the *set* of propositions which constitute the research programme.

Let us say that such a series of theories is *theoretically progressive (or 'constitutes a theoretically progressive problemshift')* if each new theory has some excess empirical content over its predecessor, that is, if it predicts some novel, hitherto unexpected fact. Let us say that a theoretically progressive set of theories is also *empirically progressive (or 'constitutes an empirically progressive problemshift')* if some of this excess empirical content is also corroborated, that is, if each new theory leads to the actual discovery of some *new fact*. Finally, let us call a problemshift *progressive* if it is both theoretically and empirically progressive, and *degenerating* if it is not. [16]

These conventions do not allow the 'tacking' of a previously unrelated theory on to an existing structure because, Lakatos claims, for mature science the auxiliary hypotheses are suggested by the positive heuristic of the programme. Auxiliary hypotheses not suggested by the positive heuristic of a genuine research programme should be eliminated. [17]

This requirement as to the admissibility of auxiliary hypotheses would be clear if each research programme would correspond to exactly one set of prescriptions – its positive heuristic; but this is not the case. Lakatos permits the positive heuristic to alter while the research programme is maintained. (An adjustment to the positive heuristic could bring the new auxiliary hypotheses in line with the suggestions of the new positive heuristic.) ' . . . it occasionally happens that when a research programme gets into a degenerating phase, a little revolution or a *creative shift* in its positive heuristic may push it forward again. It is better therefore to separate the 'hard core' from the more flexible metaphysical principles expressing the positive heuristic.'[18]

Lakatos does not seem to realise that by allowing the positive heuristic of a given research programme to alter, his criterion for the elimination of tacking is severely weakened. Given that the positive heuristic may change, then *any* auxiliary hypothesis may be justified, simply by changing the positive heuristic of a programme.[19]

Now, if neither the auxiliary hypotheses nor the positive heuristic is constant for a given research programme, then programmes must be identified by the elements of the hard cores; because if one is to adjudicate between the development of differing programmes over time, it must be between the *constant* elements of the programmes that one judges. But it is impossible to identify the hard core of a programme in any unambiguous way; for the hypotheses which some practitioners regard as being indispensible may be regarded by others as being up for exchange.

It is implicit in the methodology of scientific research programmes (MSRP) that one classifies under a common programme only those practitioners who make identical decisions as to which propositions are included in the hard core (as to which propositions they will not alter). In trying to make such a classification it becomes clear that the set of propositions which constitutes the hard core of any programme may have elements in common with the hard cores of rival programmes. Indeed, it would be surprising if this were not the case.

The intractability of the concept of the hard core becomes apparent if one practitioner is considered to make a decision to discard one programme in favour of a rival, when the difference between the programmes is only one element in the hard core. Would it not, then, be legitimate to say that the practitioner has replaced an element in his/her hard core? If one admits that a practitioner's hard core can change, why not then say that the elements of the hard core are changeable?

This is not merely a matter of selecting the appropriate words. The all-or-nothing language of Lakatos encourages a misleadingly simple classification of theories and a misleadingly simple representation of the choices open to participants in a debate between theories.

The misleading implications of the classification can be seen in the attempts by Latsis to apply the Lakatosian methodology to the theory of the firm.[20] Latsis identifies two rival programmes. The first, which is contrasted with behaviouralism is labelled 'situational determinism'. This, the dominant approach to the explanation of business behaviour, goes back to Adam Smith.

The programme of situational determinism is characterised by the economic unit making decisions which are uniquely determined by the objective of the unit and its external environment. The positive heuristic of the programme prescribes the construction of static, uniquely-determined, models.

The hard core of the neoclassical programme may be put forward in the following four propositions:
(i) Decision-makers have correct knowledge of the relevant features of their economic situation.
(ii) Decision-makers *prefer* the best available alternative given their knowledge of the situation and of the means at their disposal.
(iii) Given (i) and (ii), situations generate their internal 'logic' and decision-makers *act appropriately to the logic of their situation.*
(iv) Economic units and structures display stable, co-ordinated behaviour.[21]

The debate in the 1920s as to the equilibrium output for a firm in a perfectly competitive market serves to illustrate the misleading simplicity of this formulation. The firm under Marshall's free competition is not faced with the uniquely-determined equilibrium characteristic of situational determinism. The size of the firm (as in Adam Smith and, though this is less clear, in J. S. Mill) is not uniquely determined by the model.[22] Clearly, Marshall's theory of the firm does not fit the research programme of situational determinism.

A less clear-cut problem is posed by the classification of Pigou. Until the mid 1920s, Pigou seems to have accepted Marshall's model of free competition in which firm size is not uniquely determined. However, in 1928, Pigou invested his equilibrium firm with a U-shaped, long-run average cost curve. As a result of this move, he could accept that equilibrium for the firm in the long run occurs at that output at which long-run average costs are a minimum.[23]

According to the categories of Latsis, Pigou, by changing the gradient of his firm's long-run average cost curve at the equilibrium point, steps into the fold of the situational determinists. Pigou may be said to have discarded one research programme in favour of another, or to have changed an element in his hard core; but does not the former language suggest an all-or-nothing leap between starkly-contrasting alternatives?

Such language invites misunderstanding. Because the MSRP demands that all participants in a programme share an identical hard core, either Lakatosian history will be misleadingly simple, or so many writers will be labelled with a separate programme that their differences will be emphasised at the expense of that which they share.

Normative standards

The following study compares the relative goodness and badness of various theories as to the behaviour of firms in product markets. Theories will be distinct to the extent that they are inconsistent — whether this inconsistency lies in higher-level propositions (those from which many deductions have been made) or in lower-level propositions is irrelevant for the purposes of distinction and evaluation. The evaluation will be comparative in the sense that no absolute standard of truth will be used; but, rather, the standard used will be the degree of verisimilitude.

Any small change in an auxiliary hypothesis (that is, a lower-level hypothesis) produces a new theory whose relative truthlikeness can, in principle, be assessed. If we are to learn about the truth, we must learn about the truth precisely — and not in terms of research programmes. The study will explain the precise differences between conjectures. The study will then attempt to compare the different theories with observations.

Popper's standard of verisimilitude defines the degree to which a theory approaches the truth. He defines the truth content (falsity content) of a theory t_1 as the class of the true (false) logical consequences of t_1.

Assuming that the truth-content and falsity content of two theories t_1 and t_2 are comparable, we can say that t_2 is more closely similar to the truth, or corresponds better to the facts, than t_1, if and only if either
  (a) the truth-content but not the falsity content of t_2 exceeds that of t_1, [or]
  (b) the falsity-content of t_1, but not its truth content, exceeds that of t_2.[24]

Time horizon and organisation

Economists (perhaps more than is true of the natural scientists) suffer the burden of studying those relationships among individuals which are the subject of wide public discussion.[25] Economics can only claim to be a valuable discipline if it can point to those true consequences of economic behaviour which seem improbable to the untrained participants in public discussion.

Prior to 1660, writings within the subject area of economics propounded very little in the way of true, improbable propositions; but in the development of economics, as in so much intellectual history, the mid-seventeenth century is a major watershed.[26] By the eighteenth century the old arguments of political debate were being subjected to a process of careful reasoning.

This scientific approach is primarily to be seen in a growing appreciation of interdependencies – one of the most notable contributions from Quesnay and his 'physiocratic' school. Quesnay's Tableau traces through sequences of reactions so as to illustrate an equilibrium of aggregates. Furthermore, physiocratic writings on the imposition of taxes on goods and on restrictions on the corn trade stress the indirect effects of such action on the economy as a whole.[27] The growing awareness of the firm as a part of a general equilibrium schema culminated in the work of Adam Smith and Anne Robert Jacques Turgot in which the firm is analysed as part of a general equilibrium system. The resulting awareness of interdependencies enabled economists to point to consequences which the untrained observer would consider to be improbable. Our study begins at the emergence of this scientific approach to economics.

The study will be divided into three substantive parts. Each part will be based on a discussion of a book which is representative of a classical situation in the Schumpeterian sense. Following Schumpeter's dictum that, ' . . . every classical situation summarises or consolidates the work – the really original work – that leads up to it, and cannot be understood by itself, . . .'[28] the study will refer to the earlier literature in exploring each classical statement.

The classical statements chosen will be those recommended by Schumpeter. *The Wealth of Nations*, J. S. Mill's *Principles*, and Marshall's *Principles* provide a structure for chapters 2, 3, and 4 around which preceding and contemporaneous work is discussed. Each of these chapters considers the motivation of the firm, the definitions of costs and the nature of the cost functions employed, equilibrium and stability under competition, and equilibrium and stability in monopolistic markets.

At every point the extent to which any theory is inconsistent with earlier formulations is outlined. To the extent that there is an inconsistency, any evidence which may help in deciding the degrees of verisimilitude of the theories is presented. The type of evidence available has meant that the former task is tackled rather more convincingly than the latter.

Chapter 5 will consist of a much more cursory analysis of post-Marshallian developments. Its structure will be similar to that of the three preceding chapters and, once more, a search is made for the degree of consistency or inconsistency with the propositions in currency at the time of Marshall's death.

2 Adam Smith

Chapter 1 pointed to the mid-seventeenth century as the beginning of scientific economics. This emerging scientific approach had many facets – one of which was the attempt by writers to increase the generality of propositions.

Analysis may well outline the relationship between event x and event y; but analysis outlining a relationship between class x and class y may be more valuable in the sense that there is a possibility that, through generalisation, the truth may be more closely approached. If the process of generalisation increases the truth content, but not the falsity content, of a theory, we are moving closer to the truth.[1] The process of iterating more general statements is a vital component of the growth of knowledge.

One of the characteristics of the emergence of the scientific economics which flowered in *The Wealth of Nations* was the emphasis on classes of firms as contrasted with the emphasis by the pamphleteers on particular firms – such as the East India Company and the Merchant Adventurers. Instead of paying attention to the price charged by a particular firm operating in a particular market, hypotheses were given greater range by referring to classes of firms, classes of markets, and classes of productive factors.

The generation of hypotheses relating to classes of phenomena was complemented by a decline in the emphasis on the personality of particular firms. The type of person in charge of a firm is an elusive characteristic for the purposes of scientific classification. Eighteenth-century economists paid little attention to personality as an element in analysis and paid far more attention to the internal structure of firms and to the external constraints within which firms operate.

The firm was disembodied and became a unit in which resources congeal in the productive process. When we come to examine the equilibrium/value theory of *The Wealth of Nations* it will be shown that, in that context, the firm is little more than a passive conduit which assists in the movement of resources between alternative activities. This

11

depersonalised nature of the firm is true also of the theory of economic development embodied in *The Wealth of Nations*.[2]

This does not imply that the internal organisation of firms is irrelevant to Smith. However, the internal structure of the firm bears on the analysis in a way that the psychology of the participants in the firms does not. This is clearly the case with Smith's dicta regarding the division of labour; and perhaps even more apparent in his references to the joint-stock method of productive organisation.

Eighteenth-century English industrial organisation was characterised by the burgeoning of partnerships of unlimited liability. The so-called 'Bubble Act' of 1720 had prohibited the formation of new joint-stock companies unless especially sanctioned by act of parliament or crown charter; and this act was not repealed until 1825. However the old joint-stock companies survived.[3]

Smith was critical of these companies on the grounds that their management, playing with funds provided by investors who exercised little control, was characterised by 'negligence and profusion'.[4] It was only their monopoly privileges which enabled joint-stock companies to pursue these paths; without these privileges competition from private adventurers generally would spell their ruin. Smith's theme of the need to link industry and effort with reward is a continuing theme throughout *The Wealth of Nations*.[5] The lesson which may be drawn from the remarks on joint-stock companies is that even the pivotal hypothesis of profit-maximisation may be rendered questionable when the internal structure of firms is of this (exceptional) type.

1. THE MOTIVATION OF THE FIRM

The Co-ordinator

The charge against the joint-stock organisation is one instance within *The Wealth of Nations* of emphasis on the co-ordinating and organising roles played by business leaders.

> The directors of such [joint-stock] companies, however, being the managers rather of other people's money than of their own, it cannot well be expected, that they should watch over it with the same anxious vigilance with which the partners in a private co-partnery frequently watch over their own. . . . Negligence and profusion, therefore, must

always prevail, more or less, in the management of the affairs of such a company.[6]

One does not get from *The Wealth of Nations*, 'the over-all impression that a business runs by itself'[7]; but there is no explicit theory of entrepreneurship in *The Wealth of Nations*. Smith does not attempt to capture *the* entrepreneurial function in a simple definition as so many other economists have done. Rather he attributes a number of different roles to the business leader. Chief among these is the marshalling of resources (particularly capital) into those productive activities which appear to be most profitable. In this emphasis on the importance of capital for the process of production Smith was following the tradition of Quesnay and Turgot.[8]

Quesnay and his followers constructed their system on the basis of the influence of the yield of a net product (surplus over cost) on the level of aggregate economic activity. In a disequilibrium position, with increasing net product, part of this increase could accrue to farmers and be channeled into agricultural investment before equilibrium is restored by the capture of this surplus into the rents accruing to landowners. But Quesnay was evasive on the important question as to why competition wipes out the net product in manufacturing but not in agriculture.[9] It was in answering this question that Turgot came to stress the importance of the manufacturer in the process of the accumulation of capital.

Like the physiocrats, Turgot had no concept of *the* entrepreneurial function. He used the word entrepreneur to refer to the industrialist or merchant who heads the firm. The leader of the manufacturing or industrial firm must supply capital – essential because of the interval between the purchase of productive services and the readiness of the product for sale. This person, like his counterpart in *The Wealth of Nations*, plans and supervises the activities of the firm and is referred to variously as 'entrepreneur' or 'capitaliste'.[10]

Following in this tradition of the physiocrats and Turgot, Smith refused to produce a definition of the entrepreneurial function. He was content with a sketch of the functions of the head of a firm.

The Entrepreneur as Capitalist

Until the mid-nineteenth century, while theorists distinguished the function of a capitalist from that of a business leader, the world demanded as a pre-condition for one's playing of the latter role, that one also play the former. Marshall gives Walker the credit for first observing the cracking of this nexus.[11]

Marshall quotes Walker as saying, 'as early as 1876', that: 'It is no longer true that a man becomes an employer because he is a capitalist. Men command capital because they have the qualifications to profitably employ labour. To these captains of industry . . . capital and labour resort for the opportunity to perform their several functions.'[12]

English economists from Smith to Marshall recognised that one needed to have one's own finance if one was to be a business leader; but this did not prevent them from distinguishing the role of the provider of capital from that of the manager of a business. A distinguishing feature of the English school is that they did not use the words 'entrepreneurial function' to refer to one of the functions performed by business leaders to which they wanted to draw especial attention within the framework of their theoretical systems.

It is no criticism of ninteenth century English economics that it followed this course. The entrepreneurial function is a theoretical concept. English economists chose to erect their systems without the aid of such a concept. It is to their degree of verisimilitude that one must look in assessing those theories. From such an assessment it may emerge that theories which assume the key role of business leadership to be *x* correspond more closely to the truth than those which make no such assumption. However, the converse may also be true.

Profits

For Smith, profits to the firm refer to the residual remaining after costs of labour, rent, and raw materials have been deducted from revenue. In calculating profit, the cost of labour must include a wage cost imputed for the labour services provided by the owner-manager; and the cost of rent must include a rent cost imputed for the land services provided by the owner-manager's land.[13] The resulting residual is gross profit.

Profits are profits of stock and 'bear some proportion to the extent of the stock'[14] committed to the enterprise. From these profits of stock, interest must be paid for the use of money borrowed. 'Clear' profit (defined as gross profit minus compensation for the occasional losses 'to which every employment of stock is exposed'[15]) is twice the current (1776) rate of interest in Great Britain. (This ratio is variable across both countries and periods of time.)

The explanation of this 'reasonable' margin of profit on interest (where, by 'reasonable', Smith means 'common or usual'[16]) accruing to the owner-manager is two-fold:

(i) the risk to the borrower who, as it were, insures it to the lender; and

(ii) recompense for the trouble of employing the stock.

This two-fold explanation[17] is puzzling. For the recompense for the service of insurance and for the trouble of employing the stock should perhaps be a *wage* which the owner-managers should impute to themselves before they calculate profits. But Smith insists that profits on stock are 'altogether different' from managerial returns, and are regulated by altogether different principles.[18]

If Smith had catalogued the insurance against risk and the trouble of employing stock under the labour of the owner-manager he would still be left with some residual (positive or negative) due to fluctuations in market conditions.

> Profit is so very fluctuating, that the person who carries on a particular trade cannot always tell you himself what is the average of his annual profit. It is affected, not only by every variation of price in the commodities which he deals in, but by the good or bad fortune both of his rivals and of his customers, and by a thousand other accidents to which goods when carried either by sea or by land, or even when stored in a warehouse, are liable.[19]

Smith clearly sees that if the net revenue of a firm is apportioned between payments to labour, land, and capital there is a residual. The question as to whom this accrues and why, is still being debated today.[20]

One of the most fertile suggestions towards its solution was made by Frank H. Knight when he pointed out that the problem is essentially that costs are undertaken before the point of sale. If the price at which sale is to take place is uncertain then revenue cannot be fully imputed to productive services – not even when the services provided by the owner-manager are included. Knight chooses to confine the words 'pure profit' to this unimputable residual.[21] Smith tries to impute it to the owner-manager but, in so doing, blurs his otherwise careful distinction between income accruing to the services of capital and income accruing to the services provided by the owner-manager.

Since the publication of Knight's classic, it has been common to castigate Smith for not seeing from Cantillon the importance of the residual nature of the entrepreneurial income under conditions of uncertainty. Cantillon, writing between 1730 and 1734, anticipated

Knight in emphasising the variability in an element of the income accruing to the business leader – due to the unforeseen vagaries of market conditions. Cantillon attributed this uncertainty to the weather (governing supply in agricultural markets) and fluctuations in demand: the sale price is uncertain because the quantity to be placed on the market depends on the harvest which is yet to be reaped. The future needs and incomes of buyers are also unknown – as are the competitive actions rivals are likely to take.[22] This much is contained in Smith.

However, Cantillon is one step closer to Knight in his taxonomy. Cantillon contrasts the fixed incomes of those on contractual wages with the uncertain nature of the entrepreneurial income.[23] But, the use to which Cantillon puts this distinction, in his theories of the allocation of resources and of the distribution of income, is as confusing as that of Smith. Like Smith, Cantillon fails to acknowledge that the uncertain nature of the income of a business leader has any implications for the allocation of the resources of business leadership. Like Smith, Cantillon fails to see that given the *ex ante* uncertainty of business returns, factors will accept those contractual arrangements which best fit their propensity to bear uncertainty. In the following passage from the *Essai* the returns to business leadership are treated as a Marshallian supply price.

> All these Undertakers become consumers and customers one in regard to the other, the Draper of the Wine Merchant and vice versa. They proportion themselves in a State to the Customers or consumption. If there are too many Hatters in a City or in a street for the number of people who buy hats there, some who are least patronised must become bankrupt; if they be too few it will be a profitable Undertaking which will encourage new Hatters to open shops there and so it is that the Undertakers of all kinds adjust themselves to risks in a State.[24]

Perhaps it should be re-emphasised that the labelling of a particular aspect of business leadership as 'entrepreneurial' fails to constitute, by itself, a theory either of the firm or of anything else.

The distinction between contractual incomes and the uncertain income of the business leader proved a fruitful starting point for the deductive constructions of later theorists. Cantillon contributed this distinction; but he failed to proceed beyond the stage of taxonomy in the theory of the entrepreneur.

Motivational hypothesis

Along with his predecessors and contemporaries, Smith considered that, as a matter of fact, people are motivated by self-interest in their market dealings. The assumption of self-interest is maintained consistently throughout *The Wealth of Nations*, not merely as the conditional of an 'if . . . then' hypothesis, but also as a fact of life. His assumption of self-interest is not merely a statement of the limits to the applicability of his theory but rather it is a statement of fact. *Because* (not 'if') people are motivated in this way, one can reason in the following manner . . .

At one time it was popular to puzzle over the compatibility of this statement with the non-egoistic psychology contained in *The Theory of Moral Sentiments*.[25] Whatever one's solution to the puzzle, it is clear that Smith was consistent in his maintainance of the proposition that when people deal in markets they are motivated by self-interest.

From the time of the scholastics, the principle of the self-interest of business leaders had been equated with the proposition that they attempt to maximise net revenue.[26] While this self-interest was often condemned, it was thought to be accurate as a description of those business leaders who were sinful.

Aquinus in the *Summa* quotes Augustine reporting 'the saying of a certain actor was accepted by all: "you wish to buy cheap and sell dear" . . .'.[27] But to pay less than the just price is wicked under divine law and every person should try to' . . . attain such justice as to resist and overcome this desire . . .'. 'Hence it is evident that this common desire is not natural but due to wickedness, and hence is common to many who travel the broad road of sin.'[28]

The English merchant pamphleteers of the sixteenth and seventeenth centuries were generally free from scholastic influence and were concerned very little with the broad road of sin — at least in their economic writings. However, they agreed with the scholastic proposition that business leaders strive to maximise their net revenue.

In *A Discourse of the Common Weal of this Realm of England* (written around 1549) it is stated that merchants, ' . . . buy cheap and sell dear and won't sell to us if they can get a higher price somewhere else.'[29]

This view is repeated in the *Discourse of Corporations* (1587—89?) again with reference to merchants, that 'the marchant hath ever eie to his gaine' — 'his greatest proffitt'.[30]

On reading this pamphlet literature it becomes clear that the maximisation of net revenue is the aim not only of merchants, but of all traders. 'The chief End or Business of Trade [defined as the making and selling of one sort of goods for another] is to make a profitable bargain . . .'[31]

Cantillon and Quesnay similarly postulate that business leaders aim to maximise their net revenue. So it comes as no surprise to find Sir James Steuart referring to self-interest as 'the ruling principle of my subject'.[32] Steuart identifies self-interest with the desire of business leaders to maximise their net revenue. Steuart points out that the use of this hypothesis, while generally accurate as a description of reality, has a further justification in its utility. 'I exclude here the sentiment of charity. This alone, as I have often observed, is a principle of multiplication, and if it was admitted here it would ruin all my supposition; but as true it is, on the other hand, that could the poor fellow have got bread by begging, he would not probably have gone a-hunting.'[33]

Unlike Steuart, Smith does not choose the net-revenue-maximisation assumption for utilitarian reasons. His sole justification are the facts of the world of trade. But, in aiming for an accurate description of reality, he places severe qualifications on his profit-maximisation hypothesis.

The first qualification is that mentioned previously[34] with reference to joint-stock companies from which it is clear that, given monopoly power, the leaders of a joint-stock company do not pursue their self-interest by maximising net revenue unless they are large holders of the capital of the firm. Smith's opposition to joint-stock companies is based on the fact that they do not necessarily pursue the minimisation of unit costs implied by the maximisation of profit. They do not minimise costs because the self-interest of those in positions of power does not lead them to maximise the return on the funds invested in the company.

But even capitalists do not necessarily seek to maximise their net return. While Smith insists that: 'The consideration of his own private profit, is the sole motive which determines the owner of any capital to employ it either in agriculture, in manufactures, or in some particular branch of the wholesale or retail trade . . .,'[35] it appears ten pages later that he only holds to this statement if 'profit' is used to mean private valuation. For, even when the business leader uses his own capital, providing there is a margin between revenue and costs, the producer may pursue policies inconsistent with the maximisation of profit. Slaves are a high-cost form of labour according to Smith; but because man loves to domineer: 'Wherever the law allows it, and the nature of the work can afford it [as is the case with sugar and tobacco], therefore, he will generally prefer the service of slaves to that of freemen.'[36] The raising of corn is insufficiently profitable to support the luxury of slaves.

While there are scattered comments such that the entrants to a hazardous industry are attracted by the 'presumptuous hope of success'[37], the distinction between anticipated net revenue and net revenue measured *ex post* is never explicitly made. In *The Wealth of Nations* there is a simultaneous emphasis on the factual variability of profits, and an operating assumption that, with the exception of certain 'hazardous' trades, business uncertainty in the Knightian sense is not a major factor to be considered. It is by such an implicit operating assumption that Smith is enabled to construct a model of equilibrium in markets which is produced by business leaders entering when the rates of profit are higher than normal (and scooping some of this excess profit as expected) and leaving when the rate of profit is below normal. This process is re-told as though no thought has been given to the possibility that expectations may be confounded.[38]

2. COSTS AND COST FUNCTIONS

The division of labour

The first three chapters of *The Wealth of Nations*, containing Smith's remarks on the division of labour, are widely known. However, one aspect of this discussion deserves a further airing: the relationship between the division of labour and the organisation of industry. In particular, this section will examine Smith's theorem that, 'the division of labour is limited by the extent of the market'.[39]

This theorem has been notably fertile in its offspring. To quote one of the most successful midwives: 'That theorem, I have always thought, is one of the most illuminating and fruitful generalisations which can be found in the whole literature of economics.'[40]

Remarks on the advantages of the specialisation of labour have been recorded at least since the time of Plato. For this reason it is easy to discount the objective originality of these three chapters of *The Wealth of Nations*. A formidable list of 'precursors' can be compiled from Cannan's footnotes and Viner's introduction to Rae's *Life*. Schumpeter claims that Petty anticipated Smith on the division of labour, 'including its dependence on the size of markets'[41]. However, Petty's writings give no more than heavily-veiled hints towards the discussion we find in *The Wealth of Nations*.[42] The uniqueness of Smith's discussion lies in the prominence it gives to the relationship between the division of labour and forms of industrial organisation.

Categories of Division

Under the heading of the division of labour Smith outlines three distinct categories:

(i) division within a plant;
(ii) division within a firm but between plants; and
(iii) division between firms.

Bücher suggests that these may be called subdivision of labour, division of production, and division of trades respectively.[43] Each of these three will be discussed in turn.

That Smith chose to draw his example of the division of labour from a pin factory rather than from the nearby Carron iron works is a puzzle to T. S. Ashton; but one, he hastens to add, whose solution is obvious. 'Adam Smith was anxious to isolate the results of the application of his celebrated principle from those of the use of machinery and power. The pin trade employed only simple appliances: it was almost ideal for his purpose.'[44] This particular solution to the puzzle, far from being obvious, is incorrect.

The correct solution, as Viner indicates in his introduction to Rae's *Life*, is to be found in Smith's own explanation. Smith's example was chosen to illustrate the subdivision of labour rather than the 'less obvious' division of production. For this purpose he needed a 'trifling manufacture' whose production was confined to a single plant.

. . . in those trifling manufactures which are destined to supply the small wants of but a small number of people, the whole number of workmen must necessarily be small; and those employed in every branch of the work can often be collected into the same workhouse, and placed at once under the view of the spectator. In those great manufactures, on the contrary, which are destined to supply the great wants of the great body of the people, every different branch of the work employs so great a number of workmen, that it is impossible to collect them all into the same workhouse.[45]

The three different forms of the division of labour must be carefully distinguished when reading the first three chapters of *The Wealth of Nations*.

The meaning of the 'market'

The Wealth of Nations, like Marshall's *Industry and Trade*, uses the word 'market' to refer to an area of exchange. According to the demands of the context, this may be the area of sale of one firm, of a group of firms, or of all the firms in the economy. In Book I, chapter 3 – headed, 'That the division of labour is limited by the Extent of the Market' – Smith gives examples relating the division of trades to the growth of the economy as a whole. But the many meanings he attaches to the word 'market' elsewhere in *The Wealth of Nations* suggest the possibility that the theorem applies to the three forms of the division of labour as limited by the area of sale of a firm, of a group of firms (industry?) or of the economy as a whole.

(i) *That the subdivision of labour is limited by the sales of the firm*
With the refinement of the model of perfect competition following the death of Marshall, the factors limiting the size of firms became a matter of vital interest. If homogeneity of product is assumed, together with a large number of producers who pursue no policy but that of adjusting the quantities they dump on the market, then clearly demand does not limit the size of any particular firm. The limitation apparently must arise from the rising marginal costs encountered by the firm as it expands its output.

As will be seen, Smith's model of free competition requires neither the assumption of product homogeneity nor the assumption of 'large numbers'. Smith does not explore the issue of the determinants of the size of the firm, at least not within the context of his freely competitive model. His usual operating assumption is that the scale of each firm increases as the industry expands. The consequent higher rates of production by each firm give access to economies.

> The increase of demand, besides, though in the beginning it may sometimes raise the price of goods, never fails to lower it in the long run. It encourages production, and thereby increases the competition of the producers, who, in order to undersell one another, have recourse to new divisions of labour and new improvements of art, which might never otherwise have been thought of.[46]

It seems reasonable to ask of *The Wealth of Nations* why, if firms are competitive and have access to lower unit costs through the expansion of their sales, do they not cut their prices prior to the expansion of the general market and so expand at the expense of their rivals?

The clear answer to this question from within *The Wealth of Nations* is that the economies are due, not merely to changes in the scale of the firm, but also to changes in the firm's production function caused by the expansion. In geometrical language, the expansion of output may not merely involve a movement along a long-run average cost curve, but also a downward displacement of that curve because of inventive activity occasioned by the process of expansion. Smith was aware that people learn by doing.

For Smith, the process of the division of labour is occasioned by the continued development of manual and organisational skills and of technical knowledge, rather than by a firm realising that it is marginally profitable to undertake certain activities the possibility of which it was always aware. The firm does not cut its price so it can learn by trying to increase its output because it does not know that it will learn anything and thereby lower its costs.

The historical nature of these decreasing costs explains why they are consistent with a competitive equilibrium. However, Smith does not offer any alternative to increasing costs as an explanation as to the determinants of the allocation of output among the firms in a market. The increasing cost solution was first offered by Cournot; and Marshall provided an alternative which is consistent with the model of *The Wealth of Nations*.[47]

(ii) *That the division of trades is limited by the demand for the product*
This subheading is perhaps a more accurate summary of the text of Book I, chapter 3 of *The Wealth of Nations* than is that offered by Smith. His thesis is that people can only work full time at a particular trade if there is a sufficient demand at the natural price to keep them fully employed. In the diagram, the full time specialisation of a nail-maker can only occur if the demand of x nails at a price ρ_1 represents the rate of output of at least one nail-maker when working full time at the making of nails. From this illustration it is clear that the advantages arising from the division of trades are contingent on the possibilities the specialist has for sale. To secure the widening of markets, Smith advocates the abolition of barriers to competition, improvements in transportation, and the expansion of colonial settlements and of foreign trade.

The localisation of productive activity as a means of market expansion was advocated by Edward Gibbon Wakefield in his schemes for the British colonies. The schemes were designed to limit the area over

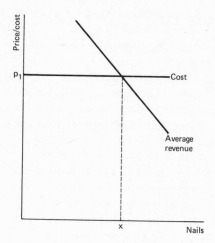

Demand for the Product

which productive activities took place in order to lessen the costs of trade between producers. The facilitation of trade would enable the division of trades with the attendant advantages outlined in Book I of *The Wealth of Nations*.[48]

Stigler has also written an article inspired by Book I, chapter 3.[49] Stigler proposes that we view the firm as engaging in a series of distinct operations, each exhibiting varying cost functions – when cost is expressed as a function of the total 'output' of the firm. As the demand for the final product expands it becomes profitable for firms to specialise in those operations which are subject to decreasing average costs. He predicts that vertical disintegration is the typical development in growing industries, while vertical integration will be the typical development in declining industries.

If there are no economies arising from the integration of processes (that is, that the cost functions of the various processes are independent), as Stigler assumes for simplicity, then it is difficult to see why a process exhibiting uniformly increasing returns and undertaken by more than one firm should not be specialised, no matter what the rate of sales of the final product happens to be. Stigler specifically discounts the defence of the high cost of inter-firm transfers but suggests that, 'at any given time these functions may be too small to support a specialised firm or firms'.[50] Given his assumptions, it is hard to see why this could be so. If the specialised firm can undertake the process and offer it at a price lower than the cost of production to the integrated firms, why should the specialised firm not be established?

Apart from this *a priori* objection, it is not clear from observation that vertical disintegration is the typical development in growing industries and vertical integration the typical development in declining industries.

Herbert Spencer's 'law of increasing heterogeneity and definiteness in structure and function'[51] predicts (although the reasoning is rather unclear) increasing specialisation of business tasks into separate organisational units as the economy grows over time. (Stigler's theory implies this proposition.) Beatrice Webb's father (a substantial, mid-Victorian entrepreneur) dismissed Spencer's law in this wise: 'Words, my dear, mere words. Experience tells me that some businesses grow diverse and complicated, others get simpler and more uniform, others again go into the Bankruptcy Court. In the long run and over the whole field there is no more reason for expecting one process than the other.'[52]

The more careful observations by Laffer of corporations in the United States for the period 1929–65[53] yield much the same generalisation.

(iii) *That the division of labour is limited by aggregate demand*

In his chapters on the division of labour Smith was not so much concerned with the division of industry-wide markets among firms as with the ways in which the expansion of sales increases the wealth of nations, and the effects of changes in costs on the long-range movements in the prices of commodities. For these purposes Smith was not overly concerned to distinguish between movements within a given production function and changes in the production function. Indeed, he explicitly outlines reasons for the interdependence between increases in sales and the technical progress which may result from that increased scale of production.[54]

It is the interdependence between the expansion of the aggregate demand for goods and the expansion of aggregate output which Allyn Young explores in his famous article;[55] and it is from this article that the various models of 'balanced growth' of the past fifty years have received their inspiration.[56]

3. EQUILIBRIUM AND STABILITY UNDER COMPETITION

The successors to Adam Smith have spent much time and effort unravelling his theories of value. This section will not attempt finally to dispose of the myth that *The Wealth of Nations* contains a labour theory of value, that task already has been accomplished;[57] rather it will be concerned to outline the theory of the firm which underpins the analysis.

Smith's discussion of market price and natural price is conducted on the assumption that conditions of free competition prevail. The meaning and implications of this assumption will be explored in the following section. This section will examine the relationship between market price and natural price.

In the late seventeenth century and early eighteenth century there came into currency in France and Britain a distinction in analysis between the price to be observed in markets (market value or price) and the unit cost of production (intrinsic, fundamental, or natural value). While many writers adopted this distinction, its significance for analysis depended on the problem the writer was addressing.

Nicholas Barbon[58], one of the first to propose the distinction, suggested that the value of things to some 'little' extent reflects the cost involved in their production. 'Little' empirical content is conveyed by this proposition. The market conditions likely to facilitate the approximation are not specified and no mechanism is suggested as to how deviations of price from unit cost should initiate stabilising activity — even if that is what the author proposed.

In his *use* of the distinction between 'intrinsic' value (measuring the quantity and quality of labour and land used in production) and market price, Cantillon did not advance beyond Barbon. Cantillon assumes that market price in some way reflects intrinsic value and then proceeds further to explain intrinsic value by means of his famous par between land and labour.

Achille Nicholas Boisguilbert[59] and Sir James Steuart[60] produced theories in which the relationship between real value and price (the relationship reflecting the incentive to produce) plays a key role in the equilibrium and disequilibrium of the aggregate level of productive activity. However, neither of these writers developed an interesting theory of the firm to underpin this analysis of aggregate equilibrium.

More interesting, for our present purpose, are those writers who used the distinction to generate hypotheses concerning the allocation of resources between alternative productive activities. In this connection the work of Joseph Harris and Turgot will be discussed along with that of Smith.

Equilibrium and stability

The concepts of equilibrium and stability are central to a discussion of the theory of value outlined in *The Wealth of Nations*.[61] An equilibrium position is one from which there is no tendency for change. This study will speak of the stability of equilibrium in the sense of Samuelson's perfect stability of the first kind: an equilibrium position is stable if from any initial conditions all the variables approach their equilibrium values in the limit as time becomes infinite.[62] To determine normal or natural values (as with Smithian natural value) certain variables are assumed constant and natural values can then be computed as functions of time.

The Wealth of Nations outlines the concept of natural price in the following way: 'When the price of any commodity is neither more nor less than what is sufficient to pay the rent of the land, the wages of labour, and the profits of the stock employed in raising, preparing, and bringing it to market, according to their natural rates, the commodity is then sold for what may be called its natural price.'[63] Unlike Cantillon's intrinsic value, Smith's natural price is not constant through time as in some stationary state, rather it is an equilibrium value moving through time. Indeed, the digression concerning the variations in the value of silver (in Book I, chapter 11) is concerned to explain such changes in natural price over the course of the centuries.

However, within the context of his discussion of the allocation of resources between industries (in particular, Book I, chapter 7) Smith implicitly assumes that natural price (unit cost) is constant for changes in output within the neighbourhood of the equilibrium rates of production. This does not mean that Smith assumed a production function with constant returns to scale. In the digression on silver, Smith expresses input costs and technical progress as functions of scale. The temporary assumption that natural price is constant for changes in output within the neighbourhood of equilibrium rates of production is used to simplify the discussion of equilibrium and stability. For this reason, while considering Smith's discussion of the allocation of resources between activities, it is possible to imagine Smith's natural price as a Marshallian long-period supply curve, as in the diagram.

Smith's natural price is defined as unit cost plus unit normal profit computed at the market rate. Profit is not classed as a cost but is included in the supply price along with the costs. The inclusion of profit on capital as an element in natural price was not acknowledged before Turgot and Smith. Turgot is clear that unless the owners of capital gain as good

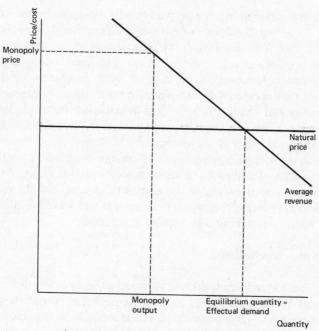

Smith's Natural and Monopoly Prices

returns in a particular venture as they could in another, they will not devote their capital to that particular venture.[64]

Smith relates this return to the stock of capital. It is not the return which governs the decision of the capitalist, but the *rate* of return on capital invested. With *The Wealth of Nations* that rate of return on capital (the supply price of capital) is used to calculate input unit supply prices before these are summed to compute a product's natural value. This step is rightly praised by Meek: 'The most significant theoretical advance which Adam Smith made over the work of his predecessors was undoubtedly his inclusion of profit on capital as a constituent element in the supply price of commodities.'[65]

It was noted above that for the analysis of resource allocation between activities, *The Wealth of Nations* assumes that natural price is constant for changes in output in the neighbourhood of equilibrium rates of production. The constancy of the natural price of output implies that its constituent parts (the natural prices of factors) are also constant. So no changes in factor prices occur except those necessary to cause a movement towards equilibrium from a disequilibrium position. The natural prices of factors do not change between equilibrium positions.

This latter requirement is not particularly stringent in the case of labour — whose natural price is determined independently of commodity markets. Nor is it upsetting in the case of capital; for *The Wealth of Nations* provides us with few clues at all as to the determinants of the rate of profit. However, in the case of land, chapter 11 of Book I explicitly outlines the relationship between the scale of production of a commodity and changes in rent. It is in this case that the temporary assumption in Book I, chapter 7, of constant natural prices of factors that the greatest leap of the imagination is needed.

The demand function represented on the diagram is positioned independently of influences in the commodity market. Smith does not outline precisely the form of the demand function; but the negative relationship of quantity demanded to price is an hypothesis utilised at many points throughout *The Wealth of Nations*.[66]

Stablisation Mechanism

Harris, Turgot and Smith share in common a theory of the allocation of resources between industries in which equilibrium occurs when the market price (the price observed) is equal to the natural price. Galiani was another mid-eighteenth century theorist who outlined a clear notion of an equilibrium allocation of resources between industries. His *Della Moneta* (1751) argues that the equilibrium stabilises in response to disturbances as the system tends towards an equilibrium position. The analyses of Turgot and Smith are similar in this respect.

Galiani supposes that a country entirely Mohammedan is converted to Christianity. This creates an increased demand for wine which consequently rises in price. Given that they seek to make profit 'from the base incentive of sordid gain', merchants will begin to import wine. An equilibrium position may soon be resumed, but, often, ' . . . so many additional people go into this branch of industry, impetuously but too late, attracted by the first reports and the first examples, that its value falls below what is just; and then all begin to withdraw, each one paying the penalty for his rashness, and the just limit is reached again.' Galiani mentions the aquatic analogy which later becomes a commonplace in the literature of value analysis. 'From this two important consequences flow. First, that it is not necessary to consider the first developments in a case, but the permanent and fixed conditions, and in that there is always order and equality; just as water in a vessel, if disturbed, returns to the due level after a confused and irregular fluctuation . . .'[67]

The equilibrium system outlined by Harris has as a condition of equilibrium that the price equals intrinsic value plus a margin of profit.

Men's various necessities and appetites, oblige them to part with their own commodities, at a rate proportionable to the labour and skill that hath been bestowed upon those things, which they want in exchange: If they will not comply with the market their goods will remain on their hands; and if at first one trade be more profitable than another, skill as well as labour and risques of all sorts, being taken into account; more men will enter into that business, and in their outcrying will undersell one another, till at length the great profit of it is brought down to a *par* with the rest.[68]

Turgot and Smith outline an equilibrium of resource allocation in which the market price is in equilibrium (corresponding to Marshall's market-period equilibrium) and the market price equals the natural or necessary price (corresponding to Marshall's long-period normal).

In explaining his condition for equilibrium of the market price, Smith's language gives rise to confusion. 'The market price of every particular commodity is regulated by the proportion between the quantity which is actually brought to market, and the demand of those who are willing to pay the natural price of the commodity, or the whole value of the rent, labour and profit, which must be paid in order to bring it thither.'[69] In other words, the market price is a function of the proportion between the quantity which would be demanded at the natural price and the quantity supplied during the time period under consideration.

This statement, quite unexceptionable in a chapter explaining the relationship between market price and natural price, is criticised by J. S. Mill.[70] Smith was interested in establishing this relationship because he was concerned to explain the equilibrium of resource allocation between industries. Mill demands clarity in the explanation of market price: he demands that the condition for market price equilibrium be that the quantity demanded equal the quantity supplied.[71]

Neither in *Réflexions* nor in *The Wealth of Nations* do equilibrium conditions require that the rate of return on capital be equal between industries. (*Ex post* and *ex ante* profit are not distinguished.) Even given free competition – an assumption implicit in Turgot and explored at length by Smith – equilibrium in resource allocation is consistent with those differences in profitability which are explained by extraordinary factors. These extraordinary factors are the varying degrees of agreeability[72] or of risk[73] which may require or encourage a capitalist to accept a higher or a lower return than normal. Risk is an attraction to the Smithian capitalist, but a disincentive to that of Turgot.

As with *Della Moneta*, *The Wealth of Nations* illustrates the stability of the equilibrium quantity of production. If, because of a public mourning, the quantity of black cloth supplied is less than the equilibrium quantity, market price will be higher than the natural price. The rate of profit in that industry will rise. Traditional suppliers or (given knowledge and mobility) new rivals will move to capture some of this profit. The returns to labour and capital will remain above their natural rates until resources flow into the activity and equilibrium is re-established. The new equilibrium will be characterised by an equality between the market price of the commodity and the natural price of the commodity, equality between the market prices and the natural prices of the factors, and equality between the rates of profit on capital between industries (making allowance for variations in risk and agreeability).

The stabilising resource flows seem to be such that factor proportions are kept constant—at least when this story of resource allocation is being told. The flows of resources may take place within the structure of the existing firms, or may take the form of new firms entering. There is no limit to the size of firms.

However, there may be impediments to these stabilising resource flows; and it is in outlining these barriers to the attainment of equilibrium that the process of decision-making within the firm is elaborated. The impediments to the free movement of resources constitute Smith's definition of monopoly.[74] Within *The Wealth of Nations* 'monopoly' is usually taken to mean a barrier to the attainment of equilibrium. Sometimes the word is restricted to those barriers to the free flow of resources which could be removed by government action. The next section will explore these elements of market structure.

Free competition

The term 'free competition' is used in *The Wealth of Nations* to refer to that process whereby a party (unimpeded by government) acts to achieve a position which is incompatible with that desired by a rival. For Smith, the significance of free competition consists primarily in its being the conduit by which resources move to the equilibrium allocation outlined in the previous section. Rivalry can either come from a firm established in the industry or from a firm moving into this area of competition. If there is only one producer or if there is an agreement between established firms the internal competitive process may be thwarted. A government franchise may prevent rivalry from outside the group of established firms. Whichever way the flow of resources is impeded, the restriction is labelled by Smith as 'monopolistic'. The Smithian category of monopoly is not restricted to a single firm industry, but encompasses any means by which the process of rivalry is lessened.

It is important to recognise that the concepts of free competition and monopolistic restriction relate to the competitive process and to the corresponding resource flows. The extent to which this process is free is a matter of degree; and, conversely, so is the extent of monopolistic restriction. For this reason it is impossible to outline the conditions required by *The Wealth of Nations* before competition could be said to exist. It is also difficult to specify the degree of competition which must exist before resource flows are stabilising. For resource flows take place over time and a monopolistic barrier operating at the present (for example, an agreement by established firms) may be inoperative next year (when new rival firms may enter the market). However it is possible to outline those factors which tend to facilitate or to impede the competitive process.

The number of competitors is likely to influence the degree of freedom of competition in that with fewer competitors collusion is facilitated.

The inhabitants of a town, being collected into one place, can easily combine together. The most insignificant trades carried on in towns have accordingly, in some place or other, been incorporated; and even where they have never been incorporated, yet the corporation spirit, the jealousy of strangers, the aversion to take apprentices, or to communicate the secret of their trade, generally prevail in them, and often teach them, by voluntary associations and agreements, to prevent that free competition which they cannot prohibit by bye-laws. The trades which employ but a small number of hands, run most easily into such combinations.[75]

The smaller the number of producers, the easier it is to combine. Combination, both tacit[76] and by means of bye-laws, can limit the possibility of rivalry between established firms. This facilitation of combination is the only way proposed by Smith by which small numbers can restrict the process of free competition.

In discussing the inequalities of wages and profit occasioned by the Policy of Europe,[77] Smith often mentions the effect of policy in 'restraining the competition in some employments to a smaller number than might otherwise be disposed to enter them.' But this evil is placed alongside those evil policies which 'increase the number beyond what it would naturally be'. In this context the policy which creates 'small numbers' refers to limitations on the supply of productive services, and the number of competitors is taken as a proxy for this supply.

While we are given no theory placing limits on the size of firms, we must suppose that Smith is referring to small-scale craft workshops in which case an increase in productive services is normally associated with an increased number of firms. Whatever the rationalisations made, 'small' is used in the sense of 'fewer than would exist under equilibrium conditions', and not in any sense by which numbers would tend to affect the degree of freedom of competition.

Combinations are often sufficient to prevent competition from established members of the industry; but such combinations are unlikely to be sustained unless competition both from abroad and from new local competitors can be prevented. Smith often castigates the government for establishing such barriers to the free flow of resources. Even in cases approximating neo-classical large numbers (as in the case of livestock rearing in eighteenth-century England) such restrictions are labelled as 'monopolistic'.

In times of moderate plenty, the importation of foreign corn is loaded with duties that amount to prohibition. The importation of live cattle, except from Ireland, is prohibited at all times, and it is but of late that it was permitted from thence. Those who cultivate the land, therefore, have a monopoly against their countrymen for the two greatest and most important articles of land produce, bread and butcher's meat.[78]

Book I, chapters 7 and 10 creates the impression that government policy is responsible for all those immobilities which produce disequilibrium allocations. Turgot creates the same impression, referring to 'statuts sans nombre dictes par l'esprit de monopole'[79]; and many early nineteenth-century English economists convey a similar attitude.

There is modern evidence to suggest that today non-government barriers to entry are significant.[80] But it is important to remember both the ease of raising finance in eighteenth-century England,[81] and the ubiquity of government franchises – many of which had survived since the times of the Tudors and Stuarts.

One other impediment to free resource movement mentioned by Smith should be noted: lack of knowledge. Producers who can keep a secret of their extraordinary profits may lessen the threat from rivals for the duration of the secret. Or, even if the profits are known, they may be sustained so long as the process of production is kept secret.[82]

Perfect Competition

It is possible to interpret the above discussion as indicating the stability conditions for a Smithian stable equilibrium. Resource allocation will only move towards equilibrium given factor mobility, perfect knowledge, and price elasticity of the supply of factors. Given this interpretation[83] *The Wealth of Nations* may be seen as an important predecessor of the model of perfect competition which emerged at about the time of the death of Marshall. However, Smith's model of equilibrium differs from the model of perfect competition in two important respects.

In the first place, the structural assumptions made in *The Wealth of Nations* are far less demanding than those of the model of perfect competition. Smith's model is consistent with product differentiation and does not require large numbers of competitors. Providing that there are no impediments to free movement of resources, market price will continually be gravitating towards the natural price – which itself is some equilibrium moving through time. Occasionally words are used implying boundaries to the areas of competition (the concept of the industry), but the concept of the industry is not essential for the analysis.

The analysis of intrinsic value (cost based) and market price (determined by supply and demand) in Cantillon's *Essai* is, compared with that of *The Wealth of Nations*, notably free of any analysis of the decisions made by the participants in the market. Because the *Essai* contains no analysis of monopoly, no contrast is drawn between the intrinsic value/market price analysis and that of monopoly. It is this contrast in *The Wealth of Nations* which reveals the disaggregative foundations of Smith's value analysis. But, as with Smith, we should be careful not to say of Cantillon that he 'reasoned on the hypothesis of the most perfect of perfect competitions'.[84] Like Smith, Cantillon's intrinsic-value-equals-market-price equilibrium is consistent with a wide range of assumptions regarding market structure. In outlining the bargaining process involved in the determination of market price, Cantillon explicitly refers to market price often depending 'upon the eagerness or easy temperament of a few Buyers or Sellers (d'un petit nombre d'Acheteurs, ou de Vendeurs)'.[85] He immediately follows this with an example of this bargaining process in which the buyers number four.

The second important difference between Smithian competition and the model of perfect competition is that in *The Wealth of Nations* the significance of the natural value / market value equilibrium analysis lies not in the characteristics of equilibrium but in the role played by the 'stability conditions'. Hicks notes the relationship between stability conditions and laws of change.

The laws of change of the price-system, like the laws of change of individual demand, have to be derived from stability conditions. We first examine what conditions are necessary in order that a given equilibrium system should be stable; then we make an assumption of regularity that positions in the neighbourhood of the equilibrium position will be stable also; and thence we deduce rules about the way in which the price-system will react to changes in tastes and resources.[86]

Marshall's praise of the value analysis contained in *The Wealth of Nations* is recorded in the *Principles*.[87] Like Marshall, Smith is concerned to outline the way in which the allocation of resources will alter through time. The question is posed: given a situation in time t, what will be the situation in time-period $t + 1$? In attempting to answer this question, Smith stresses the nature of impediments to the mobility of resources (monopoly) and the ways in which those impediments are overcome. This approach may be contrasted with the theory of perfect competition which concentrates on stating the conditions required for equilibrium. The advantage of the dynamic emphasis of Smith and Marshall is that it may yield predictions as to what will happen and when.

An equilibrium solution yields no proposition whose truth content is easily testable. Statements relating an equilibrium position to observable phenomena are usually invalid inferences from the theory. It is not correct to say that the natural price is some sort of average of the market prices observed. Such a statement will only be true if the 'shocks' caused by changes in the 'parametrical' variables are of a particularly regular type.

Rather, the analysis of the equilibrium position(s) is only one step in the direction of a testable hypothesis. Once equilibrium conditions have been stated, it is necessary to outline the stability conditions which determine the direction (and possibly the rate) of change in the variables. If these stability conditions are so vague that they merely predict that the system will move from one equilibrium position to another, then the prediction yielded by the model is merely as to the direction in which variables will change.

However, if by a careful estimation of the stability conditions, the model can predict accurately the rate at which variables will move over time, the truth content of the model will have been greatly increased; for the model will then predict the values of variables at specific points in time.

It will emerge, as the study proceeds, that the careful articulation of stability conditions is a leading characteristic of the English classical school. By adopting this approach, Adam Smith and Alfred Marshall have moved the theory of value towards greater verisimilitude.

4. MONOPOLY

In the light of the preceding discussion, it may seem strange that Smith's theory of monopoly comes in for such a battering at the hands of the commenters.

Schumpeter declares of *The Wealth of Nations*: 'There is no theory of monopoly. The proposition (Book I, chapter 7) that "the price of monopoly is upon every occasion the highest which can be got" might be the product of a not very intelligent layman – taken literally, it is not even true.'[88] De Roover[89] claims that Smith ignored price elasticity of demand in this remark. Cannan's forthright style also finds vent: 'Smith seems to have been strangely forgetful of the meaning of "monopoly" when he declared that the rent of land was "naturally a monopoly price". By derivation and in ordinary usage a person who has a monopoly of anything is one who is the only person who has the power of selling it.'[90]

If the word 'monopoly' is considered to mean that impediment to the free flow of resources which permits a differential between market price and natural price to persist, the above objections lose their force. Moreover, Smith was not merely being perverse in using the word in this way. In the centuries before 1776 the disputants in debates on English economic policy had expended enormous energy over just this issue of semantics.

When Smith mentions that the price of monopoly is the highest price that can be got, he is referring to a situation in which the supply of resources is limited (by monopolistic restriction). As can be seen from the diagram,[91] given any such quantity, a price may be charged between the natural price (average cost of production) and the price to be read from the demand curve. It is the latter which, Smith predicts, will rule. The price will be the highest that can be got for the limited quantity.

In the light of Cournot it may seem unsatisfying that Smith does not predict the rate of production. The rate of production of Smithian monopolists would depend on their degree of monopoly power and the extent to which they were trying to maximise their net revenues. Smith often returns to the theme of their high costs of production. He condemns monpolisitc restriction for the redistribution of income it occasions, for its high costs of production, and for the poor allocation of resources between activities which results. These ill effects arise from the impediments to resource flows and the consequent margin between market price and natural price (average cost). In explaining these impediments to resource flows the category of the single seller with a government franchise is treated as a speical case.

Pre-Smithian analysis

From the time of Aristotle, writers have related the structure of markets to the prices charged. Aristotle is thought to be the originator of the analysis of monopoly (defined as a single seller). His stories of engrossment in *Politics*[92] and his condemnation of their unjust pricing in *Ethics*[93] were both repeated by the schoolmen who contrasted the price set by a monopolist with the just price. The just price was, in some sense, the competitive price.

In the sixteenth century monopsony (although not labelled as such until Joan Robinson) was condemned. Sir Thomas Moore noted that fewness of sellers (for which he invented the word 'oligopoly') may cause the price to be above the competitive level. Lessius (1554—1623) drew the world's attention to the importance to the monopolist of preventing the appearance of new alternative sources of supply.[94]

Throughout the seventeenth century the debate over English monopoly legislation was a key facet to the power struggle between the crown (trying to maintain its power to grant monopolies) and parliament. Very few participants in the debate were sufficiently bold as to defend something labelled a monopoly. So the debate over what was evil became a debate as to the meaing of the word 'monopoly' whose evil character few dared to question.

Heckscher draws our attention to what he calls 'one of the most far-reaching discussions on monopolies throughout the mercantilist era'.[95] In his report on the two so-called free-trade bills before the House of

Commons in 1604, Sir Edwin Sandys uses language sounding as a pre-echo of *The Wealth of Nations*.

The name of monopoly, though taken originally for personal unity, yet is fitly extended to all improportionable paucity of the sellers in regard of the ware which is sold. If ten men had the only sale of all the horses in England, this were a monopoly; much more the Company of Merchant Adventurers, which, in effect not above two hundred, have the managing of the two third parts of the clothing of this realm, which might well maintain many thousand merchants more.[96]

But it must be stressed that statements such as this are rare in the seventeenth-century literature. Most of the public debate centered around whether the sellers in the company colluded on price and thereby constituted a single seller. The ethico-legal interest in the behaviour of monopolies was, during the time of the scholastics and up until the eighteenth century, aroused by the high prices such organisations could charge at the expense of consumers rather than at the poor allocation of resources which might result. That such evil can only be sustained because of an absence of rivals seems an obvious inference to draw. It is also one which makes the game of cops and robbers relatively easy. It is far more difficult to spot the causes of impediments to resource flows than to spot a single seller.

Apart from this legalistic discussion of monopoly and Becher's attempt to link large numbers (that is, too many) with unregulated competition ('polypolium')[97] the exploration of the effects of numbers of participants in the market process on price yielded little fruit until the eighteenth century.

Sir James Steuart

Steuart's *Principles* seems to be one of the first works written in English to analyse the concept of competition. Here the failure of the eighteenth century to distinguish static from dynamic concepts is clearly illustrated. For Steuart, competition is the process of rivalry: 'The term *competition* is relative to, and conveys the idea of emulation between two parties striving to compass the same end.'[98] Steuart is interested in competition because he is interested in the process by which market price is settled. The numbers of buyers and sellers influence this process. Rivalry from new producers is ignored; so that competition can exist between buyers only if there is more than one buyer, and competition between sellers only if there is more than one seller. If both sides of a market have more than one competitor, competition is double competition. If a single buyer is confronted with more than one seller or if a single seller is confronted with more than one buyer, competition is single. (Bilateral monopoly is not mentioned.) Competition is a matter of degree, for it may be classified as small, strong, or weak;[99] but it is unclear whether these classifications correspond in a uniform and positive way with the number of rivals.

In the process by which market price is settled, competition between sellers will put a downward pressure on the initial (high) offers of individual sellers; and the competition between buyers will act as an upward pressure. In the course of this process there will be 'vibrations' (variations) in the relative power of buyers and sellers; but if buyers or sellers 'unite' the vibrations will cease and united sellers will be able to set prices according to the demand. Demand is a negative function of price; and the form of the function (elasticity) will place limits on the extent to which price will rise or fall.

Turgot

For the future of the analysis of market structure and value, Turgot's contribution is vital. Turgot defines 'valeur estimative' as the degree of esteem which a man attaches to the different objects of his desires.[100] Turgot proceeds to provide a solution to the problem of the rate of exchange between two isolated persons (given two goods). The final outcome will lie between the esteem values of the two individuals. In particular, it will be the mean of the two esteem values.[101] This determinate solution for isolated exchange anticipates that of Menger.[102]

It is particularly frustrating that the article in which these propositions occur was left incompleted by Turgot because Turgot's writing on multiple exchange in *Réflexions* seems to contrast the bargaining process of isolated exchange with the more quickly determined outcome of multiple exchange. The difference between these two cases is not absolutely clear; and different interpretations are possible.[103]

However, it often happens that several Individuals have wine to offer to the man who has corn: if one of these is not willing to give any more than *four quarts* for a *bushel*, the Proprietor of the corn will not give him his corn if he comes to learn that someone else will give him *six quarts* or *eight* for the same *bushel*. If the first man wants to have corn, he will be forced to raise the price to the level of the one who offers more. The Sellers of wine gain on their side from the competition between the Sellers of corn: no one decides to part with his commodity until he has compared the different offers that are made to him of the commodity which he needs, and he gives preference to the highest offer. The value of corn and wine is no longer haggled over by two isolated Individuals with reference to their reciprocal needs and resources; it is fixed as a result of the balancing of the needs and resources of the whole body of Sellers of corn with those of the whole body of Sellers of wine.[104]

We noted above that Turgot was not particularly concerned with the analysis of monopoly. But in the above quotation it can be seen that he was edging towards the later schema of market classification. He is far less concerned than Smith with the time dimension of the adjustments towards equilibrium, and with what may be interpreted as stability conditions — factors (principally 'monopolistic' restrictions) which impede the adjustment towards equilibrium.

So, by the beginning of the final quarter of the eighteenth century the division of approaches between British and French economists, which was to last at least another century, was beginning to jell. The British were concerned to explore the impediments hindering the attainment of competitive equilibrium. The French were concerned to classify markets according to the number of participants and to state the conditions of equilibrium for each market category as elegantly as possible.

3 J. S. Mill

This chapter will focus on those writers of the English classical school who followed Adam Smith. The scope of the chapter is defined by the method of analysis and the writers' choice of problem rather than by the time period. Those writers are included whose work elaborates the theory of the equilibrium and stability of resource allocation contained in *The Wealth of Nations*. The work of contemporary writers (such as Cournot, Dupuit and Ellet) who developed the seminal ideas of Turgot and elaborated the static equilibrium conditions for various categories of markets will be discussed in chapter 4.

The work of these writers in developing conditions for the static equilibrium for various market categories was facilitated by the discovery that the appropriate technique is that of marginal analysis (the differential and integral calculus). Von Thünen utilised the marginal analysis; but his static analysis was not applied to a classification of market structures. For this reason he straddles both the group of writers discussed in this chapter and that group to be discussed in chapter 4. Accordingly, his work will be mentioned in both chapters.

The discussion will again revolve around a 'classic' statement; and once more Schumpeter's suggested classic will be adopted: J. S. Mill's *Principles* will be used as the classic statement on which to hang the discussion.

In his preface to the *Principles*, Mill states that he has attempted to bring *The Wealth of Nations* up to date. He does this by including in his book the valuable work which has been presented since 1776.

Much of the most valuable work on the theory of the firm produced by the writers discussed in this chapter was suggested by the analysis of the concrete problems raised in political debate, and by detailed observations. However, the treatises of the classical economists were dominated by the Ricardian model. In one of his *Five Lectures on Economic Problems* Stigler convincingly argues that, in writing these treatises ' . . . classical economists have employed an apparatus which is different, and in modern eyes inferior, to that which they employed to analyze concrete problems . . .'.[1] Some of these concrete studies were undertaken in response to the burning political issues of the day. Senior's report to parliament on the plight of the hand-loom weavers[2] (rightly praised by Stigler) and Torrens' careful discussion of the monopoly power of unions[3] are examples.

The spur to good analysis provided by facts confronted the younger Mill rather indirectly. Mill did not present evidence and argument on specific economic problems to parliament as McCulloch and Senior had done; but he did absorb much factual material through reading records of the observations of others. This can be seen from the numerous empirical studies cited in the *Principles*.

It has been argued that direct experience caused Say to criticise Adam Smith's proposition that all profits are in proportion to the capital invested. J. S. Mill's modification of the profit-maximisation hypothesis to allow for the influence of custom seems to spring from direct observation. Both with the influence of custom and with Babbage's information on economies of scale, observation suggested to Mill a conjecture as to the implications of the observation for the structure of industry.

In extending and applying Adam Smith's equilibrium and stability analysis, Mill further increases the empirical content of the Smithian model. Mill states that the actual prices to be observed in markets will be those for which the quantity supplied equals the quantity demanded; and he points out that, when applying Smith's cost-based natural value to products produced jointly, the propositions regarding natural value apply only to the products taken jointly.

William Thornton finds that Mill's explanation of market price is not sufficiently precise to explain the actual behaviour of firms. Thornton's experience of business decisions[4] caused him to extend and to modify this part of Mill's analysis.

Marshall, who provides the classic statement for chapter 4, meets Thornton's criticisms of Mill by discussing the immediate determinants of the firm's supply decision. In pursuing this suggestion from Thornton, Marshall pushed the equilibrium and stability analysis of Adam Smith towards a yet greater degree of verisimilitude.

1. THE MOTIVATION OF THE FIRM

Profits de capitaux and profits industriels

The theory of profits contained in *The Wealth of Nations* is outlined in chapter 2. Despite its confusion certain points are clear. Profit (along with rent and wages) is one of the elements of national income accruing to the capitalist class (the other two classes being the landowners and the labourers). Profits are related to the amount of capital employed and cover interest, payments to the borrower to cover the risk of the loss of the capital, and recompense for the trouble of employing the stock.

Say was highly critical of Smith's 'neglect of the distinction between the profits of superintendency, and those of capital'.[5] Say's criticism was not that Smith did not distinguish between interest and returns to business leadership. Smith had been careful to distinguish interest from returns for the trouble of employing the stock. Indeed, this distinction was not original to Smith. It is evident in certain English writings of the seventeenth century.[6]

Say's criticism was as to causal connection. Smith had claimed that all the elements of profit are profits of stock — having a value related to the value of the stock invested — although this value does vary between enterprises and between activities. Say claimed that while *interest* is related to the amount of capital invested, *profits industriels* are not a function of the amount of capital invested but of the skill, activity, and judgment of the business leadership.

> No wonder he [Smith] found himself thus perplexed; their value is regulated upon entirely different principles. The profits of labour depend on the degree of skill, activity, judgement, &c. exerted; those of capital, on the abundance or scarcity of capital, the security of the investment, &c.[7]

It has been suggested that this difference between Say and Smith may have been due to differences between the industrial environments observed by the two writers. Knight mentions von Mangoldt as suggesting that the personality of the manager was more important to French than to English industry.[8] Hoselitz suggests that Say's personal entrepreneurial experience may account for his views.[9]

Whatever the explanation as to why Say was 'ahead' of his English counterparts, it is clear that rapid expansion (involving changes in the products and the methods of production) in the English manufacturing sector brought into prominence certain industrial leaders and inventors — the stuff of school texts on the English industrial revolution — and it is not surprising that this emphasis on personality should eventually percolate into the analytical literature.

The eighteenth-century literature (both English and French) had placed little emphasis of the importance of the personality and ability of particular business leaders. After Say, the importance of entrepreneurs lies in the uniqueness of their decisions. Each decision bears the imprint of the entrepreneur's personality and ability.

[Gross profit, though] it does not vary much from employment to employment, varies greatly from individual to individual, and can scarcely be in any two cases the same. It depends on the knowledge, talents, economy, and energy of the capitalist himself, or of the agents whom he employs; on the accidents of personal connexion; and even on chance. Hardly any two dealers in the same trade, even if their commodities are equally cheap, carry on their business at the same expense, or turn over their capital in the same time.[10]

The tone of this passage is markedly different from that of Smith and Cantillon. The eighteenth-century writers acknowledge that profit rates vary markedly between firms but attribute this to differences in the environments those firms encountered. Mill, following Say, asserts that an important factor governing the rates of profit between firms is the personality and ability of the business leader.

It was not until two decades after Say that this view was promoted in the English literature and it took yet more time before it was incorporated into the conventional (English) wisdom. One reason for this delay is that the heavyweights north of the channel in the first three decades of the nineteenth century were interested in other matters. While Ricardo and Malthus were vitally interested in the movements in the rate of profit over time and in response to protection, and were concerned to establish that rates of profit are equal between various employments, they were just not interested in the question as to why they should vary between firms.

In the published correspondence between Say and Ricardo, there is no record of dispute between the two as to the determinants of the component parts of a firm's profit. In Say's notes to the French translation of Ricardo's *Principles*, Say mentions the disagreement in the appropriate places; but does not claim that this disagreement affects the validity of the Ricardian model.[11] Both Say and Ricardo accepted the Smithian proposition that secular movements in the rate of profit may be gauged roughly by secular movements in the rate of interest. The reason for this absence of dispute is probably that both realised that Ricardo's acknowledgement of Say's point might warrant a footnote in the *Principles* but it would scarcely be fundamental to the model.[12] The irrelevance of Say's classification of the component parts of profits for the Ricardian model largely explains the English reluctance to discuss Say's entrepreneurial income. The economic debate in England was absorbed with the propositions contained in Ricardo's *Principles*.

During the early 1820s certain English economists[13] reiterated the Smithian point that the imputed wages of the owner manager should not be classified under profits. William Ellis[14] addressed himself to the semantic question and chose to equate the word *profits* with the rate of interest – because ownership of capital is rarely combined with the requisite talent for conducting business; but, apart from his new proposal for the use of words, he did not contribute to the analytical debate.

Thomas Tooke suggested that English economists should adopt Say's classification and distinguish between 'profits industriels' and 'profits de capitaux'.[15] Tooke attempts to outline the determinants of the rate of interest, and to outline the difference between the rate of interest and the rate of profit. In particular, certain factors may influence the supply and demand of funds but not the supply and demand of expected profitable opportunities.

Samuel Read concentrates on semantic issues – and follows the suggestion of Ellis that the word *profits* should be restricted to the ordinary rate of interest.[16] Read's view is that the returns to business leadership should be called *wages* because they are due to labour – even though the principles governing the 'wages of masters' are quite different from those governing the 'wages of inferior labour' – as in the Ricardian model.

J. S. Mill, in his *Essay on Profits and Interest*, later published as one of the *Essays on Some Unsettled Questions* (but written in 1829–30) sees the analytical issues clearly and formulates a defence for Ricardo. In contrast with the view of Smith and Read, Mill argues that the wages of superintendence may be considered as part of gross profits because they are governed by the amount of capital employed rather than by the degree of hardness or skill of the labour of superintendence. The profits of an enterprise equal the rate of profit in that particular trade multiplied by the amount of capital invested. From this one can deduct the rate of interest to determine the wages of management. Such wages vary with the amount of capital rather than with the amount of managerial skill and effort because, 'the trouble of managing a business is not proportionally increased by an increase of the magnitude of the business'.[17]

Scrope, who had reviewed Read's book in the *Quarterly Review*

(January 1831), classifies profits into various component parts; but, like Read, he does not provide an analytical reason for this classification. Ramsay is not so unhelpful. He points to the usefulness of the French distinction between profits of capital (interest) and profits of enterprise. He adopts a compromise between the Ricardo/early Mill view that the profits of enterprise are a function of the amount of capital employed and the Say/Storch view that the skill of the entrepreneur also counts. 'Thus the profits of enterprise constitute a revenue of a two-fold nature, depending primarily on the amount of capital, and varying with it, but at the same time liable to rise or fall within certain limits, according to the intellectual qualifications of those who put it in motion.'[18]

By the time J. S. Mill came to write his *Principles*, the hegemony of the Ricardian model was broken. The old ubiquity of Ricardian issues was no longer evident. Writers were again enquiring as to the component parts of the profits of a particular firm. To what extent are they attributable to the size of the capital stock, and to what extent to the particular entrepreneur? By what rules do the various participants in a firm distribute the revenue? In answering these questions in the *Principles*, Mill was far more eclectic than he had been when writing the earlier essay on profits. Certainly Say's influence (perhaps partly via Tooke and Ramsay) and that of Senior are evident.

According to the J. S. Mill of the *Principles*, the gross profits from capital must suffice for three purposes: 'They must afford a sufficient equivalent for abstinence, indemnity for risk, and superintendence. These different compensations may be either paid to the same, or to different persons.'[19]

Abstinence

While Senior has no claim to objective originality in this respect, he is often remembered as the exponent of an abstinence theory of interest. Part of the profits of a firm are needed to 'compensate for the sacrifice of immediate personal gratification'[20] those who forgo present consumption in order to provide a firm with the finance (and resources) for provision of capital. Interest theories are outside the scope of this study; and there is a good secondary literature on the topic.[21]

Indemnity for risk

Schumpeter castigates J. S. Mill for wishing, 'to make risk-bearing an entrepreneurial function alongside of "direction". But this only served to push the car still further on the wrong track.' . . . 'It should be obvious, so soon as we have realized that the entrepreneur's function is distinct from the capitalist's function, that the entrepreneur, when he employs his own capital in an unsuccessful enterprise, loses as a capitalist and not as an entrepreneur.'[22]

If Mill is guilty of this charge, then so too are many of the leading economists who discussed the question between the time of Adam Smith and that of J. S. Mill. Say states that the function of risk-bearing depends on institutional relationships.[23] However, he claims that under contemporary institutional relationships, the entrepreneur was the first capitalist to lose his contribution to the firm's stock. Presumably, other providers of capital would only lend if the person responsible for the success of the venture were prepared to undertake at least the same degree of risk as themselves. If the firm makes a loss, 'he [the entrepreneur] loses, if he has anything to lose: or if he has nothing, those lose who have given him their confidence'.[24] This implies that the entrepreneur undertakes risk-bearing not as one capitalist among many, but as the most vulnerable capitalist.

While both Say and Mill held this institutionalist view, others seem to be much more ready unreservedly to attribute the risk-bearing function to a particular factor of production. Read is quite clear in his Cantillon-type division of functions. The master, not the capitalist, receives a residual and must receive a premium to be encouraged to do so.[25] Most who discussed the bearing of risk considered that those who do bear the risk will need a premium to do so – although few were influenced by the work of Hermann's *Staatswirtschaftsliche Untersuchungen* (1832) or by that of von Thünen who followed his lead. Von Thünen proposes that we distinguish between insurable and uninsurable risks. Uninsurable risks are generally borne by the entrepreneur. Such an entrepreneur will generally risk all his savings in his own firm and (in return for such a gamble) will require some recompense.[26]

Mill's analysis of the risk-taking function is identical to that of Say. While Mill states that the capital of the entrepreneur is normally at greater risk than that of the passive capitalist, Mill is at pains to emphasise that the apportionment of risks varies between firms. It is one of the great themes of Mill's *Principles* that, unlike the laws of production, the laws of distribution are largely dependent on human statute and institution.[27] In his chapters on income distribution, the possibilities of various arrangements of property rights and risk-bearing are explored – as in his interest in various co-operative ventures and profit-sharing schemes. However, he always maintains that to entice persons to undertake great risk, it is necessary to offer them some premium.

It is notable also that in the writings of the classical economists the risk being referred to is always a passive risk. The risky situation is not created by the entrepreneur. Given that the *ex post* profits are not known *ex ante*, some scheme must be agreed upon as to the relative vulnerability of capital contributions. The returns to the maker of decisions is not discussed under the heading of risk, but under the heading of returns to entrepreneurial skill.

Remuneration for superintendence

In *The Wealth of Nations*, Smith was at pains to distinguish the wage cost an owner-manager imputes for his labour services from the margin of profit on interest which accrues to the owner-manager. The former income is related to general wage rates, whereas the latter is regulated by the amount of capital employed in the firm and the rate of return on capital in that employment.

Say emphasises the wage component in the income of the entrepreneur but, in contrast with Smith, emphasises the unique skills of particular entrepreneurs and the premium wage which this enables them to earn. He considers this wage to be regulated by supply and demand. The supply of entrepreneurial talent is limited by lack of capital (a prerequisite to the performance of the entrepreneurial function) or by lack of ability to borrow capital from others. The entrepreneur must also possess the art of superintendence and administration as well as the ability to make calculations of the future and to devise expedients to meet new contingencies.[28] To the extent that individuals possess these qualifications they will be rewarded in business. To the extent that they do not, they will receive low rewards and leave – thus regulating the supply of entrepreneurial talent.

This contribution from Say was accepted by Mill as the quotation above confirms.[29] However, Mill offers a hint that: 'The extra gains which any producer or dealer obtains through superior talents for business, or superior business arrangements' . . . are of a very similar kind to other forms of rent.[30] This hint was further developed by Marshall.

Marshall mentions Senior and Mill, Hermann and von Mangoldt among the economists 'of the last generation' who explored the relationship between rent and profits.[31]

Quasi rent and profits

Various generalisations of the concept of rent paved the way for Marshall's notion of quasi rent. Von Mangoldt defined rent as any surplus over costs[32]; but earlier writers pointed more tentatively to the notion of land rent as a scarcity price (that is, one for which price and the unit cost of production are not of the same money value) or drew analogies between land rents and payments to skilled labour more than sufficient to reimburse training costs.

Credit for the initiation of this development is usually given to Storch. His statement of this generalisation[33] contains all that Mill was ever prepared to concede.

Storch was followed in Britain by Bailey, Senior and Mill. But one 'minor' British writer (Craig) writing before Storch noted that scarcity may have a time dimension and, further, that in certain cases the relevant time dimension is the time taken for producers to increase the capital stock thereby bringing selling price in line with unit cost of production.[34] Such propositions place Craig within striking distance of Marshall on quasi rent.

John Craig's *Elements of Political Science* claims that, because of the constant re-purchasing of circulating capital: 'A common rate of profit does not so readily establish itself over all the employments of fixed, as over those of working capital.'[35] He proceeds to explain that every time money returns from working capital, there arises the opportunity of laying it out in a different speculation if its former placement proved unprofitable. Thus, fixed capital can earn a rate of profit out of line with the norm for a much longer period than can working capital. In this respect fixed capital is like land. But eventually the returns to fixed capital will be constrained by the cost of new capital equipment; and this constraint does not apply to the rent of land.[36]

2. COSTS AND COST FUNCTIONS

During the period under consideration some progress was made in the process of distinguishing the functional relationships between the costs of production incurred by a firm and the scale of the firm, technical progress, input prices and the growth of the economy over time. While some improvement in the formulation of these relationships is discernible compared with *The Wealth of Nations*, much remained to be clarified.

Historical returns

The West–Malthus–Ricardo proposition of historically diminishing returns in agriculture is discussed in most of the standard texts. Most of the English classical economists admitted that such diminishing returns (however defined) could be counter-balanced to some degree by technical progress in agriculture, but thought that this was unlikely. This latter point is prominent in the writing of J. S. Mill and in that of Senior.

However, the tendency of the agricultural sector to diminishing returns can be contrasted with, 'another category (embracing the majority of all things that are bought or sold) in which the obstacle to attainment consists only in the labour and expense requisite to produce the commodity.'[37] Even though these commodities may incorporate some agricultural inputs, their natural prices will tend to be stable over time except to the extent that they will decrease due to technical progress. While these historical issues dominated the discussion of cost functions among the English classical economists, some attention was devoted in analysis of concrete problems and in Mill's *Principles* to the cost functions of the firm.

Cost minimisation

Most of the English writers assumed implicitly that competition and the quest for profits encourage firms to minimise the cost of producing their output. However, English economists of this period saw few implications in this for the mix of inputs a firm would use. The controversy over the possibility of the technical progress of the industrial revolution creating unemployment of labour certainly indicates an awareness of the possibility of the substitution of capital for labour. As early as 1804, Lauderdale states:

> That the profit of stock employed in machinery is paid out of a fund that would otherwise be destined to pay the wages of labour is evident; because if the proprietors of all the capital so employed, would combine to charge a greater sum for the use of the machines than the wages of labour supplanted, they would be instantly set aside, and the same portion of the revenue of the nation again employed in the payment of wages that was so directed before the machines were invented.[38]

This statement forms part of Lauderdale's discussion of the unemployment issue in which he illustrates that a firm will choose that input combination which minimises its costs. But his point that a firm will substitute factors in response to a change in relative factor prices was rarely used in the later extensive discussion of 'the machinery question'.

Ricardo, in his chapter on machinery in the *Principles*,[39] admits that a rise in the wage rate causes factor substitution and consequent unemployment; but J. S. Mill seems to neglect this possibility altogether when discussing this issue.[40]

By far the most modern performance on the issue of factor substitution in the period under consideration is that of von Thünen. The first eighteen chapters of Book One of *Der Isolierte Staat*[41] are devoted to a discussion of alternative factor mixes for a uniform product. Methods of production may alter as one substitutes grain for town-produced goods. The relative profitability of the methods depends on relative input prices which vary as one changes location.

Later, in chapters 13 and 17 of Book Two, Part I, von Thünen approaches the problem of the optimal combination of labour and capital, given that the two are substitutes in production. His solution to the problem is partly obscured by an odd model of capital formation, in which capital production depends solely on the number of man-hour inputs. Looking through this smoke-screen, his solution is reasonably clear.

At the laying out of a new estate the advantage of the capital-producing worker calls for an increase in the number of employed wage-workers up to the point that the increment brought about by the last worker employed is absorbed by the wages which he receives. Likewise it is to the advantage of capital-producing workers to raise the capital investment to that point where no higher revenue is forthcoming. But because one worker can be replaced by capital and conversely one unit of capital can be replaced by more workers, then at the margin at which capital and labour are to be used beneficially the cost of the work through human effort and the cost of work through capital must be at equilibrium, . . .[42]

Fixed costs and opportunity cost

Writers in the period under consideration were edging their way towards the later concepts of opportunity cost and of fixed cost. It was shown above[43] that Storch, Senior, Mill, and von Mangoldt, generalised the concept of rent and drew an analogy between rent and profit. J. S. Mill aids our understanding of rent by referring to rent as a scarcity price. A scarcity price is a price paid so as to lure a scarce resource from its highest-paid alternative.[44] It can be seen that Mill's notion of a scarcity price is very close to the modern notion of opportunity cost. However, Mill denies that land rent is a scarcity price in the case where there is sufficient land to maintain a rentless margin.[45]

The idea that a firm may have fixed costs which do not influence particular policy decisions may be interpreted as an application of the principle of opportunity cost. The possibility may also be seen with the aid of elementary calculus. A constant term in a function will not enter the first derivative of the function. For this reason, Cournot notes in 1838 that if their total costs do not vary with output, then monopolists will charge the same price as if they produced without cost.[46]

The idea of the irrelevance of fixed costs is found in the work of Cournot's contemporaries among the works of those German and English writers who discussed concrete examples of business policy.

In 1826, von Thünen's concern with the determinants of business decisions caused him only to consider as costs those opportunities forgone as the result of a particular decision. For example, horses used for fieldwork in the summer may be used for the transportation of grain at low cost in the winter. The only additions to cost occasioned by such transportation are the shoeing, the wear and tear on the wagon, and the greater quantity of feed consumed by the horses.[47] Lardner's book on *Railway Economy* recommends a similar attitude to sunk costs.[48]

Senior's *Letters on the Factory Act* (1837) outlines the likely effects on cotton manufacturing of legislation restricting working hours. If cotton prices were to remain constant and working hours were reduced by one hour per day, Senior reasons, ' . . . *net* profit would be destroyed – if they were reduced by an hour and a half, even *gross* profit would be destroyed. The circulating capital would be replaced, but there would be no fund to compensate the progressive deterioration of the fixed capital.'[49]

In his *Report on the Unemployed Hand-Loom Weavers*, Senior notes that a weaver will keep working so long as the price is sufficient to cover the value of new material and the workman's wages;[50] and in his 1850–1 lectures he makes a similar point by means of a numerical example of an investment project. 'It repays the labour, but not the abstinence of its producer. And yet even on these terms, if he can get no better, he must continue to produce; for his buildings and machinery are valueless for any other purpose.'[51]

Torrens' *On Wages and Combination* uses similar reasoning to argue that, in times of excess capacity, French manufacturers may cut their prices of goods exported to England so long as they cover the costs of their floating capital.[52]

Economies and diseconomies of scale

Stigler alerts us to J. S. Mill's discussion of the economies of the firm in two articles. Stigler points out that in Book I, chapter 9 of Mill's *Principles*, 'is the first systematic discussion of the economies of scale of the firm to be found in a general economic treatise'.[53]

Adam Smith's discussion of the division of labour had suggested a source of economies of scale; and meditations on *The Wealth of Nations* provided a fruitful springboard for the writers before Mill.[54] According to Mill, division of labour is a major source of economies for the reasons given by Adam Smith. But whether Mill is referring to average cost or marginal cost as a negative function of scale is unclear. He makes statements of the following ambiguous form: 'As a general rule, the expenses of a business do not increase by any means proportionally with the quantity of business.'[55]

Mill quotes at length from Babbage's study of the *Causes and Consequences of Large Factories*. Babbage had noted that a firm will benefit by having a scale sufficient to employ specialists at their specialty on a full-time basis. It will raise costs to employ specialists to spend part of their time on tasks for which they are comparatively less well suited.[56]

Deriving from Rae, Mill reports another source of scale economies. If each labourer uses various specialised machines in rotation, the return on the instruments will be postponed. By allotting each labourer to one machine (or set of tools) the labourer can exhaust the instrument more rapidly, thus bringing its yield forward in time with a consequent higher rate of return.[57]

Babbage gives three sources of scale economies which Mill chooses not to reproduce.[58]

1. That a larger firm may generate sufficient by-products that, rather than adding to waste, their further processing for sale becomes possible.

2. A large (established) firm has a name which potential customers will trust; and, besides, its financial power will cause its customers to hesitate before suing it for the sale of a faulty product.

3. A large manufacturer with considerable capital, can afford, says Babbage quoting with approval the report of a committee of the House of Commons, 'to try the experiments which are requisite, and incur the risks, and even losses, which almost always occur, in inventing and perfecting new articles of manufacture, or in carrying to a state of greater perfection articles already established.'[59]

In his *Essays on Some Unsettled Questions*, Mill had claimed that, 'the trouble of managing a business is not proportionally increased by an increase of the magnitude of the business.'[60] Indeed, at one point in the *Principles* Mill implies that increased scale enables economies of management to be reaped. The reason given is that in small firms: 'The principal in the concern is either wasting, in the routine of a business, qualities suitable for the direction of it, or he is only fit for the former, and then the latter will be ill done.'[61]

But Mill also says that the magnitude of such savings is often exaggerated, since many small-scale producers compensate for their administrative inefficiency by accepting a low return so that they can continue to be their own master.[62] Moreover, managerial diseconomies are even a possibility, owing to the 'more watchful attention, and greater regard to minor gains and losses, usually found in small establishments.'[63]

Cournot's discussion of scale economies when compared with that of Mill's *Principles* is, characteristically, both less specific and more precise. Cournot clearly places *marginal* cost as a function of output. Marginal cost may be an increasing (in the case of agricultural lands, mines and quarries), decreasing, or constant function of the output of the firm.

For what are properly called *manufactured articles*, it is generally the case that the cost becomes proportionally less as production increases, or, in other words, when D increases $\phi'(D)$ [marginal cost] is a decreasing function. This comes from better organization of the work, from discounts on the price of raw materials for large purchases, and finally from the reduction of what is known to producers as *general expense*.[64]

It is notable that Cournot mentions pecuniary economies and diseconomies which are largely neglected by Mill. When discussing the cost advantages of large-scale compared with small-scale farming, Mill mentions 'the greater cheapness of buying things in large quantities'; but he estimates that this (among the other advantages of large-scale farming), 'does not seem that they ought to count for very much.'[65]

Mill was well aware of the structural implications of his analysis of economies of scale. He proposes an 'unfailing test' by which one can ascertain at which scale average costs are minimised. 'Wherever there are large and small establishments in the same business, that one of the two which in existing circumstances carries on the production at greatest advantage will be able to undersell the other.'[66] Mill admits in his discussion of competition that, particularly in retailing trades, such ability to undersell may not be utilised; but, generally, the firm with lower unit costs will undercut the price of the firm without access to economies because of its sub-optimal or super-optimal scale.

Stigler has undertaken an empirical study inspired by Mill's 'unfailing test'.[67] Stigler proposes that the range of optimal firm sizes within each industry may be determined by comparing the percentage of the industry's assets in each asset class in various years. Those asset classes in which the share of the industry's assets are stable or increasing are optimal. The various factors influencing optimal size might be tested by means of multi-variable regression techniques.

3. VALUE AND EQUILIBRIUM

The English classical economists' analysis of the causes of value largely consists in variations on a theme by Adam Smith. That theme is the analysis of value within the context of resource movements among competing products. Equilibrium exists when the quantity being produced equals the effectual demand, bringing the market (observed) price into line with the natural price. Impediments to the attainment of equilibrium are analysed under the heading of monopoly.

While the later English classical economists varied this theme, the theme remains unmistakeable even though the elaborations are sometimes substantial. Many words were expended on the problem of the relationship between the supply and demand approach and the cost of production approach; but this debate reveals differences in verbal emphasis rather than differences in analysis. In fact, if one reads the writings on value by the British economists from Smith to Cairnes for their analyses (that is, the form of their functional relationships), rather than for the number of times that they mention 'demand' compared with the number of times that they mention 'cost', then the extent of their agreement is remarkable. While the supply and demand framework is used to discuss changes in market price, natural price analysis is usually divided into three categories.

Mill presents these categories as:

I. Commodities in which the obstacle to attainment consists only in the labour and expense requisite to produce the commodity;

II. Commodities for which increased production necessitates a greater cost; and

III. Commodities naturally or artificially limited in supply.[68]

Ricardo, while confining detailed attention to cases I and II, mentions each of these three categories in his *Principles*. However, it was probably Bailey who first presented the classification in this systematic way.[69]

Before proceeding to examine each of these three categories and the controversy over the demand and supply framework, a few points should be made by way of clarification.

The first is that the criteria of classification are restricted to the form of the cost functions and the barriers to entry. They do not include the number of producers. This is not to say that the number of producers is irrelevant to the consideration of value. Most writers were agreed that the fewer the competitors, the more likely is it that they will agree to limit production. The use of the supply and demand framework is often said to be contingent upon 'a plurality both of competing dealers and competing customers',[70] or even upon 'the whole supply [being] in the hands of a very large number of small holders, and the demand [being] caused by the wants of another set of persons each of whom requires only the same very small quantity.'[71]

But the reasons given for such assumptions are variously that large numbers militate against restrictive agreements, that large numbers lessen the possibility of quirky results caused by discontinuities in the demand or supply functions,[72] or, merely, as in the case of Babbage, that 'experience' indicates that price is higher with a few sellers when compared with very many.[73]

Secondly, while the words 'market' and 'commodity' are freely used, they are not defined; and the conceptual problems surrounding their use are rarely raised. Cairnes questions Adam Smith's use of the word 'market', when the latter uses it in the context of supply and demand determining market price.

It is not quite clear from the passage in what sense he uses the word 'market', whether as a sort of abstract term to comprise all places where things are bought and sold, or as signifying some one particular or given place of this kind. I am, for my part, disposed to understand him in the latter sense; indeed the former would hardly have satisfied the requirements of the problem he had to consider . . .[74]

Cairnes proceeds to claim that, in the latter sense, Smith's statement regarding the proportion of supply and demand is 'untrue', because overseas markets can cause changes in the prices ruling in British markets even though neither local demand nor local supply alters. Cairnes' scruples in this matter are rare, if not unique, among the British classical economists.

Competition among markets was ignored in much the same way as was product differentiation within the market. While product differentiation was acknowledged in industry studies or in inductive work, it was largely ignored in the treatises. Mill places the influence of vulgar finery on price differentials between retail establishments in the same sentence as the influence of indolence, and claims that these influences are largely absent from competitive markets.[75] Senior's report on the hand-loom weavers acknowledges that better quality cloth fetches higher prices[76] (hardly a surprising proposition); and Babbage mentions the need for a firm to vary price and quality in order to suit the tastes and finances of its customers.[77]

Thirdly, as Mill notes, economists, particularly English economists prior to the publication of Mill's *Principles*, stressed the effects of competition and ignored those of custom. 'This is partly intelligible, if we consider that only through the principle of competition has political economy any pretension to the character of a science.'[78] That is, given the hypothesis of competition, the economist is able to reason towards propositions of scientific precision; but the final propositions are themselves hypothetical. In making this oft-quoted observation, Mill was not contrasting competition with monopoly; but was contrasting a competitive situation with one in which the psychology of the market participants produces non-maximising behaviour.

> I am not speaking of monopolies, either natural or artificial, or of any interferences of authority with the liberty of production or exchange. Such disturbing causes have always been allowed for by political economists. I speak of cases in which there is nothing to restrain competition; no hindrance to it either in the nature of the case or in artificial obstacles; yet in which the result is not determined by competition, but by custom or usage; competition either not taking place at all, or producing its effect in quite a different manner from that which is ordinarily assumed to be natural to it.[79]

The dominance of custom over competition is most often met in the retail trades where prices are often found exceeding the minimal average cost at which production is possible. Such situations exist because of the non-maximising behaviour of buyers (deriving from ignorance, laziness or conceit) and of sellers. Large retail margins encourage the entry of new firms thereby reducing profit per trader; but they do not encourage reduction of prices. Competition implies a strong valuation of monetary gains over those of ease or pleasure. 'An enterprising competitor, with sufficient capital, might force down the charges, and make his fortune during the process; but there are no enterprising competitors; those who have capital prefer to leave it where it is, or to make less profit by it in a more quiet way.'[80]

The framework of supply and demand

Until recently it was fashionable to praise Say, Malthus, and Lauderdale for maintaining that demand influences value in the face of the assertion by Ricardo and the Ricardians to the contrary. Yet it is not clear to what extent the participants in this debate differed from each other.

Say seems mainly to be concerned with the determinants of market price (over which no one denied the influence of demand), but also considers the determinants of the Smithian natural price. As far as the latter is concerned, Say acknowledges that, 'there are many articles that would not rise in price in consequence of the competition [between buyers], which some people affect to be allarmed at . . .'.[81] This indicates that Say considers demand only to influence long-run price for those commodities whose supply is limited by monopoly or for those commodities which can only be produced with increasing cost.[82]

Lauderdale's dogmatic insistence on the generality of the supply and demand framework appears to contribute little; but Malthus, for all his confusion of exposition, seems to have more to offer. In particular, Malthus insists that the demand and supply framework is applicable to the determination of natural price. This is so because changes in cost influence price via their influence on the profitability of production and, thereby, on the quantity supplied.[83]

There has been some debate as to whether Ricardo accepted this point or not. For the goods which Bailey classified as produced under conditions of equal competition, Ricardo emphasised that 'the real and ultimate regulator of the relative value of any two commodities, is the cost of their production.'[84]

In making this assertion, Ricardo was merely upholding the Smithian model against the criticism of Say. The only apparent difference on this issue between Ricardo and Smith is that Ricardo eliminates rent from the costs which determine the natural price. In his notes on Malthus'

Principles[85], Ricardo seems to admit that cost only regulates price via its influence on supply, as he does in a letter to Say: 'You say demand and supply regulates the price of bread; that is true, but what regulates supply? The cost of production, – the quantity of utility imparted to bread by industry.'[86]

If this is as far as we can go in defending Ricardo against the charge that he failed to appreciate the insights of Malthus, J. S. Mill aids in defending the Ricardians against a similar charge. In a remarkably pungent piece of abuse published in 1825, the young Mill, still under predominant Ricardian influence, wrote, 'an exceptionally clear exposition of what the Ricardian theory of value really asserted.'[87] Mill is attacking a reviewer of the 'new' (Ricardian) school of political economy.

We have already remarked, that the second of the three propositions which the Reviewer puts into the mouth of the new school, 'that demand and supply have no influence on prices and values except in cases of monopoly, or for short periods of time', never was maintained by them at all. They not only allow that demand and supply have *some* influence on value, but they assert that nothing else has any influence whatever, except in as far as it may be calculated to affect either the demand or the supply. When they say that cost of production regulates value, it is only because cost of production is that which regulates supply. If there be two commodities, produced by equal cost, what is the reason that they exchange for one another? The reason is, because if one of the two bore a higher value than the other, when the cost of production is the same, the profits of the two producers would be unequal, and it would be the interest of one of them to withdraw a portion of his capital from his business and transfer it to the other; thus *increasing the supply* of the dearer commodity, diminishing that of the cheaper, until the equality of values is restored: and restored, as the reader will observe, not in contradiction to the principle of demand and supply, but in consequence of it.[88]

John Mill proceeds to quote from his father's *Elements*, 2nd ed., p. 88, that the ultimate cause of value is cost, but that the immediate cause is demand and supply, to confirm his defence of the new school.

Apart from an odd comment in his private notes on Senior's *Political Economy*[89], all of J. S. Mill's later output is consistent with the above passage. It is possible to quote from Scrope,[90] Longfield,[91] and

Ramsay,[92] to show that they also accepted Malthus' position. Senior clearly did also and somewhat laboured his view that Ricardo did not.[93]

Equality or ratio?

J. S. Mill convinced British economists that equilibrium in a market requires the equality of the quantity of the good demanded with that of the quantity supplied. This precision contrasts with earlier vague statements concerning the ratio of demand to supply.

Mill was not the first to claim that the quantity demanded and the quantity supplied are functions of price. Sir James Steuart had made that claim as early as 1767.[94] However, Mill did emphasise to economists north of the channel that equilibrium entails not a ratio of demand to supply but equality of quantities. At prices above equilibrium, the quantity demanded will be less than the quantity supplied whereas at prices below equilibrium, the quantity supplied will be less than the quantity demanded. As price tends towards equilibrium the quantity supplied tends towards the quantity demanded.[95]

Prior to Mill, Thomas Cooper's *Lectures on the Elements of Political Economy* had claimed that when the quantity demanded equals the quantity supplied, price will be stationary; when quantity demanded is greater than quantity supplied, price will rise; and when quantity demanded is less than quantity supplied, price will fall.[96] Cournot proposed that the quantity demanded and the quantity supplied are functions of price and that the equilibrium condition is that these two quantities be equal.[97]

These precursors compel us to exercise caution in attributing great objective originality to the formulation in Mill's *Principles*: but certainly the clarity of Mill's explanation far exceeds that of his predecessors, and this clarity facilitated the acceptance of his formulation.

Joint products

Mill's solution to the problem of the pricing of joint products does seem to be objectively original. Adam Smith's proposition that natural price equals unit cost (plus allowance for profit at the going rate) is inapplicable to products whose costs of production are shared. 'It sometimes happens that two different commodities have what may be termed a joint cost of production. They are both products of the same operation, or set of operations, and the outlay is incurred for the sake of both together, not part for one and part for the other.'[98]

A particularly advanced book-keeping manual of the late eighteenth century advised merchants, in the case of such joint products, to enquire into the success of the whole operation.

When we import a cargo of different kinds of goods which could not well be separated, such as iron and deals; of which the one is necessary for ballast, and the other to complete the lading, it is proper to join them in one accompt, and compute the profit or loss on the whole together. Here we open an accompt of goods from Gottenburgh, and distinguish the iron and deals in inner columns, which is better than to open one accompt for iron, and another for deals. Perhaps there might be gain on the one and loss on the other; but as we were obliged to import both together, it is the success of the whole that we should inquire into.[99]

Such joint production means that cost of production does not regulate the value of each, only their joint value. 'Since cost of production here fails us, we must revert to a law of value anterior to cost of production, and more fundamental, the law of demand and supply.'[100] So the amount of both will be produced up to the point where excess profits from the process are eliminated. The value of each product will then depend upon demand and supply.

Case I: Commodities in which the obstacle to attainment consists only in the labour and expense requisite to produce the commodity
The value of Case I commodities occupies a crucial position in the Ricardian model; and, as was argued in chapter 2, constant costs is the assumption implicit in the value and equilibrium analysis in *The Wealth of Nations*.[101]

In the Ricardian model it is assumed that constant costs exist in the manufacturing sector.[102] Such an assumption entails regarding Case III (monopoly) commodities as 'exceptional'. In doing this, Ricardo has a strong supporter in J. S. Mill. Mill quotes a 'happy illustration' by De Quincey in which the latter guesses that in ninety-nine cases out of a hundred, the prices of goods in a randomly-chosen shop will be determined by their cost of production.[103]

The price to which Mill and Ricardo are referring is the Smithian 'natural price' and not the price to be observed at a particular moment in time in a particular market. Mill continues the tradition of *The Wealth of Nations* in saying that an average of market values over a 'sufficient' number of years will serve as an estimate of natural value.[104] Cairnes corrects this statement (which, if not a tautology, is a mistake), on the grounds that, 'the commodity may exist under conditions which do not supply any controlling principle to its fluctuations, and consequently do not develop any tendency in these to revolve around a central point.'[105]

It was mentioned previously[106], that Ricardo so constructed his model that rent is excluded from the elements of natural price. This move by Ricardo was one of the dimensions to the debate between Ricardo and Malthus as to the causes of value. However, outside the Ricardian model of secular income distribution, rent clearly does enter into costs, if by rent one means the payment for land necessary to attract it from its best alternative use.

No one can deny that rent sometimes enters into cost of production. If I buy or rent a piece of ground, and build a cloth manufactory on it, the ground-rent forms legitimately a part of my expenses of production, which must be repaid by the product. And since all factories are built on ground, and most of them in places where ground is particularly valuable, the rent paid for it must, on the average, be compensated in the values of all things made in factories.[107]

Is it possible to be more precise as to what these writers mean when they refer to constant costs? It seems that Ricardo considers price to be regulated by the marginal producer in manufacturing as well as in agriculture; but in manufacturing, costs are constant between producers and so all producers are on the margin of profitability.[108] Unlike J. S. Mill, Ricardo was not concerned with the amount of output produced by each firm – although not even Mill was clear as to how output is increased if the market price rises. Under what conditions will existing firms expand their production? Under what conditions will the increased output be provided by new firms entering the industry? These questions as to the relationship between the supply functions of firms and the supply functions of the industry were tackled by Cournot,[109] but not by any of the British economists in the period under consideration.

Senior suggests that manufacturing is subject to increasing returns which offset the historical tendency for the prices of raw materials to rise. Such increasing returns may be attributed to the use of, 'better instruments and a greater division of labour'.[110] However, such increasing returns are not *merely* downward displacements of cost functions due to technical progress, because the shape of the respective cost functions in manufacturing compared with agriculture is the reason given as to why an increase in taxation on manufactured products will cause an increase in price greater than that of the tax increase per unit, while an increase in taxation on agricultural products will cause an increase in price less than that of the increase in unit tax.[111]

While it is difficult to know what Senior meant in saying that manufacturing is subject to increasing returns, the model generally used for the value and equilibrium of manufactured commodities was that of constant costs. The precursor of this model in *The Wealth of Nations* was used in those circumstances in which no barriers to the free movement of resources existed. This assumption continues with the economists under consideration.

Ricardo refers to Case I commodities as those, 'on the production of which competition operates without constraint.'[112] This is contrasted with monopolistic restrictions on the free flow of resources; but the phrase 'competition without constraint' is not otherwise defined. Neither is this phrase explained any further by Bailey who uses it to characterise one of his three categories of price determination. Senior makes matters more explicit. He talks of 'equal competition', by which he means conditions under which any person contemplating production can set up with the same costs as the established producers.[113] This means that the only obstacle to supply is the unit cost of the established natural price – implying the 'universal accessibility' of all factors to all producers,[114] or 'equal advantages' between all producers and potential producers.[115]

The worth of this careful classification and analysis by Senior was neglected for much of the nineteenth century – until Richard D. Ely jolted the memories of those who attended the twelfth annual meeting of the American Economic Association.[116] In more recent years, Marion Bowley has performed the role of Senior's standard-bearer.[117] But neither of these notable writers has sufficiently emphasised the continuing tradition of analysis beginning in *The Wealth of Nations*, and incorporated in all British value theory up to 1836, in which year Senior gave the analysis form, and gave the assumptions precision.

Case II: Commodities for which increased production necessitates a greater cost
The idea that increasing costs are associated with expanding agricultural production was not new in 1815 (the idea is quite clear in Sir James Steuart's *Political Oeconomy*[118]); but the debate over corn prices occasioned by the end of the Napoleonic wars certainly rekindled attention in the idea. Increased production of 'corn' could be got either

by the use of poorer, previously uncultivated, land (the extensive margin), or by the addition of extra units of labour and capital to the existing area of cultivation (the intensive margin). Similar arguments were applied to the extractive industries.

In such circumstances, price will equal the cost of production to the producer who is only marginally profitable. In his attempt to achieve a consistent taxonomy of value theory, Bailey attributed the gains of the intra-marginal producers to a monopoly: 'the possessor of the cheaper means of producing it [such a commodity] has evidently a monopoly to a certain extent . . .'. 'The same causes will be in operation [as with monopoly], but instead of the value of the article having no assignable boundary, it will be limited by the watchful competition, which is ever ready to act upon it the moment it has exceeded a particular point.'[119]

In Bailey's classification, Case II becomes a type of monopoly; but it is not classified as a monopoly because,

(i) the price is limited by those extra factors which are on the margin of entry; and
(ii) the marginal producers are making no excess profit.

Senior follows Bailey, but classifies Case II as one of his four species of monopoly, with the qualification that it is a 'qualified monopoly' or 'unequal competition'.[120] Senior's analysis of price determination in this case is the same as that of Ricardo with the exception that the position of Senior's margin is determined by the extent of demand, which, in the Ricardian case, is determined by the extent of the supply of labour and capital.

Since Senior's classificatory criterion for monopoly is the imperfect accessibility of all factors to all producers (or unequal advantages) it is only natural that, given no application of the principle of opportunity cost, the intra-marginal gains in agriculture should be called monopoly gains.

J. S. Mill refuses this classification of monopoly, but calls these intra-marginal gains 'rents'. His reason for so doing is that the price is governed by cost.[121] He reserves the word 'monopoly' for circumstances in which the supply either is absolutely unable to be increased, or in which the supply is 'artificially' limited as a result of discretion over price by the producer. Unless all land (as on an isolated island) is fully used, rent payments are not determined by an unalterable or a discretionary restriction of production, but by the marginal cost of production.[122]

Mill's taxonomy is hardly very neat. Land which is better than a specified quality is absolutely limited in quantity and attracts a payment according to its relative scarcity for the same reasons and to the same extent as 'those wines which can be grown only in peculiar circumstances of soil, climate and exposure'.[123] One may, for reasons of public policy, wish to distinguish such prices determined by natural scarcity from those which result from a deliberate interference with the flow of resources. The latter resource allocation 'problem' might be solved by government policy, whereas the former cannot. But this is not Mill's reason for refusing to classify land rent as a monopoly return.

One may argue that there is an analytical distinction between intra-marginal rents to agriculture and other forms of monopoly gains with the aid of Senior's notion of inequality of advantage. In the case of intra-marginal land rents, there is likely to be a fine gradation of rents, because the array of degrees of inequalities of access is likely to be fairly continuous. At least, it is continuous under the assumptions of the Ricardian model, which envisages certain producers cultivating rentless land at the margin.

These land rents may be contrasted with other cases of monopoly gains where the array of degrees of inequality of advantage may be quite discontinuous. In the extreme case of a government grant to the sole trade in a particular commodity (like the spice trade of the Dutch East Indies which earlier tracts had found such a convenient example), the differential of advantage can be quite extreme. It is this degree of equality of advantage which Senior chose to emphasise.

Case III: Commodities naturally or artificially limited in supply
In our survey of the value and equilibrium analysis we have seen that, in terms of analysis, the differences between the various classical economists are not great. However, the classical economists differed markedly in their empirical judgments as to the importance of monopolistic restrictions.

It was noted above that Ricardo, while mentioning the presence of monopolistic restrictions, chose to base his model on the proposition that the prices of manufactured goods are governed by the principle of competition without constraint.

It is this proposition which constitutes one of the chief grounds for the attack on Ricardo by Bailey.[124] Bailey devotes his final five pages to the attack of such, 'false simplification in matters of fact'. Both Senior[125] and Tooke[126] support the charge.

Bailey and Senior seem to adopt this position for two reasons.

(1) They both desire analytical neatness. Both are concerned, one might say that they are concerned above all, with precision of expression and completeness of classification. Bailey and Senior both claim that the prices of most products reflect a monopoly element in that they contain agricultural products or minerals among their raw materials. Ricardo's model ignores such problems.

(2) Both Bailey and Senior are concerned (and this is explicit in their methodologies), to formulate generalisations which broadly fit the facts. Both emphasise the distortion of reality inherent in reliance upon the constant cost case.

Instead of scarcity, of, in other words, monopoly, or protection from competition, being an unimportant source of value, and the com-modities which owe their value to it forming a very small part of the mass of commodities daily exchanged in the market, we have seen that it is a most extensive source of value, and that the value of many of the most important articles of interchange must be referred to this as its origin.[127]

In fact, if one reads Bailey's book, one sees nothing of the sort. No empirical information is given. We are merely offered Bailey's opinion. But his opinion is that the empirical evidence is overwhelming.

But what of the *analysis* of Case III?

The analysis of monopoly's as 'a limitation of the free flow of resources permitting a differential between market price and natural price to persist',[128] was maintained by all of the classical writers, with variations. J. S. Mill is representative of this on-going stream. However, it is Senior who stands out for his careful definition and clarification.

The references to monopoly in Ricardo's *Principles* faithfully follow the path established in *The Wealth of Nations*. An exception to this faithfulness is Ricardo's reference to seasonal shortages of corn as a monopoly. Mill, following Ricardo, mentions such shortages as an example of a price determined by supply and demand and not by simple cost of production. But Mill refuses to call it a monopoly.[129] Ricardo prefers to say that a monopoly has a time dimension. The extent to which producers enjoy a monopoly depends not only on the extent to which resource flows are restricted, but also depends on the time taken to release such impediments.

'The corn and raw produce of a country may, indeed, for a time sell at a monopoly price; but they can do so permanently only when no more capital can be profitably employed on the lands, and when, therefore, their produce cannot be increased.'[130]

This emphasis on (belief in?) the inability of monopolistic restrictions to persist, while not an explicit theme in the writings of Ricardo, was maintained by certain other British economists of this period.

McCulloch's ambivalence towards the activity of trade unions sprang from a conflict between his sympathy for their aims and a belief that such combinations were, in the end, powerless in the face of market forces.[131] Cairnes is more outspoken. In his chapter on trade unions, he argues that unions cannot raise the rate of wages for any period of time; and, similarly, that Adam Smith's claim that employers conspire successfully to depress wages is wrong – such attempts are futile.[132]

On the issue of the monopoly power of unions, Torrens' essay is the most careful. He attempts to outline those few circumstances in which such power might be effective in securing a rise in wage rates.[133]

In contrast with the work of Cournot, the English classical economists (even those such as Bailey and Senior who stress the ubiquity of monopolistic restrictions of the free flow of resources), utilise the value and equilibrium framework of *The Wealth of Nations*, which suggests that a monopolistic restriction is a situation of disequilibrium. Disagreements arise as to the likely permanency of such a disequilibrium.

Bailey's discussion of Case III suffers from a lack of clear definitions: it lacks the type of clarity which gives Senior's work such precision. However, Bailey does have some interesting remarks on the differences between a single-firm and a multi-firm monopoly. A single-firm monopoly can restrict output; but a multi-firm monopoly will find such a line of policy to be impracticable: ' . . . for although it might be to the advantage of the whole body if the quantity of the monopolized article were proportionately reduced to each holder, yet as, by the supposition, there is no combination of interest, every individual finds it beneficial to dispose of all that he possesses. To destroy any part of it, would be to injure himself for the benefit of his brother monopolists.'[134] So each firm will produce every unit of output for which the rate of profit equals or exceeds normal.

Following the publication of *The Wealth of Nations*, the extent of a monopoly had been regarded as a matter of degree – depending on the extent to which barriers impeded the free movement of resources. Senior's classification of monopoly types is based on the degree to which such barriers exist. In particular, the classification is based on the relationship between the cost functions of established firms compared with the cost functions of potential entrants to the industry.

Senior shows that the monopolistic impediments of the English classical economists are based on the absolute cost advantages of established firms. Further, he classifies the various forms this impediment may take, and the corresponding effects this is likely to have on price. Senior has a four-fold classification in his *Principles*, one class of which was discussed above under Case II.[135]

(1) Senior's first case is: 'Where the monopolist has not the exclusive facilities [possibly due to a patent] as a producer, and can increase with undiminished, or even increased facility, the amount of his produce.'[136] In this case, the price charged will be constrained by the (minimum efficient scale?) production costs of rival producers. The price set may be less than such average costs because, by charging a lower price, the monopolist will expand sales and possibly gain access to economies of scale.

(2) 'Where price is checked neither by the hopes nor by the fears of the producer, where no competition is dreaded and no increased supply can be effected.'[137] An example is a particular type of wine. Price cannot be below unit production cost but will not be constrained by an attempt to gain access to scale economies as the amount of land available to produce the wine is strictly limited. The only constraint on price will be the ability and the willingness of consumers to pay.

(3) Type three embraces 'those cases in which the monopolist is the only producer, but, by the application of additional labour and abstinence, can indefinitely increase his production'.[138] Again, the possibility of gaining access to scale economies may limit the price charged. Price will probably exceed unit production costs and will be constrained by the ability and willingness of consumers to pay.

Thornton's attack

William Thornton's volume, *On Labour*,[139] and J. S. Mill's response in the *Fortnightly Review*,[140] have become classics in the history of economics. They are famous principally for Thornton's attack on the doctrine of the wages fund and for Mill's subsequent capitulation, from which many date the downfall of the English classical system.

However, our attention will be directed towards Thornton's attack on Mill's formulation of the proposition that price is in equilibrium when the quantity demanded equals the quantity supplied. Thornton gives examples of discontinuous functions for which equilibrium will exist when Mill's condition of equality is not satisfied; and examples of such functions for which Mill's condition, while necessary for equilibrium, is not sufficient to yield a unique solution.[141]

However, Thornton's criticism is more probing than a mere catalogue of awkward cases. Thornton reminds his readers that the theory of supply and demand rests on the assumption, 'that the goods supplied or offered for sale are so offered unreservedly, the owner or owners being content to let them go for what they will fetch.'[142] But this condition is almost never met. 'It rarely happens that they [the buyers] are prepared to take more than a very small portion of the entire stock. Ninety-nine times out of a hundred his supply of goods is immensely greater than the quantity immediately demanded at the price at which he offers them. But does he lower his terms? Not at all. He has reserved his price.'[143]

In his reply, Mill concedes that Thornton is right in pointing to exceptional cases. These do not invalidate the law, but merely help us in defining the limits to the applicability of the law.

These concessions by Mill fail to meet the nub of Thornton's very real objection. His objection is that the applicability of the law is almost nil as every sale is a unique contract between a buyer and a seller.

Once goods are taken to market, the producer will sell them providing the price covers marginal selling costs. But clearly price usually exceeds this lower limit. In fact, the dealer nominates a set-up price. 'His object is to get in exchange for his whole stock the largest aggregate price which he can get within the period during which it will suit him to keep part of his stock unsold.'[144]

The dealer does not ask the highest price which he thinks his customers would consent to pay rather than go without the goods because he fears being undersold by a rival producing for the same market. He cannot charge a higher price than his rival – except to noncompetitive buyers. If a firm has a competitor it will need to content itself with the highest price at which it will not be undersold. 'All dealers, while considering at what price they shall offer their goods, consider each for himself the actual state and future prospects of the market.'[145] The lowest price so chosen becomes the market price. But it is rare that any of these estimates will be ruinously low, because of the tacit understanding between traders as to the sort of price needed to sell the amounts they wish to sell in this planning period.

Thornton's propositions as to the determinants of market price were to prove influential. Mill's *Principles* had presented the condition for equilibrium in market price, but it had not analysed the determinants of the quantity supplied in the market period nor the behaviour by which market price is settled.

Thornton suggests that any such analysis must take into account that supply decisions will be based on uncertain estimates of future demand conditions. He offers little comfort for the theorist. 'There is no regularity about competition – competition is not regulated at all. If it can properly be said to depend on anything, it depends partly on individual necessity, partly on individual discretion; and as for the first of these there is proverbially, and for the other manifestly, no law, so likewise is there no law of competition.'[146]

The suggestions by Thornton were later to be used by Marshall in his theory of market price. The great importance of Thornton's value analysis consisted in directing attention to the determinants of market price – the prices to be observed in markets. It is to the theory of market prices and of movements in market prices that we must go if we are to test price theory against the standard of observations.

4 Alfred Marshall

This chapter covers the period from 1870 until the death of Marshall while including some discussion of the work of Cournot, Dupuit and Ellet which was postponed from chapter 3. Once again, the chapter will be based upon Schumpeter's chosen classical statement for the period.

> First and last, Marshall was, and felt himself to be, the great *English* economist of the period. But this does not alter the fact that Marshall's great work [the *Principles*] is the classic achievement of the period, that is, the work that embodies, more perfectly than any other, the classical situation that emerged around 1900.[1]

Few would dispute Marshall's claim to be the classic writer of the period – particularly if the reference for the choice is the theory of the firm. However, Marshall's work is peculiarly elusive for the historian of ideas. Even more than the mature Mill, his sources of stimulation are so varied and his product such a complex tapestry that no single model structure dominates. It is impossible to nail Marshall with a single paradigm.[2]

Marshall was fond of emphasising his debt to the English classical school as well as to the German historical school, von Thünen and Cournot. At the beginning of this chapter, it is important to outline the relationship between Marshall and Cournot; for it is the use of the method of Cournot which provides the boundary of demarcation between the writers of the English classical school and the giants of the period now being discussed: Walras and Marshall.

1. THE INFLUENCE OF COURNOT

Both Marshall[3] and Walras[4] have publicly acknowledged their respective debts to the work of Cournot. Cournot's application of the differential calculus to the function expressing the quantity of a product demanded as depending on its price so as to derive the conditions under

70

which a firm will maximise its statically conceived profits was important both for the work of Marshall and for that of Walras.

There is no direct evidence pointing to Cournot's possible influence either on Dupuit or on Lardner. Indeed, it is likely that Dupuit did not read Cournot's principal work on economic theory, the *Researches*. Dupuit's work on public utilities which spawned his theory of price discrimination was more immediately practical in its aim than that of Cournot; and René notes that the form of Dupuit's analysis is not strikingly similar to that of Cournot.[5]

On the question of Lardner's debt (either to Dupuit or to Cournot) we have more cause to be cautious. Lardner's manual of *Railway Economy* was read by Jevons before the latter wrote his *Theory*;[6] and the book is praised by Marshall.[7] The book would deserve a prominent place in the present study whether or not its diagram of static profit-maximisation for a monopolist was subjectively original. Hicks considers that 'it is definitely possible' for Lardner to have borrowed from Cournot. 'For at the time Lardner wrote his book (1850) he was living in Paris, and so was Cournot; and there was at least this link between them, that in 1835, three years before he wrote the *Recherches*, Cournot had translated a book on Mechanics by Lardner into French.'[8]

As to the possibility of Lardner's debt to Dupuit, we may entertain a strong presumption. On page 197 of *Railway Economy*, Lardner recommends a series of articles on railway costs which appeared in the *Annales des Ponts et Chaussées* and other periodicals written by M. Julien of the Paris and Orleans Railway. Now one of the most important of these articles[9] was in the very issue of the *Annales* which contained Dupuit's, 'De la mesure de l'utilité des travaux publics'. It is in this article that Dupuit describes precisely in words and illustrates with an example the bell-shaped total revenue curve of Lardner's *Railway Economy*. Lardner's other references to the *Annales* indicates that he was a regular reader of the journal in the years of Dupuit's contributions.

Ekelund guesses that Lardner probably was acquainted with the work of Cournot and Dupuit;[10] but Hooks disagrees.

There is no indication that Lardner was aware of the work done by Dupuit on utility, for he does not explicitly employ the utility theory of value in his demand analysis. Rather, he seems to rely on a concept of empirically estimated demand schedules in his discussion of the effect of price changes on quantity demanded.[11]

In an attempt to be more specific as to Cournot's influence on the theory of the firm embodied in the work of Marshall and Walras, four aspects of Cournot's treatment should be considered:

    A. The use of the differential calculus and the treatment of time;
    B. Market structure;
    C. The nature of industry equilibrium; and
    D. The applicability of concepts to empirical work.

A. The use of the differential calculus and the treatment of time

It is often, but truly, said that the use of mathematical methods by economists has yielded great gains in the precision with which 'old' propositions could be stated. In using a strictly deductive method, Cournot had to spell out many of the assumptions needed to arrive at his results. In doing this, he produced models from which the element of time is banished.[12]

Marshall's method of operation was to follow Cournot's lead in the use of mathematics; but because the element of time was difficult to handle with the calculus (and Marshall considered time to be crucially important), the results of the mathematics would then be qualified to take account of the future and of the past. This method of working can be seen most clearly in the *Principles*, as, for example, in the Theory of Monopolies (Book 5; chapter 14). Here Marshall sets out his version of Cournot on monopoly and then proceeds to qualify the theory by, among other things, an elaboration of the statement that the monopolist will consider his profits over a period of time.

Marshall refers to the obligation he owed to Cournot, ' . . . as regards the *form of thought* and von Thünen as regards the substance.'[13] During Marshall's working life, it appears that his affection for Cournot faded while his affection for von Thünen strengthened. An early note by Marshall on von Thünen has recently been published, and the editor, J. K. Whitaker, rightly observes that: 'There is little here to suggest why Marshall came to feel that he had been strongly influenced by Thünen.'[14] By 1898, Marshall, referring to the *Economics of Industry* (1879), is more enthusiastic — claiming that he settled the outlines of his distribution theory under the good guidance of von Thünen. 'Von Thünen worked out his theory with several curious subtleties, and some perversities but he gave a good lead by suggesting symmetrical relations between labour and capital; the earnings of each being defined by the last profitable application of each at the margin.'[15]

However, Marshall's indebtedness to von Thünen over his symmetrical treatment of labour and capital and the substitutability of factors at the margin hardly seems sufficient to account for the fulsome praise von Thünen receives vis-a-vis Cournot in a fragment reprinted in *Memorials*.[16]

This preference for von Thünen over Cournot seems to be due, not to their relative influence on Marshall's analysis, but rather, in the first place, to von Thünen's readiness to deal with the detailed problems of business life compared with the heroic abstractions of Cournot, and, secondly, to von Thünen's 'ardent philanthropy'. Cournot lacked both the discipline of the facts evident in von Thünen's work and the generous heart evident in von Thünen's ethics.

B. Market structure

Not only did Cournot explicitly formulate the assumptions behind his various equilibrium solutions but, further, these assumptions constitute a sharp break with the assumptions of the English classical school as outlined in the previous chapter. In particular, Cournot's classification of markets according to the number of sellers (and its subsequent development by Edgeworth and Pareto) is an important departure. These writers say little of the determinants of industry structure; and a particular structure, once assumed, is not allowed to change by activity within the market.

By assuming a given market structure, Cournot obviates the need to analyse market behaviour through time – behaviour which may possibly alter the number of sellers. Marshall's interest in the determinants of market structure is congruent with his view of the effects of the behaviour of firms through time. In pursuing these interests, which he shared with Adam Smith and J. S. Mill, Marshall parted from the tradition begun by Cournot, established by Pareto, Walras and Edgeworth, and continued by Chamberlin, which treats the number of sellers as a means of classifying markets – allotting a different analysis to each market classification.

It is important to appreciate the relationship between a writer's concern with static equilibrium (rather than behaviour through time) and the assumption of a given number of firms. If a market, and all the firms within it, are in equilibrium then the number of firms may be counted using Jevons' law of indifference.[17] But, if a number of firms is assumed for a disequilibrium situation, it is possible that, in moving towards equilibrium, that number may alter. The establishment of a taxonomy of models according to the number of firms presupposes that the models are of the equilibrium type. If that were not so the taxonomy may be ambiguous.

From this point of view it is difficult to label the Walrasian analysis 'general' in the sense of Samuelson. Samuelson states that whether equilibrium is partial or general, the *method* of economic statics always entails certain *cet. par.* assumptions.

The only difference lies in the fact that in the general equilibrium analysis of, let us say, Walras, the content of the historical discipline of theoretical economics is practically exhausted. The things which are taken as data for that system happen to be matters which economists have traditionally chosen not to consider as within their province. Among these data may be mentioned tastes, technology, the governmental and institutional framework, and many others.[18]

Walrasian models do consider the interrelationships between all *prices* within an economy; but all the subjects of economic investigation are not included as variables. The objective functions of firms and the elements of industrial structure have been variables discussed since before the eighteenth century. This is not to say that the assumption of a given market structure is illegitimate, but merely that such an assumption rules out certain questions which have traditionally interested students of economic behaviour.

C. The nature of industry equilibrium

One major departure by Marshall from many of the other leading theorists of the period was over the relationship between the equilibrium of the industry and the equilibrium of the firms within the industry. The models of Cournot, Walras, and Edgeworth held, as a condition for equilibrium of the large group, that all the firms within the group should be in equilibrium. It is appropriate to mention Marshall's attitude to this issue at this stage even though a fuller discussion is postponed until later.

Marshall's observations of business behaviour led him to observe that individual firms within an industry are always expanding or contracting; and, further, the fortunes of individual firms will wax and wane even when the demand and supply conditions for the industry as a whole are constant. The observation of these facts of business life caused Marshall to outline conditions for equilibrium of the industry which do not require equilibrium of the firms within the industry. When he required a micro analogue for equilibrium of the industry he used the expositional device of the representative firm. But more of this shortly.

D. The applicability of concepts to empirical work

In his Preface to *Researches*, Cournot observes that, ' . . . the public is so tired of theories and systems that now the demand is for so-called 'positive' matter, that is, in political economy, custom-house abstracts, statistical documents, and government reports, such as will throw the light of experience on the important questions which are being agitated before the country, and which so greatly interest all classes of society.'[19]

Cournot approves of this empirical trend, but adds that theory (as distinct from systems) should always have some part, 'small though it may be', in the study of political economy in setting out the general form of the important functional relationships. Throughout his book, Cournot follows this elected path of dealing with functions of a general form; but occasionally he does note some problems of statistical measurement.[20]

Cournot's method of partial equilibrium (the term comes from Pareto) is more easily amenable to applied work than the sets of simultaneous equations contained in Walras' *Elements*.

Walras recognises the legitimacy of ranking the importance of certain variables in equilibrium analysis.

It is all the more legitimate to do this when we pass from the static to the dynamic point of view, or, better still, when we pass from the realm of pure theory to that of applied theory or to actual practice, for then the variations in the unknown quantities will be effects of either the first or the second order, that is to say, effects which need or need not be taken into consideration, according as they arise from variations in the special or the general data.[21]

In 1874, Walras wrote a letter to the elderly Cournot in which Walras linked Cournot's interest in probability to the latter's willingness to proceed beyond pure theory to create tools for applied work: 'Notre méthod est la même, car la mienne est la vôtre, seulement vous vous placez immédiatement au bénéfice de la loi des grand nombres et sur le chemin qui mène aux applications numériques. Et moi, je demeure en deça de cette loi sur le terrain des données rigoureuses et de la pure théorie.'[22]

To a yet greater extent than Cournot, Marshall tried to fashion tools for applied work. While not ignoring the notion of general equilibrium (as in Note XXI of the Mathematical Appendix to the *Principles*), Marshall used notions of competition, equilibrium and monopoly power which, he considered, were of far more use in applied work than the tools of Cournot and Walras.

In 'The Old Generation of Economists and the New',[23] Marshall looks to the new generation of economists to measure the functions the form of which had been established during his lifetime. But Marshall defends the English classical economists (with the exception of Ricardo) from the charge that they neglected the study of facts.

> Such a charge seems to me baseless. Most of them were practical men with a wide and direct knowledge of business affairs. They wrote economic histories that are in their way at least equal to anything that has been done since. They brought about the collection of statistics by public and private agencies and that admirable series of parliamentary enquiries, which have been a model for all other countries, and have inspired the modern German historic school with many of their best thoughts.[24]

Marshall learned from Roscher and Knies the lesson that generalisations regarding economic behaviour are, to some extent, contingent on historical, cultural and industrial circumstances. It was on these grounds that he criticised the method of the English classical school. He charged that their intimate but narrow knowledge of the City caused them tacitly to assume that ' . . . the world was made up of city men.'[25]

One of Marshall's favourite sayings, and the one which he placed on the title page of *Industry and Trade*, was: 'The many in the one, the one in the many'. Throughout *Industry and Trade*, Marshall proposes generalisations relating to particular industries or groups of industries. Since the death of Marshall the investigation of subsets of firms has become more common. Such studies may seek to establish the extent to which their findings are part of a more general pattern – 'the many in the one' – and the extent to which they constitute a subgroup – 'the one in the many'.

2. THE MOTIVATION OF THE FIRM

Throughout the period under consideration it progressively became clearer that the people who made vital decisions within businesses often contributed little or none of the capital under their control. Francis Walker's observation that the ownership of capital was no longer needed for one to fulfil the role of entrepreneur seems to have been a seminal influence in promoting this recognition.[26]

Certain terminological changes were adopted during the first few decades after the 'marginalist' revolution. Previously it was recognised that any individual could earn income both in the form of interest and in the form of wages. But the departure by the conventional economists from the 'magnificent dynamics' led to a change in the use of words such as 'labourer', 'capitalist', and 'landowner'. Instead of being a system for classifying people, these words came to denote the various functions one could perform in the productive process. While J. B. Clark acted as the propagandist largely to effect this, more than terminological, change, the change is implied by Walras' distinction between productive services and the owner of the capital from which the services are derived.

> Let us call the holder of land, whoever he may be, a *landowner*, the holder of personal faculties a *worker*, and the holder of capital proper[27] a *capitalist*. In addition, let us designate by the term *entrepreneur* a fourth person, entirely distinct from those just mentioned, whose role it is to lease land from the land-owner, hire personal faculties from the labourer, and borrow capital from the capitalist, in order to combine the three productive services in agriculture, industry or trade. It is undoubtedly true that, in real life, the same person may assume two, three, or even all four of the above-defined roles.[28]

In perfectly competitive equilibrium, each firm, Walras noted, will be earning what are now called 'normal profits'. Because Walras regards forgone alternative profit as a cost, he states that each firm in perfectly competitive equilibrium will be making neither a profit nor a loss.[29]

Edgeworth was never prepared to allow this Walrasian proposition to pass unqualified. In his review of *Éléments*,[30] it seems that Edgeworth did not understand the Walrasian notion of costs; for he advises Walras to seek a more precise statement after considering the Jevonsian notion of the 'disutility of labour'. However, in later statements Edgeworth acknowledges that the Walrasian proposition is roughly true – with the qualification that a particular entrepreneur might choose to receive less than his marginal product in order that he might remain as master of his own firm.[31] But he still seems to object that Walras does not allow the entrepreneur's payment to be called a gain. This objection seems to indicate a refusal to follow Walras' functional definition of 'entrepreneur'.

The work of J. B. Clark repeatedly emphasises the Walrasian propositions that, in perfectly competitive equilibrium, each contributor of productive services will be paid the money value of its marginal product, and that, in equilibrium, the entrepreneur (using the word in its functional sense) receives nothing.[32]

J. B. Clark's equivocation over whether 'co-ordination' was, or was not, the sole entrepreneurial function, together with his concentration on the case of the stationary state, stimulated much work at clarification among younger American economists. Clark had elaborated the proposition that pure profits arise from the economy not being in equilibrium. In equilibrium the product is exhausted; but in disequilibrium receipts are unlikely to equal planned payments for the use of productive services. In explaining the distribution of the product out of equilibrium, younger American economists were attracted to the ideas of earlier German economists – Hermann, von Thünen and von Mangoldt.[33]

The taking of risks

Of the American economists who attempted to relate J. B. Clark's analysis of distribution in the static state to the economy out of equilibrium, Davenport may be taken as being representative.[34] Davenport regards profit as, ' . . . the residual compensation falling to independent business activity after such apportionment as is possible has been made for rent, interest, wages, and other outlays.' . . .'Thus, profit goes, truly, to him who takes the risk, but does not, therefore, go as compensation for the risk or in proportion to it.'[35]

In opposing this view of the entrepreneurial function as the bearing of risks, Schumpeter maintains that it is the capitalist who bears the risks, not the entrepreneur.[36] This difference between Schumpeter and his senior American colleagues derives primarily from a difference in their time horizons. Schumpeter was concerned with the process of competition over 'decades', in which firms both begin their lives and die. If the firms' asset values are to decline it is clearly those performing the role of capitalists who suffer most. But the Americans were concerned with short-run problems of disequilibrium and the question as to which function they should assign the 'unimputed' residual. The entrepreneurial function was their solution.

The Americans wished to allow for sources of capital which did not partake of the residual (the fixed interest lender). But most of them agreed that, of risk-takers, 'the most prominent, though not the only, species is the investor in joint stock companies'.[37] Hawley amplifies this statement by noting that labourers and business organisers (who have contributed no capital to the concern) stand to lose if the firm is not successful.

In more recent times, Weston[38] has argued along these lines, noting that the uncertainty of business income implies that some incomes will be contractual while others will be determined as residuals. He defines profit as the difference between *ex ante* expectations and *ex post* reality in business income; but he refuses to impute the residual to some 'entrepreneurial' factor. As to whose income is a residual and to what extent one's income is determined residually are matters contingent on contractual relationships.

In chapter 3 it was noted that Say and Mill held this view that the distribution of risk-bearing was a matter for particular institutional relationships. In the period under consideration in this chapter Wicksteed[39] and Marshall followed this view – thinking it unnecessary to 'impute' the element of residual in each income to any one productive service. Marshall held that, 'in the modern industrial world'[40], most residual income accrues to capitalists; but he does note other possibilities, for example, profit-and-loss sharing schemes, some *de facto* form of which exists 'between almost every business and its employees . . .'.[41]

Frank Knight considered this view held by Marshall to be too strictly empirical to yield any useful generalisation; but Knight also considered that to say that almost every income contained an element of profit was to be too abstract. For this reason he distinguished between incomes which are basically contractual and those which are basically residual.[42]

The exercising of control

Knight certainly wishes to impute residual incomes to a factor called entrepreneurial: that which bears risks in the face of an unpredictable business environment; and he plays all manner of semantic games to achieve the result that those who choose to specialise in the assumption of risk are those who exercise control over the firm in its uncertian environment.

In the joint-stock company, when all managers are on contractual incomes, it looks as if the shareholders operate as entrepreneurs. Knight says that these entrepreneurs exercise *control* over the company, if control is understood to mean the selection of those who make the decisions.

> The paradox of the hired manager, which has caused endless confusion in the analysis of profit, arises from the failure to recognise the fundamental fact that in organized activity the *crucial* decision is the selection of men to make decisions, that any other sort of decision-making or exercise of judgment is automatically reduced to a routine function.[43]

Even if one accepts Knight's (rather odd) definition of control, one may still question the proposition that those who bear the risks in a joint-stock company select those who make the decisions.

On the issue as to who controls firms (as with that as to who earns the residual), Marshall is firmly empirical. In both the *Principles*[44] and in *Industry and Trade*,[45] Marshall notes that while shareholders usually gain the residuals in modern corporations, control over general policy is in the hands of salaried managers: 'The expansion of Joint Stock Companies has resulted in the general democratization of the ownership, as distinguished from the control, of business.'[46]

The Maximisation of net revenue

The Cournotesque theory of static equilibrium for the firm requires that, in the period under consideration, the firm will maximise its net revenue. Walras is less explicit as to the motivation of firms; but his monopoly model as well as his stability mechanism in his exchange-and-production model assume static profit maximisation.

Marshall and Schumpeter, with their mutual emphasis on the judgment, energy and imagination required to produce the most successful businesses, take account of the time horizon governing business decisions. For Cournot and Walras, a firm will maximise its profits on the basis of an objective calculation from certain given technological and price constraints. For Marshall and Schumpeter, the expansion of a firm *through time* is largely a product of the type of people within the firm who make the important decisions.

Marshall maintained that the alert, risk-embracing businessman was a peculiarly time-bound phenomenon of England in the nineteenth century, and that this type was dying.[47] However, he thought that certain characteristics of large businesses lead to vitality. The increasing size of businesses[48] causes scientific methods to be substituted for empirical. Further, the growth of communication between businesses creates an appreciative audience for the technical expertise and the imagination involved in the employment of advanced methods.[49] But, despite these offsetting factors, the trend was towards the stifling of the vigorous business leadership.[50]

> The owner of a business, when contemplating any change, is led by his own interest to weigh the whole gain that it would probably bring to the business against the whole loss; but the private interest of the salaried manager or official draws him in quite another direction. For the trouble of a new experiment will come largely on him. If it fails, he will have to bear much of the blame; and, if it succeeds, only a very small part of the consequent gain will accrue to him. So the path of least resistance, of greatest comfort and least risk to himself is generally that of not striving for improvement himself, and of finding plausible excuses for not trying an improvement suggested by others, until its success is established beyond question.[51]

3. COSTS AND RENTS

For a person trained in mathematics, Marshall was peculiarly casual when defining terms, and peculiarly inconsistent in his use of terms once defined. His explanation was that he wanted to use words to mean what the business world took them to mean. Nowhere are these inconsistencies more apparent than in Marshall's use of the various terms relating to costs.

From his early article on Mill, Marshall was clear that by a firm's 'costs', he meant the money outlays in the form of expenses.[52]

> When considering costs from the point of view of the capitalist employer, we of course measure them in money; because his direct concern with the efforts needed for the work of his employees lies in the money payments he must make. His concern with the real costs of their effort and of the training required for it is only indirect, though a monetary assessment of his own labour is necessary for some problems, as will be seen later on.[53]

Opportunity costs

In chapter 3 it was shown that the notion of opportunity cost was widely used in the middle third of the nineteenth century in writings which were considering the allocation decisions made by firms. Cournot, von Thünen, Lardner and Senior use this piece of common-sense quite explicitly.[54] The common business sense they use is that an outlay is only relevant to a particular decision if it varies as a result of that decision. However, in the period under consideration, generality was claimed for the concept and it was given a clear definition.

Historically, the idea derives from the Austrians – and, in particular, from von Wieser. Von Wieser, assuming that the supply of productive services is fixed, looks at the value of forgone products. Marshall was quite happy to use this notion of opportunity costs in his *Principles* from the sixth (1910) edition.

The whole value of his [a businessman's] business connection to him when working it is a notable instance of Conjecture or Opportunity *value*. It is mainly a product of ability and labour, though good fortune may have contributed to it. That part which is transferable, and may be bought by a private individual, or by a large amalgamation of firms, must be entered among their costs; and is in a sense a Conjecture or Opportunity *cost*.[55]

But in this form of forgone products, the notion does not incorporate those costs which influence the supply of productive services.[56] To generalise the concept, a definition in terms of forgone opportunities is necessary. D. I. Green generalised the concept in this way and coined the term 'opportunity cost' in 1894.[57] The proposition that economic agents will minimise the value of forgone opportunities is derived from the many models of resource allocation which assume consistency of preferences in the Walras-Samuelson tradition. Indeed, the Walrasian equations are almost free of motivational postulates. They merely propose that quantities demanded and quantities supplied are functions of prices; and, in this respect, supplies of productive services are similar to supplies of commodities.

This axiomatic view of behaviour has its counterpart in the notion of opportunity cost. Indeed, Hicks is not exaggerating when he states that: 'Walras' equations give the most exact version that has ever been given of the "opportunity cost" element in value; . . .'[58]

Marshall resolved early in his career to devote his time to the building of structures rather than to attacking the work of others. One result of this decision is that we know little of his attitudes to the ideas of his professional contemporaries.

However, the proposition that the businessman will minimise opportunity cost implies that all possible alternatives are known and that they can be ranked so that the best may be chosen. Except as an outcome which firms tend to approximate (in the long run), Marshall is always hesitant to propose that firms behave in this way. Rather, he considers the behaviour of businesses to be based on uncertain estimates of the probable results of alternative possibilities.

Time-period analysis

For the purpose of outlining his theory of equilibrium price, Marshall divides the influence of time into four periods. He refuses to offer a clear criterion of demarcation and this refusal is deliberate.

> Of course there is no hard and sharp line of division between 'long' and 'short' periods. Nature has drawn no such lines in the economic conditions of actual life; and in dealing with practical problems they are not wanted. . . . If it is necessary for the purposes of a particular argument to divide one case sharply from the other, it can be done by a special interpretation clause: but the occasions on which this is necessary are neither frequent nor important.[59]

The time-period analysis is an abstraction aimed at clarification. Shove explains the use of this classification when talking of the long-period supply and demand curves: 'They may serve a useful purpose by provisionally isolating for separate and preliminary analysis some of the forces making for change at a particular moment and indicating the direction of their pressure.'[60]

Marshall talks of these influences as affecting the market quantity supplied at any particular moment. Secular influences (due to the gradual growth of knowledge, of population and of capital) do not concern the present study so much as the market period, the short period, and the long period influences.

A firm deciding on its production policy for the immediate future will be confronted by more stringent constraints than if it were deciding what it would produce in the distant future. Accordingly, it is possible to classify the decisions a firm makes according to the severity of the constraints which bind those decisions. Under Marshall's classification the market period is that period in which stocks cannot be increased; the short period is that period after which the stocks of goods for sale can be increased but not the stock of all types of capital goods; and the long period is that after which the stock of all capital goods can be increased. Furthermore, it is possible to imagine each firm making plans for each of the three periods, with a degree of interdependence between the price and production policies planned for each of the three periods. Because a plan is paired with each of the three periods (defined with reference to the nature of production constraints) it is possible to speak of a decision relating to a period, for example, a long period decision is a decision concerning the plan a firm has for its activities after that time has elapsed in which it is impossible to expand or to modify the plant of the business.

At any moment of time the firm may make price and production decisions given the constraints both of the market and of its past (long-period and short-period) decisions.

It is some idealised model such as this that Marshall seems to have had in mind when discussing his time-period analysis.[61]

Prime and supplementary costs

In chapter 3[62] it was noted that many writers, when discussing decision-making by firms made the point that the only 'costs' relevant to the decision are those which vary as a result of making the decision. This distinction (common enough among businessmen) was called, in Marshall's borrowing from the language of businessmen, the distinction between prime costs (which are relevant) and supplementary costs (which are not).[63]

If prime costs are defined as the best opportunity forgone as the result of making a particular decision, then the concept is seen to be simply an application of opportunity cost. It is this definition which Marshall seems to have in mind when he states that the 'line of division' between prime and supplementary costs is 'often blurred'; that particular expenses may, depending on the decision being considered, sometimes be regarded as direct (prime) and sometimes as supplementary costs.[64]

However, Marshall often wishes to apply his prime cost/supplementary cost distinction to his three-time-periods analysis. When he does this, he sometimes speaks as if prime costs were costs relevant to short-period plans while, for long-period plans, supplementary costs are also relevant.[65] If he were using the above definition consistently, prime costs would be, by definition, those which are relevant to *any* business plan. According to this definition, it is not the planning horizon considered which distinguishes between direct and supplementary costs, but rather it is whether the cost varies or not as a result of making a decision.

On p. 360 of the *Principles* Marshall says that 'supplementary costs are taken to include' (he is not defining the term by establishing its bounds) those costs which vary with output given that the decision to keep the plant operating has been made.[66]

But, as if to assert that he agrees with the present writer's definition given above, Marshall does call capital costs 'necessary' if a firm is making a decision concerning capital expansion;[67] and, in similar circumstances, he even refers to such costs as 'prime'.

> But in view of an order for a large number of locomotives to be delivered gradually over a series of years, some extension of plant 'specially' made for the purpose, and therefore truly to be regarded as prime marginal costs would almost certainly be carefully considered.[68]

Marshall, using words which are borrowed from the business vocabulary, preferred to let the context explain his particular meaning rather than to use the terms consistently. In the remainder of this chapter the distinction between prime costs and supplementary costs will be understood to be that outlined by the present writer – a distinction which is at least as true to Marshall as any other single distinction.

Quasi-rent

Of those writings noted in chapter 3[69] as exploring the relationship between rents and profits, Marshall specifically acknowledges Senior, Mill, Hermann and von Mangoldt.[70] Even though the generalisation of the concept of rent had been proceeding throughout the nineteenth century, it was not until the 1890s that the generalisation of rent to encompass returns to factors other than land became widespread. Perhaps J. B. Clark and Pareto were the most influential authorities on this subject – apart, that is, from Marshall.

In a letter to J. B. Clark regarding the difference between interest and profit, Marshall states that his work on the subject dates from 1868 when he was stimulated by McLeod's criticism of the proposition that cost determines value. McLeod had claimed that the price of iron determines wages and profits – a statement with which Marshall agrees, providing that it refers only to the short run.[71]

In *The Pure Theory of Domestic Values*[72] Marshall is edging towards the concept of quasi-rent. The concept emerges in *The Economics of Industry* (1879).[73]

Marshall's concept of quasi-rent suffers from the same sources of misunderstanding as his distinction between prime and supplementary costs. Indeed, the reason for the confusing interpretations often given of quasi-rent is that Marshall used it to refer to the surplus of revenue over prime costs. If prime costs is given the meaning proposed in the previous section (that is, one unrelated to the idealised time periods analysis), then quasi-rents clearly arise *ex post*. A decision is made and prime costs are estimated. The activity resulting from the decision is implemented. Then the surplus of revenue from the activity over (*ex ante*) costs is quasi-rent.

Two quotations from Marshall's article, 'On Rent', should establish this view. But note the last phrase in the second paragraph where Marshall suggests that, *in the absence of a direction to the contrary*, the reader should assume that quasi-rent is the excess of revenue over costs relevant to short-period plans.

> *Producer's Surplus* is a convenient name for the genus of which the rent of land is the leading species. Producer's Surplus is the excess of the gross receipts which a producer gets for any of his commodities over their prime cost; that is, over that extra cost which he incurs in order to produce those particular things, and which he could have escaped if he had not produced them.[74]
>
> ... If the surplus is derived from buildings or other implements which can be quickly made, but last long, it does not enter for moderately long periods;[75] and it is best described as a quasi-rent when there is no speical mention of the period under discussion.
>
> But on the other hand, the income derived from such machinery and other plant as is both quickly made and quickly destroyed enters into cost for all but very short periods. It is therefore best described generally as profits; though when very short periods come under discussion, it has to be regarded as a quasi rent.[76]

Given the present writer's interpretation of prime costs, it is clear that, as regards any particular decision, quasi-rents are irrelevant. The decision to pursue a particular line of behaviour is taken providing the discounted expected receipts exceed the discounted expected costs. But if a plant has excess capacity then prime costs relating to say, short-period plans, will be much lower than prime costs for a long-period plan which envisages the complete replacement of plant. In this case, short-period plans will be expected to yield receipts which, when discounted, at least offset discounted expected expenditure.[77]

Marshall's work on business decisions (the extent to which they are constrained by past decisions and the extent to which they are influenced by future expectations), may be seen as the final flowering of many seminal ideas planted throughout the nineteenth century. Earlier controversies on the relationship of interest to profits, the generalisation of the concept of rent, as well as the absorption of the, uncontroversial, distinction between prime and supplementary costs all contributed. As regards the influence of future expecations, it is probable that W. T. Thornton's book[78] stimulated Marshall (as it had stimulated J. S. Mill). While some of Marshall's contemporaries (Jevons, Auspitz and Lieben, Davenport and Wicksteed) considered the influence of expectations of the future on present policies of firms, few can doubt that, in this field, Marshall was the tallest poppy.

4. COST FUNCTIONS AND SUPPLY FUNCTIONS

At the outset of this section, mention must be made of an outstanding, but still rather neglected, contribution by the American Charles Ellet Jr. In an article published a few pages at a time over many issues of the *Journal of the Franklin Institute* dating from 1842,[79] Ellet constructed a cost function for railway transportation from detailed observations marshalled with the aid of a powerful reasoning. He proceeded to test this equation against a large variety of differing types of railways, and found that it fitted remarkably well.

In the period 1920–50 it was generally true that professional economists argued about the form of cost functions instead of using data to estimate them. Marshall's contemporaries tended to assume some form without even *a priori* argument.[80] Against the performance of his contemporaries and his immediate successors Marshall's own efforts in this respect are quite outstanding. For, while his empirical observations are not available for verification, we have records of the efforts he devoted to the assimilation of factual information relating to the operation of business enterprises.[81] In his search for such information, that relating to costs was given a high priority.

The Cournot-Viner view of the firm as adapting its rate of output given a blue-print of technological possibilities has caused economists to direct their cost studies largely to the relationship between output and the cost of production. While Marshall was concerned with this relationship, he also attached importance to other influences on costs as will be shown below. In the Marshallian schema, cost functions have more variables than merely cost and output.

The relationship between cost and output under the Cournot-Viner schema translates easily into supply functions. For each price the relevant dc/do function is single-valued – yielding a determinate quantity to be supplied by the firm maximising its net revenue. Marshall's cost-output functions cannot be translated into supply functions in this way for three reasons.

In the first place, Marshall constantly emphasises the empirical importance of the 'parametrical' variables in the cost function, $c = c\ (o, \ldots \ldots)$. If one accepts this empirical judgment, it would be misleading to draw inferences about the relationship of price to quantity supplied without a consideration of these variables.

Secondly, the Cournot-Viner view of the firm as a quantity-adaptor[82] is not particularly helpful when supply is not a single-valued function of price. Marshall does not restrict his functions in this way,[83] and so generally prefers to speak of the supply price of a particular quantity rather than the quantity that will be supplied at a particular price. The supply price (for the industry) is that price which will just maintain industry output at its present rate.

Thirdly, even if quantity supplied is a single-valued function of price, the choice between quantity supplied and price as the independent variable is still more than a formality. If quantity is a negative function of price (which Marshall claims for many manufacturing firms and industries in the long period), then by treating price as the independent variable one would get the nonsense result that by lowering price, a larger quantity would be supplied.

Marginal costs

While talking in this general way, a point regarding Marshall's terminology should be clarified. Marshall often used the phrase 'marginal cost' to refer, not to dc/do, but to the prime costs of an extra lump of production.[84] That is, he used 'marginal' to refer to Δ rather than to d or to δ. This usage of words reflects Marshall's desire to picture the decisions of firms (but not of groups of firms) as relating to discrete changes.

> That part of their production with regard to which such persons are on the margin of doubts as to whether it is worth while for them to produce it at the price, is to be included together with that of the

persons who are in doubt whether to produce at all; the two together constitute the marginal production at that price. The producers, who are in doubt whether to produce anything at all, may be said to lie altogether on the margin of production (or, if they are agriculturalists, on the margin of cultivation). But as a rule they are very few in number, and their action is less important than that of those who would in any case produce something.[85]

Short-period adjustments for the firm

Marshall's statements of the tendency towards diminishing returns are based on the classical writings dealing with the response of agricultural production to the application of increasing amounts of non-land inputs in an 'old country'. Like those classical statements, Marshall's discussion is not clearly defined.[86]

The ambiguity in Marshall's discussion is particularly marked when he is referring to long-period input/output ratios in manufacturing industry. Pigou proposes that, for this case, Marshall's 'increasing', 'decreasing', or 'constant' returns should be replaced by increasing, decreasing or constant supply price;[87] and this suggestion has generally been adopted.

But whether Marshall is talking of historical returns to agriculture or of short-period adjustments, the tendency to diminishing returns is given a more precise meaning. While Marshall vacillates between average and marginal product, he is consistent in referring to product rather than revenue when speaking of returns. Marshall is also careful never to say that returns (however defined) are always declining; but rather he says that they will always decline eventually if the variable input is increased sufficiently.

> If a manufacturer has, say, three planning machines there is a certain amount of work which he can get out of them easily. If he wants to get more work from them he must laboriously economize every minute of their time during the ordinary hours, and perhaps work overtime. Thus *after they are once well employed*, every successive application of effort to them brings him a diminishing return.[88]

J. B. Clark both clarifies and generalises Marshall's statement. His 'law of diminishing productivity' refers explicitly to marginal product,[89] and it was generalised to refer to *any* homogeneous variable factor when applied to a fixed factor. [90] Clark holds that the law, if stated in the form that diminishing marginal returns will *eventually* occur, is universally true.[91] If defined in this way, and providing it is applied to factors which are of imperfect (but not zero) substitutability, Wicksteed claims that the 'law' is, ' . . . really no more than an axiomatic statement of a universal principle that applies equally to all forms of industry, . . .'[92]

If imperfect substitutability is defined so that Wicksteed's 'axiomatic principle' follows, then the 'law' seems to tell us little: its universality merely depends on the empirical question as to the existence of imperfect substitutes (as defined). In fact, writers have been extraordinarily careless in specifying the conditions needed for this law to hold.[93]

Short-period adjustments for the industry

Marshall's statement of the tendency to diminishing returns is not directly used to explain the increasing supply price for firms in the short period. In fact, he does not offer an explicit generalisation with respect to the supply schedules of firms in the short period. Auspitz and Lieben showed in 1887 how individual marginal cost/supply curves could be added to produce an industry supply curve.[94] The method is to sum the quantities supplied over all the firms for any given price. But Marshall does not envisage determinate reactions from all firms within an industry. All we are offered is a bald empirical generalisation relating to the *industry*, that there exists an ' . . . almost universal law that the term Normal being taken to refer to a short period of time *an increase in the amount demanded raises the normal supply price*.'[95]

Such a proposition need not have referred to demand considerations. Referring only to the supply side of the market, it could have read that, starting from a position of industry equilibrium, producers will only be willing to expand production if offered a higher price.

In support of this empirical generalisation we are offered the illustration of fishing entrepreneurs who, given a short-period time horizon, cannot train new sailors nor order new ships. To increase output, therefore, fish producers must consider offering higher wages to encourage sailors to work longer hours and must consider ' . . . what old fishing boats, and even vessels that were not specially made for fishing, can be adapted and sent to fish for a year or two'. They will only be prepared to pay such higher prices for inputs or have recourse to such inferior quality inputs if they are offered a higher price for the resulting increase in output.[96]

Long-period adjustments for the firm

Samuelson states in the *Foundations*, that, ' . . . the so-called method of *partial equilibrium* consists of nothing more than a liberal sprinkling of zeros into the equations of general equilibrium.'[97] Earlier in this chapter,[98] it was shown that models which are generally regarded as 'general equilibrium' also sprinkle zeros in place of certain variables which other investigators consider important. When it comes to the determinants of long-period costs, Marshall (whose qualifications for making such empirical judgments were probably better than any of his contemporaries) chose to discuss many variables which others did not even mention. The early Walrasian assumption of constant returns to scale (implied by production functions homogeneous of the first degree) removes even the rate of output as a variable which influences unit costs.

In this subsection only the relationship between unit costs and the firm's output and type of product will be considered. Other determinants of unit costs will be considered in the following two subsections. By a firm's long-period costs we mean the unit costs a firm expects to incur when considering long-period plans. By considering costs *ex ante* one is able to consider the influence both of products and of scale on unit costs. Any *ex post* observations of costs must confront the problem of the influence of capacity utilisation which, as Marshall reminds us,[99] is a separate problem.

In planning for long periods, the firm will consider the expenses of (i) circulating capital; (ii) wear and tear, and depreciation on fixed capital; (iii) interest and insurance on all capital; (iv) labour costs; and (v) the gross earnings of management.[100] The latter item is composed of the supply price times quantity of the capital contributed by those who run the business, the supply price times quantity of business enterprise and energy, and the supply price times quantity of that 'organization by which the appropriate business ability and the requisite capital are brought together'.[101]

The relationship between long-period unit costs and the output of any firm differs as between mining and agriculture on the one hand, and manufacturing on the other.[102] Marshall claims that there may be economies of scale in mining and agriculture; but that these are unlikely to be so empirically significant as to play much part in the determination of the size of individual businesses. Consequently, he concentrates his discussion on manufacturing industry.

Marshall was, of course, aware that access to economies of scale due to production is determined by plant size whereas scale economies due to marketing generally relate to the size of the business as a whole.[103] But this distinction, while clear in *Industry and Trade*, is given very little prominence in Marshall's earlier writings, where generally there is assumed to be a one-to-one correspondence between firm and plant. The economies or diseconomies to be gained by the aggregation of plants within a single unit of control came to assume importance in the vigorous debate (particularly in the US) over the desirability of trusts. The *Principles* was written while this debate was still in its infancy.[104]

A second reason why Marshall devoted so little attention to the difference between plant and firm economies may be that he did not envisage multi-plant control as a means of escaping the diseconomies associated with large plants. Marshall did not consider that long-period cost curves were U-shaped.[105] If there is no forward-rising section to the average cost curve, there is no need to resort to multi-plant control to escape the forward-rising section.

It is possible to find U-shaped long-period cost curves in Mill's *Principles*.[106] Wicksell used this U-shaped average cost curve to show that product exhaustion would occur in long-run competitive equilibrium; because each firm would be producing that output at which long-run average costs were a minimum.[107] Pareto considered U-shaped long-run average cost curves to be general,[108] as did Marshall's pupils, S. J. Chapman and T. S. Ashton in their empirical study. Ashton and Chapman claim that there is a 'determinate *mechanical* unit of maximum efficiency' which may be overcome if a business has many plants of the determinate size. But such an arrangement does not mean that diseconomies will not occur.

> The *subjective* unit of maximum efficiency, as it might be termed, is the unit which would be brought about by *personal* forces working within a given environment of objective conditions, when the latter are supposed to impose no limit of themselves. A straitened supply of initiating, organising and directing ability, for instance, is bound at some point to evoke decreasing returns in a business . . .[109]

Marshall assumes that technological real economies of scale generally are limited; but he does not envisage technological diseconomies of scale occurring at high rates of output.

> Thus, so far as the 'productive' side of business is concerned, it may be concluded that – though the volume of output required for maximum efficiency in proportion to capital is increasing in almost every

industry – yet, at any given time and in any given condition of industrial technique, there is likely to be a point, beyond which any further increase in size gives little further increase in economy and efficiency.[110]

The reasons Marshall gives for these real economies are those cited by Mill and Babbage.[111]

Like Babbage, Marshall notes that the larger firm can insure itself against risky activities by engaging in a variety of activities;[112] and, like Cournot,[113] Marshall mentions pecuniary economies. Indeed: 'The economies of highly organized buying and selling are among the chief causes of the present tendency towards the fusion of many businesses in the same industry of trade into single huge aggregates; and also of trading federations of various kinds, including German cartels and centralized co-operative associations.'[114]

When it comes to the influence of marketing and superintendence, Marshall equivocates. In general, the larger firms have great, and constantly increasing, advantages over smaller firms due to economies in marketing.[115] This is particularly true of multi-product firms in which case a company's 'own goods advertise one another'.[116] However, in certain 'specialty' trades, the firm's market may be very difficult to expand: further sales might be particularly expensive.[117]

The existence of diseconomies of scale is most probably caused either by transport costs or by managerial difficulties in those trades where such diseconomies do occur.

There are advantages to be gained from specialisation in management.

On the other hand the small employer has advantages of his own. The master's eye is everywhere; there is no shirking by his foremen or workmen, no divided responsibility, no sending half-understood messages backwards and forwards from one department to another. He saves much of the book-keeping, and nearly all of the cumbrous system of checks that are necessary in the business of a large firm; and the gain from this source is of very great importance in trades which use the more valuable metals and other expensive materials.[118]

Long-period equilibrium for the firm

In his chapter on monopoly, Cournot states that, in the case of manufactured articles, marginal cost for the firm (the statement seems to confuse marginal cost with average cost[119]) is generally a decreasing function of the firm's output. That Marshall reserved forward-rising long-period average cost curves for certain special cases indicates that he, too, shared this empirical judgment.

When Cournot comes to his chapter on 'Unlimited Competition' his firms are confronted with horizontal average revenue curves. For any firm k, first order profit-maximising conditions require that $\rho = \phi k(Dk)$ (price equals marginal cost), while the second order conditions require that, for a constant price, $\phi'k(Dk)$ be increasing at the equilibrium output. So the second order conditions cannot be satisfied if the firm is producing with $\phi'k(Dk)$ decreasing: in that case the output for the firm is indeterminate. If one observes a firm with $\phi'k(Dk)$ decreasing at its current rate of output, either one is observing a disequilibrium situation (further concentration within the industry is likely to occur), or the marginal revenue curve for the firm is forward-falling. Such a marginal revenue curve is attributed by Cournot to the absence of unlimited (large numbers) competition.[120]

Cournot outlines these two possibilities in the following paragraph.

It is, moreover, plain under the hypothesis of unlimited competition, and where, at the same time, the function $\phi'k(Dk)$ should be a decreasing one, that nothing would limit the production of the article. Thus, wherever there is a return on property, or a rent payable for a plant of which the operation involves expenses of such a kind that the function $\phi'k(Dk)$ is a decreasing one, it proves that the effect of monopoly is not *wholly* extinct, or that competition is not *so* great but that the variation of the amount produced by each individual producer affects the total production of the article, and its price, to a perceptible extent.[121]

In a letter to A. W. Flux, dated 7 March 1898,[122] Marshall explains that he devoted a good deal of his energy between 1870 and 1890 to seek for a more satisfactory answer to the problem raised by Cournot in the previous paragraph. Marshall seems to have two criticisms of Cournot's treatment.

Marshall's first objection is to the internal consistency of Cournot's argument. This criticism, which Whitaker refers to as, ' . . . a slip one can only attribute to a lapse of memory',[123] is that Cournot failed to realise that a forward-falling long-run average cost curve (as with Cournot, there is some confusion as to whether Marshall is referring to average or to marginal costs) would enable one firm to capture the whole market.

Whitaker is too hasty in his judgment of Marshall's memory. It would be surprising if a person could spend a large part of twenty of the best years of his life solving a problem the statement of which he then forgets. Marshall probably well understood Cournot's attempt to reconcile increasing returns with competiton as represented by the diagram at note 120. But Marshall's objection is that the 'equilibrium' there depicted is no equilibrium at all; for the firm with a head start will not accept some 'share of the market' marginal revenue curve, but will cut its price so as to exclude all competitors and so retain the *whole* of the market for itself.

> Some, among whom Cournot himself is to be counted, have before them what is in effect the supply schedule of an individual firm; representing that an increase in its output gives it command over so great internal economies as much to diminish its expenses of production and they follow their mathematics boldly, but apparently without noticing that their premises lead inevitably to the conclusion that, whatever firm first gets a good start will obtain a monopoly of the *whole* business of its trade in its district.[124]

Marshall claims that 'nearly every' producer is a monopolist in a particular market.

> Everyone buys, and nearly everyone sells, to some extent in a 'general' market, in which he is on about the same footing with others around him. But nearly everyone has also some 'particular' markets; that is, some people or groups of people with whom he is in somewhat close touch: mutual knowledge and trust lead him to approach them, and them to approach him, in preference to strangers.[125]

Marshall uses the word 'market' such that its sense varies with the context.[126] Every producer has a number of customers which he regards as his special market; whereas all customers for the product (when broadly defined) belong to the 'general market' – to which every producer belongs.

In the case of standardised commodities, the particular markets are formed by trust and understanding between buyer and seller. But in such markets this 'goodwill' is rarely sufficient to command a premium on price. 'He does not generally expect to get better prices from his clients than from others.'[127] The goodwill distributes buyers among sellers within the market.[128]

Because goodwill in markets for standardised commodities does not command a premium on price, it is hard for those firms which fail to take advantage of scale economies to survive for long periods of time. For example, steel firms operating under increasing returns will probably not be able to survive.[129]

However, special markets may be formed not merely by goodwill, but also by producers catering to special tastes. Such special markets are slow and expensive to acquire;[130] and the firm's output will be limited by a steep demand curve for its particular market as well as by its own supply curve.[131] The latter may be steeply rising if selling costs are considered.

Over successive editions of the *Principles*, Marshall seems to become slightly less keen on the proposition that a producer will be able to charge a premium on normal expenses by producing for a special taste. Following the third edition, a section to this effect was deleted from the *Principles*.[132] But Marshall maintained his opinion that production for special tastes may explain why producers are able to produce with forward-falling average cost curves and still be profitable in the long run.

Marshall's second criticism of Cournot's reconciliation of competition with increasing returns is that Cournot's solution has 'no near relation to reality.'

You say that, *a propos* of Increasing Returns, you are inclining to lay stress on the incomplete utilization of existing productive facilities. That is of course one of my chief hobbies. My confidence in Cournot as an *economist* was shaken when I found that his mathematics *re* I.R. led inevitably to things which do not exist and have no near relation to reality. One of the chief purposes of my Wanderjahre among factories, etc., was to discover how Cournot's premises were wrong.[133]

Marshall objects to Cournot's hypothesis that a firm's costs depend solely on the product it is producing and its rate of output. Such: 'Abstract reasonings as to the effects of the economies in production, which an individual firm gets from an increase of its output are apt to be misleading, not only in detail, but even in their general effect. This is nearly the same as saying that in such case the conditions governing supply should be represented in their totality.'[134] Marshall considers that Cournot's bag of *ceteris paribus* contains certain *variables* which are crucial to a right understanding of the long-period equilibrium for the firm.

It has already been noted that Marshall stresses that costs differ among firms within any industry because the opportunities (including opportunities for sales) and the resources available vary among firms.[135] In explaining the variability of firm size to be observed within any industry, Marshall mentions the resources available to firms.[136] But he particularly emphasises factors internal to the firm. The ability of its decision-makers to make sound judgments, the luck they have and the efficiency of the managerial structure are all important factors in determining the costs of any particular enterprise.

Until the fifth edition (1907) of the *Principles* Marshall considered that, for any business, the judgment and managerial efficiency of the founder would probably decline in his later years; and after his death, ' . . . the guidance of the business falls into the hands of people with less energy and less creative genius, if not with less active interest in its prosperity.'[137] This led Marshall to draw his famous analogy between the life cycle of trees in the forest and the life cycle of businesses.

However, from the sixth edition (1910) of the *Principles* Marshall qualifies his life-cycle thesis. If businesses are organised on the joint-stock principle they may expand rapidly when young (particularly if they pioneer new productive methods),[138] but the declining phase of the 'cycle' will be transformed into one of stagnation.[139] Private firms have their rate of expansion limited by financial constraints and by the time they take to develop particular markets. Before they reach that scale where all scale economies are exhausted they may be in decline – the effort needed to maintain goodwill and keep costs low may no longer be forthcoming. But under joint-stock organisation, financial constraints are much less pressing and the energy of decision-makers and managers is not so dependent on a few people. If the product is standardised and the organisation is joint-stock the industry may be monopolised.

It seems therefore that, if there were no other difficulty in the way of the unlimited expansion of a strong manufacturing business, each step that the firm took forwards in supplanting its rivals, would enable it to produce profitably to itself at prices below those which they could reach. That is, each step would make the next step surer, longer and quicker: so that ere long it would have no rivals left, at all events in its own neighbourhood.[140]

Given these conditions, Marshall seems to predict that there exists a long-period equilibrium for the firm whose output is equal to the output of the industry. But not all products are standardised, not all firms are joint-stock and not all industries are free from any technical progress. Marshall does not define a long-period equilibrium for the firm. Furthermore, at any moment in time, the producers of any product are likely to present an array of unit costs. If, for any moment, the firms are ranked from those with the lowest unit costs on the left to those with the highest on the right the result, if drawn continuously, is a particular expenses curve. This will always be forward rising – because of the ranking procedure – regardless whether the long-period industry supply schedule is forward falling or forward rising.[141]

The long-period supply schedule for the industry

As was noted above[142] Marshall's supply schedules do not tell us how much the industry will supply at any given price. The reasons for this should be clear by the end of this section; but from the beginning we will enquire as to the minimum price at which producers will be willing to produce a particular quantity rather than the quantity they will be prepared to produce at a particular price.[143]

The minimum price at which a group of producers is prepared to produce in the long period must cover the estimated average costs of the highest cost producer. So the long-period supply curve for the industry represents how these average costs alter as industry output expands. In the previous section the internal determinants of a firm's costs were explained. But Marshall says that a firm's costs are a function of *industry* output.

> We may divide the economies arising from an increase in the scale of production of any kind of goods, into two classes – firstly, those dependent on the general development of the industry; and, secondly, those dependent on the resources of the individual houses of business engaged in it, on their organization and the efficiency of their management. We may call the former *external economies*, and the latter *internal economies*.[144]

Very few commenters are prepared to defend the expositional clarity of Marshall's discussion of externalities. In his discussion, Marshall seems to use the phrase to refer to the functional relationship between the costs of one firm and the costs of other firms. Macgregor observers that these functions can be of three distinct types.[145]

(i) A firm's costs are a function of the general industrial organisation of the country. These externalities take such forms as improved transport, communications, subsidiary industries; and they should be treated parametrically when dealing with partial equilibrium analysis.

(ii) A firm's costs are a function of the organisation of a particular geographical centre for the trade of which it is a member. It is tempting to say that the localisation of a skilled labour pool and of subsidiary trades, and of the ease of marketing if located near similar producers should also be treated parametrically; for they relate to agglomeration rather than to the size of the industry as such. But if the industry is located at a centre (due to agglomeration economies), its *growth* may yield externalities which come under heading (iii).

(iii) A firm's costs are a function of the organisation (in particular, the size) of a particular trade. It is only this third category which should be treated as a determinant of the shape of the long-period industry supply schedule. Under this heading will be included Marshall's examples of the expanded manufacture of tools and machines with their attendant scale economies as well as the expansion of collection and distribution trades, to the extent that the expansion of these subsidiary trades depends on the expansion of the particular industry whose supply schedule is under consideration.[146]

Marshall's long-period supply price is not merely dependent on present period output and its allocation among firms. It is also dependent on the time at which the production takes place. This follows from the proposition that certain external economies are not reversible in time. Once output has expanded and the external economies reaped, such economies (for example, the establishment of a transport network or labour training) will remain an advantage for a longer period of time than the time horizon of a long-period plan.[147]

Marshall usually assumes that the supply price relating to any point on his long-period supply schedule is that which existed when the corresponding rate of output was in fact produced. Given that the output of most industries is thought to expand over time, each supply price relates to a single planning period. It is understandable that Schumpeter accuses Marshall of not constructing a true supply curve (that is, a series of conditional-static-sequences), but rather an historical record of how supply prices have altered as industry output and time have changed.[148]

Perhaps an even more basic deficiency of the Marshallian analysis is that, even given the time to which a particular level of output will relate, the determinants of costs are so many and the connections between them so various, that it would be impossible to predict the supply price. In particular, Marshall gives little guidance as to which firms will produce any increase in output.

Robertson[149] criticises the treatment of Frisch[150] on the grounds that, if the established firms are encountering increasing costs in the long period, an increase in output may be met by extra firms replicating the productive efforts of existing firms. But the implication of Marshall's treatment of the representative firm[151] is that any increase in output is normally supplied by an expansion of established firms. If this inference is valid then Marshall's general opinion was that any expansion of industry output would give access to economies because of internal expansion which would generally be reinforced by net external economies; so that while long-period supply schedules *could* be of any shape, they are *generally* forward-falling.[152]

The representative firm

Marshall's concept of the representative firm is a micro analogue of the long-period industry supply schedule. The concept adds nothing to Marshall's analysis of long-period supply. In that it is a heuristic device adding no content to the prior ideas which it is designed to elucidate, Robbins' comment that it is an 'afterthought' is certainly apt.[153]

Assessed as an expositional tool, the representative firm must be regarded as a failure. Against the onslaught by Robbins, the concept crumbled remarkably quickly. Marshall's exposition of the long-period industry supply curve implies very little regarding the firms in the industry – they may be increasing or decreasing in size, entering or leaving the industry as the output of the industry expands. The representative firm is a construction by which the student may seek to understand the behaviour of the industry. If it is too complicated to imagine the industry's supply price falling as the industry expands, then one can imagine a firm as a scaled-down version of the industry undergoing similar changes.

It is just this simplification which Robbins considers to be unhelpful – indeed he considers it to be quite misleading. 'The whole conception, it may be suggested, is open to the general criticism that it cloaks the essential heterogeneity of managerial ability – just at that point at which it is most desirable to exhibit it most vividly.'[154]

Macgregor presents a diagram which assists in the understanding of the properties of the representative firm.[155]

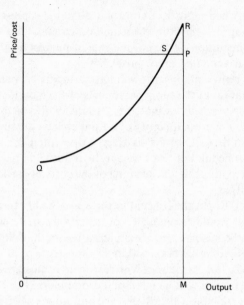

The Representative Firm

Industry supply = OM.
Price = MP.
QR = particular expenses curve.
SR = high-cost producers with long-period average costs greater than price. Unless these firms lower their costs they will decide to leave the industry when long-period plans come to be revised.
QS producers have long-period average costs less than price.
MP = price-'determining' cost.
S = representative conditions.

The representative firm may be used in three ways:

In the first place, its output will alter if and only if the output of the industry alters. Any change in output will be in the same direction for the representative firm as for the industry. So if the industry output is to increase, this must mean that price exceeds the representative firm's unit normal expenses of production.

Secondly, a firm's long-period supply price (average of normal expenses) includes income forgone by investing capital in this particular enterprise. So when industry output is stable, the representative firm must be earning its opportunity income on capital. This opportunity income is the definition of the normal rate of interest or, if earnings of management are counted in, of profit.[156]

Finally, the representative firm will have a supply curve found by the vertical summation of the supply schedules of the factors it uses, when the factor supply schedules plot the amount of the factor needed to produce a unit of a given quantity of output against the supply price of that quantity of the factor.[157] This exercise does not give any indication of the supply schedules of firms within the industry in question, but it possibly helps to illustrate the meaning of the costs of particular factors per unit of output.

For Marshall to put the concept to these uses he has to give a rough idea of how one would recognise a representative firm if one saw one. It would need to be in some sense 'representative' both of the cost and of the sales position of other firms within the industry. For this to be true it would need to be 'representative' with respect to its business ability, age, luck, size and its access to net external economies.[158]

It cannot be stated too clearly that the limitations Marshall imposed on his analysis of the long-period supply schedule are necessarily placed on his representative firm analysis. But the glory of his long-period supply analysis: his analysis of the influence of time on long-period costs and his allowance for a great variety of behaviour patterns on the part of firms within the industry, is obscured when the tool of the representative firm is used.

5. FREE COMPETITION

In the middle 1870s, Marshall laboured over a volume dealing with international trade—two segments of which were later published for private circulation by Sidgwick.[159] In this volume Marshall speaks of the economist as reasoning in ideal types. The division between 'the pure theory of domestic values' and 'the pure theory of international values' is that the former assumes perfectly free competition (that is, the perfectly free circulation of labour and capital), while the latter assumes imaginary places 'between which capital and labour do not circulate at all'.[160]

Marshall equates free competition with the process by which resources move so that the supply price of each commodity tends to equal its demand price. In referring to this free movement of resources, he treats the terms free competition and open competition synony-mously.[161]

Throughout his life, Marshall continued to base his first deductions concerning domestic values on the assumption of free competition. The epithet 'perfectly' was soon discarded so as to avoid any confusion with· the assumptions of the emerging model of perfect competition.[162]

Marshall's free competition is a direct descendent from the main-stream analysis of the English classical school; and its similarities to Adam Smith's free competition and to J. S. Mill's Case I ('Commodities in which the obstacle to attainment consists only in the labour and expense requisite to produce the commodity') are easy to see.[163]

In a preface to the second edition (1881) of *The Economics of Industry*, Alfred and Mary Paley Marshall give the following 'formal' definition of free competition.

A man competes freely when he is pursuing a course, which without entering into any combination with others, he has deliberately selected as that which is likely to be of the greatest material advantage to himself and his family. . . . Normal results in Economics are therefore those which would be brought about in the long run by this active principle, if it had time to overcome — as it necessarily would in sufficient time — custom, inertness, ignorance, and all the other *passive* elements which make up economic friction.[164]

This definition requires individual maximisation of net revenue before free competition is said to exist. As with Mill, this competitive behaviour is contrasted with behaviour dominated by custom and ignorance.[165]

Another close parallel with Mill is that the number of sellers is considered to be relatively unimportant. That the existence of free competition requires independent behaviour indicates that there must be more than one supplier, but we are told little directly on this question. The young Macgregor is more explicit — and may, perhaps, be taken as indicating his master's viewpoint. Macgregor grants that, other things being equal, fewness of numbers increases the bargaining strength of a group; but he doubts that 'under real conditions' numbers is 'the sole or preponderant aspect of the question.'[166]

Marshall holds that the key to the achieving of individual maximising behaviour is that individual businesses have freedom from constraints to expand or contract, and to enter or to leave particular activities. Examples of such constraints would be government regulations, the need to sink capital and effort and the associated risks, and *vis inertiae* —

'the opposition to change which is inherent in human nature and in human conditions'.[167] Such barriers to the free movement of factors lead to the creation of the particular markets discussed above[168] — which may or may not confer monopoly power over prices. But such monopoly power is generally limited by the independent behaviour of other firms and by the time it takes for particular markets to lose their profitability. Indeed, it is Marshall's concern with the long period which justifies the freely-competitive basis of the bulk of his analytical work.

Stress must be laid on the fact that absolute monopolies are of little importance in modern business as compared with those which are 'conditional' or 'provisional': that is, which hold their sway only 'on condition' that, or 'provided' that, they do not put prices much above the levels necessary to cover their outlays with normal profits. If they did, then competition would probably make itself felt; unless stayed by authority, as is the case with patents, copyrights, and some rights of way.[169]

It is true that profits in excess of normal are less likely to be sustained the longer the period of time one considers. For this reason, free competition is most legitimate as an hypothesis for models with a secular time horizon. But that excess profits will eventually be squeezed is a non-falsifiable proposition. The extent to which one is prepared to put one's faith in such a time horizon depends on one's judgment, and on, perhaps, one's ideology.

The law of indifference

Jevons' law of indifference states, ' . . . that in the same open market, at any one moment, there cannot be two prices for the same kind of article. Such differences as may practically occur arise from extraneous circumstances, such as the defective credit of the purchasers, their imperfect knowledge of the market, and so on.'[170] This proposition is such a commonplace that one wonders why Jevons elevated it to the status of a law and why later writers credited its statement to Jevons.[171]

The 'law' might be interesting if one were to spell out what one means by 'the same kind of article' — which Marshall attempted in his classification of particular markets. Some interest might also be derived from the law if one uses its statement to explore the types of knowledge which would be necessary for its realisation.

Edgeworth defines a normal competitive field as one which has (among other characteristics) knowledge available at almost zero cost: 'There is free communication throughout a *normal* competitive field. You might suppose the constituent individuals collected at a point, or connected by telephones – an ideal supposition, but sufficiently approximate to existence or tendency for the purposes of abstract science.'[172]

The problems associated with what has become the perfect knowledge assumption of perfect competition were not thoroughly explored until Frank Knight's dissertation, *Risk, Uncertainty and Profit* was published in 1921. Most of the writers in the present period assumed a high degree of knowledge among all economic agents – although the precise degree of knowledge was not specified. In their analyses of market equilibrium, both Walras and Marshall relied on dealers to buy if they could find a selling price below the anticipated equilibrium and sell if they could find a buying price above it. Indeed, at one stage when he is outlining the free competition model, Marshall states: 'But though everyone acts for himself, his knowledge of what others are doing is supposed to be generally sufficient to prevent him from taking a lower or paying a higher price than others are doing.'[173]

The assumption of large numbers

Cournot greatly promoted the practice of classifying a market according to its numbers of sellers. He defines *unlimited competition* in the following way.

The effects of competition have reached their limit, when each of the partial productions Dk [amount of production by producer k] is *inappreciable* not only with reference to the total production $D = F(\rho)$, but also with reference to the derivative $F'(\rho)$, so that the partial production Dk could be subtracted from D without any appreciable variation resulting in the price of the commodity. This hypothesis is the one which is realized, in social economy, for a multitude of products, and, among them, for the most important products.[174]

As a definition this seems to be clear and unexceptionable. Large numbers are sufficiently large that if a firm considers whether to change the rate at which it places output in the market, it will operate as if no change in the price of the product would result. The definition does not confuse the assumption of large numbers with the proposition that one firm among a large number will be denied access to price as a decision variable.[175]

Cournot's judgment as to the empirical ubiquity of large-numbers industries must be questionable. It is noteworthy that many writers at the close of our period held that Cournot's judgment was true of manufacturing industry when he wrote, but that it was not true of the early 1930s.[176]

Government statistics of industrial concentration normally represent nation-wide concentration rather than market concentration. For this reason, government statistics do not reflect closely changes in market concentration over time – particularly when the size of markets is changing rapidly, as occurred in the second half of the nineteenth century with improved transport and communication.

Nationwide concentration almost certainly decreased during the century preceding the 1920s; but systems of transport and communication developed during the second half of the nineteenth century expanded markets so that market concentration probably decreased up to the 1880s. However, the spate of mergers from that time up to the 1920s probably increased market concentration. It is this latter change which seems to have impressed the writers of the 1920s and 1930s. Estimates of secular changes in manufacturing concentration ratios must allow for wide margins of error. The evidence for the United States in the present century indicates a constant or slightly increasing degree of concentration.[177]

The proposition of quantity adaptor

The prime use of the large numbers assumption in the writings of Cournot, Auspitz and Lieben, and Pareto is that it causes a firm's marginal revenue to equal the market price.[178] The firm will treat prices parametrically and act as a *quantity adaptor*. Cournot seems to treat all non-monopolistic firms as quantity adaptors. The relationship between large numbers and quantity adapting becomes clearer with Auspitz and Lieben; but the first full statement is from Pareto.

Il y a lieu de faire ici une distinction fondamentale.

(α) L'échangeur subit les prix du marché sans essayer de les modifer de propos déléré. Ces prix sont modifés effectivement par son offre et sa demande, mais c'est à son insu. C'est ce qui caractérise l'état que nous appelons de *libre concurrence*.

(β) L'échangeur, seul ou d'accord avec d'autres, se livre à des manoeuvres pour changer les prix du marché. Il prend en considération les variations de ces prix pour établir son offre et sa demande. C'est ce qui caractérise l'état des *monoples*, des syndicats, etc.

In a footnote, Pareto continues: 'En langage mathématique nous dirons que: (α) Pour établir les conditions du maximum, on différentie en les prix constants; (β) Au contraire, on différentie en supposant un ou plusieurs prix variables avec les quantites que l'échangeur demande, ou offre.'[179]

The use of the assumption of large numbers in order to treat prices parametrically is still a widespread practice today. However, it is important to realise that large numbers only enables this parametric treatment of prices if the mechanism for fixing prices is of the rather odd type envisaged by Cournot and Walras.[180] They envisage that producers formulate offers contingent on prices and consumers formulate demands similarly contingent on prices. An independent authority, cognisant of these contingent offers and demands will fix the price for the period in question such that the quantity supplied equals the quantity demanded.[181]

Marshall uses the picture of the firm as a quantity adaptor as a useful abstraction when discussing the marginal productivity theory of distribution.[182] When discussing fish markets, he talks as if each firm treats price parametrically; but this treatment seems to follow from the institutional arrangements in the market, and there is no explicit assumption of a large number of producers. This is made yet more clear when, on page 374 of the *Principles*, Marshall talks of large, open markets in which price is a decision variable for firms; and where, at least in the market period, the consideration of price as a decision variable materially influences the analysis.[183]

Given that Marshall's free-competition model does not assume large numbers, but merely individual maximising behaviour by firms and the free movement of resources, it is more plausible to propose that firms treat price parametrically the longer the planning period they are considering; for in the freely competitive long run price will tend towards the average cost of an extra lump of output on long-period calculations no matter what any particular firm may do.

However, if firms treat price as a decision variable then, even given Cournotesque large numbers, firms may have demand curves with some gradient. Reder notes that, in the absence of perfect knowledge and instantaneous adjustments by consumers, firms producing a homogeneous product may charge differing prices. Whether a firm can charge a price higher than 'the general run' in such circumstances will depend on the period of time and the size of the price differential. In a market where information is costly, for example, second-hand books, or where prices are constantly changing (because of inflation), equilibrium may never be approximated and every purchase may be a bilateral monopoly bargain.[184]

Arrow develops these suggestions by Reder into a more formal model in which firms (in a large-numbers market) operate as monopolists or monopsonists under uncertainty as they adjust prices in disequilibrium situations.[185]

In sum then, for large numbers, market prices will only be treated parametrically given the odd method of price fixing envisaged by Cournot and Walras. While for long-period plans, firms will tend to treat prices parametrically whether large numbers are assumed or not − providing that the market fulfils the Marshallian criteria for free competition.

6. EQUILIBRIUM AND STABILITY UNDER COMPETITION

Equilibrium in the market period

Before proceeding to a discussion of equilibrium and stability it may be well to repeat the range of our interest with economic models. Because our attention is focussed on the behaviour of firms we shall not venture into those problems of equilibrium and stability raised by a consideration of reactions among markets. Such reactions involve analysis of a level of aggregation higher than that in which we are interested.

The historical justification for this procedure is that, while equilibrium analysis was 'generalised' to cover more than one market within our time period, stability in multiple exchange was not discussed until Hicks' *Value and Capital* (1939). This work by Hicks has since been developed by Samuelson, Metzler, Morishima, Arrow and Hurwicz, Negishi, and a host of lesser lights; but these developments have concentrated on the problems raised by the consideration of more than one market. The theory of the firm contained in this work is basically that of Walras. If only for this reason the stability analysis of Walras (which he explained in a partial setting) is worthy of consideration. It is the stability analysis of Walras as compared with that of Marshall which will act as a *cantus firmus* over these next few sections.

Thornton's criticisms of the value theory of J. S. Mill's *Principles* amounts to the proposition that, if one observes the prices of products in markets from day to day, they seem to be influenced by chance occurrences, the expectations of producers and a whole grab-bag of inter-related influences.[186] By contrast, Mill's explanation of value seems too simple. Marshall's concern with verisimilitude caused him to take Thornton seriously.

It is true that Mill does not explain this [that price expectations influence market-period supply] in his *Political Economy*. The theory of market values was considered by economists as of slight importance, until Mr. Thornton's book *On Labour* appeared. Mr. Thornton's work is not free from faults; but he has not received his due meed of gratitude for having led men to a point of view from which the practical importance of the theory of market values is clearly seen. In particular he led Mill to give an exposition of his views on the subject.[187]

Marshall proposes that, while production cannot be expanded as a result of market-period decisions, market-period supply is a positive function of price. These propositions relating to Marshall's market period are similar to Walras' first model of equilibrium of exchange.

However, there is one important difference between the two models. The Walrasian individual considers his own demand for the product at any particular price. At any price, he will be prepared to sell the difference between his endowment and his effective demand. In these circumstances, as Wicksteed emphasised,[188] a supply curve is merely a curve of net negative demand. This creates problems when one comes to stability in the market period; for it enables supply curves to be backward rising which may imply instability at points of intersection with forward-falling demand curves.

When Marshall discusses the pure theory of foreign trade he considers these points; because a country may have a significant demand for its own products. However, the *firm* producing for the domestic market has little or no demand for its own product, so it is of little use to consider its supply function as its net negative demand. 'There is not in the nature of the case any symmetry between these two sets of causes [those governing demand and those governing supply].'[189]

Marshall always speaks as if his market-period supply curve is forward rising.[190] The reason for this is that the higher the present price, the more attractive are sales in the present as compared with sales in the future.[191] The sales of any individual firm will depend on its financial position (cash flow) as well as its estimates as to future price trends. Sidgwick is more precise. He assumes, (1):

> . . . that production and consumption continue at a uniform rate throughout the year, and (2) that the commodity is not one that will deteriorate by being kept. Then, if we take any single dealer who has a stock of the commodity, we see that he will gain by selling it, unless he has reason to expect that the price at some definite distance of time will be higher than the present price by an amount more than sufficient to compensate him for his loss of interest or profit on the capital locked up in the unsold stock, together with the expense and trouble of taking care of the goods.[192]

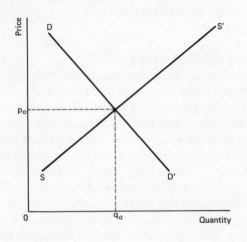

Market – Period Equilibrium

As represented by the diagram, the Walrasian condition for p_0 to be called an equilibrium price is that the quantity supplied and the quantity offered be equal at that price. This condition comes straight from Cournot,[193] or from J. S. Mill.

Marshall wishes to call p_0 the equilibrium price because it represents a price from which there will be no tendency to alter:

The price of 36s. $[\rho_0$ above] has thus some claim to be called the true equilibrium price: because if it were fixed on at the beginning, and adhered to throughout, it would exactly equate demand and supply (i.e. the amount which buyers were willing to purchase at that price would be just equal to that for which sellers were willing to take that price); and because every dealer who has a perfect knowledge of the cirumstances of the market expects that price to be established.[194]

Stability

Samuelson's 'correspondence principle' states that, '. . . the problem of stability of equilibrium is intimately tied up with the problem of deriving fruitful theorems in comparative statics.'[195] Following Samuelson's exposition, writers on exchange stability have generally been careful to specify the time paths of their variables as they converge.

This was not generally the case prior to Samuelson; but convergence in both Marshall and Walras is an adjustment process which takes place over time. Neither of them means by stability the way the demand curve cuts the supply curve.

In an early discussion by Marshall of long-period equilibrium he discusses stability in the following way.

Thus the motion of the exchange-index is in every respect similar to that of a material particle moving freely under the action of forces which attract it towards OE and OG.

. . . Then this particle will move exactly in the same manner as does our exchange-index, so that if we choose to assign to these horizontal and vertical forces any particular laws, we should obtain a differential equation for the motion of the exchange-index. This equation when integrated would give us the path which on this particular supposition the particle would describe.[196]

So Samuelson's correspondence principle did not teach us that stabilisation is a dynamic adjustment; but it did teach us that the time pattern of adjustments may influence the path to equilibrium, and may even determine whether or not the path is convergent.

Convergence in the market period

For Marshall, the path of convergence to the equilibrium price is more heavily damped the greater the degree of knowledge in the market. If all buyers and all sellers correctly estimate the equilibrium price, that price will rule throughout the trading period. If a seller tries to charge a price greater than ρ_0 no one will buy because he knows that he will be able to satisfy his wants by buying at ρ_0. If a buyer tries to buy at a price less than ρ_0 no one will sell because each seller realises that he will be able to sell all he wants at the price ρ_0.[197]

However, if expectations are imperfect, trading may take place at disequilibrium prices before revised estimates of demand and supply encourage buyers and sellers to alter the price in the direction of equilibrium.

The stabilisation mechanism is clear. When, at a price greater than ρ_0, it becomes clear to a seller that he will be unable to sell all that he wishes at the present price, he will reduce the price in the direction of ρ_0. When, at a price less than ρ_0, it becomes clear to a buyer that he will be unable to buy all that he wishes at the present price, he will raise the price in the direction of ρ_0. If the price differs from ρ_0, the actions of both buyers and sellers, as they come to learn the true demand-supply relationship for the market period, will push the price in the direction of ρ_0.

Wicksteed elaborates on this process, showing that the benefits to be derived from knowledge in such a market form an incentive to gain that knowledge.[198]

Like Marshall, Walras discusses stability in exchange when trying to establish that real market processes will approximate the equilibrium solution of his model. But Walras' process of 'tâtonnement' (which, Jaffé and Stigler suggest, is best translated as 'groping') whereby convergence occurs, does not correspond to the behaviour of any market participants. It is ironical that, in trying to establish a link between his model and behaviour in markets, Walras merely iterates the conditions under which his model will be stable.

When [the equality between effective demand and effective offer] is absent, the attainment of equilibrium prices requires a rise in the prices of those commodities the effective demand for which is greater than the effective offer, and a fall in the prices of those commodities the effective offer of which is greater than the effective demand.[199]

These stability conditions for exchange are the same as those of Marshall; but Marshall outlines a pattern of behaviour corresponding to the conditions whereas Walras does not.

Marshall does not raise the possibility of unstable equilibria in the context of his market-period discussions because all equilibria will be

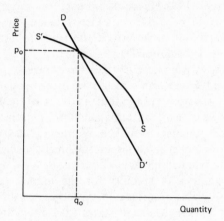

Backward – Rising Supply

stable given Marshall's propositions that demand curves are forward falling and that market supply curves are forward rising.[200] However, Walras allows his exchange supply curves to be backward rising as in the diagram. At a price close to ρ_0 the Marshall – Walras stability conditions will not lead to convergence at a price ρ_0.

In a letter to Walras,[201] Marshall claimed objective originality for the doctrine of stable equilibrium. The evidence he cited was the abstract of a paper which Marshall presented in 1873 to the Cambridge Philosophical Society.[202] Walras' statement was not published until the following year.[203] Marshall's paper does point to the possibility of both stable and unstable equilibria; but the reference, although only fleeting, is clearly to the stability of long-period equilibrium. This latter case, elaborated in the *Pure Theory of Foreign Trade*, is given a quite separate set of stability conditions from those outlined above.

Determinacy of equilibrium

An equilibrium is called 'determinate' or 'indeterminate' according as the final position is independent of the route followed or not.[204]

Edgeworth had a simple solution to the determinacy problem: allow no exchanges prior to equilibrium and, because no route is followed, the final position can not be dependent on the route. This is his 'recontract' requirement under which contracts at disequilibrium prices are regarded as purely provisional.[205] This solution suggests a way of constructing a model so as to avoid the problem of indeterminacy. However, it does not suggest the conditions under which the route followed will yield a uniquely-determined solution.[206]

In a masterly article, Jaffé clarifies the controversy as to whether Walras followed Edgeworth's means of escaping the indeterminacy problem.[207] It was not until the fourth edition of the *Elements* (1900) that Walras made it clear that trading at 'false' quantities may affect the final equilibrium outcome. Even then, Walras confines this qualification to his production model and does not say precisely why trading at false prices may create indeterminacy.

Marshall's analysis of stability for the market period envisages trading at false prices accoridng to the degree of knowledge among traders in the market. Marshall states that, providing the marginal utility of money is constant for each trader during the period , the final price will be determinate.[208]

To help clarify Marshall's position, suppose that the market period (a day) may be divided into eight hours. Suppose that a uniform daily price ρ' corresponds to a daily quantity demanded of q'. Suppose further that a uniform price for each of the eight hours $[\rho'_1 = \rho'_2 = \ldots = \rho'_8]$ corresponds to a uniform quantity demanded for each of the eight hours $\left[\left(\dfrac{q'}{8}\right)_1 = \left(\dfrac{q'}{8}\right)_2 = \ldots = \left(\dfrac{q'}{8}\right)_8\right].$

Consider good Q and money (corresponding to the subscripts q and m). If trade in good Q for each trader is very small compared with his stock of money, the marginal utility of money (Mu_m) for any trader will not alter significantly during the course of the day's trading. Suppose A and B are any two traders. The condition for equilibrium is that:

$$A\frac{Mu_q}{Mu_m} = B\frac{Mu_q}{Mu_m} = \rho_q. \qquad \ldots (1)$$

According to Marshall's stability analysis, the market will approach this condition after a number of hours. But, as $\dfrac{A\,Mu_m}{B\,Mu_m}$ is constant over time, the amount of Q traded when the equilibrium price is attained will be such that:

$$\frac{A\,Mu_q}{B\,Mu_q} = \frac{A\,Mu_m}{B\,Mu_m} = \text{constant} \qquad \ldots (2)$$

Given the condition of a constant Mu_m for each trader[209], the price and quantity traded *in the hours of equilibrium* are determinate. Further, once knowledge has been gained to attain the equilibrium price and quantities, those equilibrium values will be maintained. But it should be noted that the quantity traded over the *eight* hours is not q' but rather the sum of the pre-equilibrium hourly quantities plus $\left(\dfrac{q'}{8}\right)$ summed over the hours *after* equilibrium has been attained.

The short period

The Marshallian short-period analysis has no parallel in the work of Walras. Indeed, the short-period analysis is peculiarly imprecise. While Marshall does talk of 'normal' (equilibrium?) prices in the short period, neither equilibrium conditions nor stability conditions are proposed.

The application of a short-period analysis to a general equilibrium model would involve an heroic attempt at abstraction. Such an application would require a period of time for which the supply of all products could be altered but for which no producers could increase their stock of fixed capital.[210]

The analysis is not only vague and difficult to apply to general equilibrium models, but also it is hard to imagine a real-world analogue to the short-period normal prices. While market prices are roughly the prices one observes in markets, and long-period normal prices are those which one would observe in a stationary state, short-period normal prices lack such a corresponding reality.

To understand the role which the short-period analysis plays in Marshall's schema, it is necessary to understand the raison d'être of the time period abstraction.[211] The short-period analysis isolates the influence of short-term plans and, in particular, the influence of capacity availability on present policies and on the direction in which market prices are moving.

Marshall's proposition that short-period industry supply functions are forward rising seems to be an empirical generalisation rather than a deduction from the proposition of the tendency to diminishing returns.[212] This can be seen clearly when he is talking of the case of excess capacity. Excess capacity will worsen a firm's bargaining strength with respect to its customers.[213]

One would expect that excess capacity would, via this influence on relative bargaining strengths, force the price below the prices estimated for long-term plans. Following the normal rule, one may expect producers to maintain production so long as price covers average prime costs. But this is not the case.

> . . . they generally hold out for a higher price; each man fears to spoil his chance of getting a better price later on from his own customers; *or*, if he produces for a large and open market, he is more or less in fear of incurring the resentment of other producers, should he sell needlessly at a price that spoils the common market for all. The marginal production in this case is the production of those whom a little further fall in price would cause, *either* from a regard to their own interest or by formal or informal agreement with other producers to suspend production for fear of further spoiling the market.[214]

It should be noted that this behaviour is consistent both with independent behaviour of firms acting within special markets and with 'informal agreements' between firms acting in large, open markets. The latter, of course, does not envisage oligopolistic interdependence, but rather informal social pressure, which may operate even in a market of Cournotesque large numbers. 'It seems to be not so much of their trade policy that Marshall's typical producer moves in fear, as of their personal behaviour to him (and no doubt to his wife) when he meets them outside the chapel or in the club.'[215]

The long-period normal

Marshall usually uses the word 'normal' to express those ideas expressed by Adam Smith's 'natural' value which are strictly scientific. For Marshall, normal (as applied to the long period) refers to the equilibrium which would result if sufficient time elapsed for firms to be acting in accordance with long-period plans based on a given set of market constraints. Alternatively, it is the industry price and output which would exist at any moment, if the time taken to adjust to equilibrium were zero.[216]

The preface to the second edition of the early *Economics of Industry* maintains that the long-period normal outcome is the freely competitive equilibrium;[217] but when Marshall came to write the *Principles* he maintained that normal values are not necessarily competitive.

> Of course Normal does not mean Competitive. Market prices and Normal prices are alike brought about by a multitude of influences, of which some rest on a moral basis and some on a physical; of which

some are competitive and some are not. It is to the persistence of the influences considered, and the time allowed for them to work out their effects that we refer when contrasting Market and Normal price, and again when contrasting the narrower and broader use of the term Normal price.[218]

By 'the narrow use of the term', Marshall seems to be referring to the normal results of a particular industry – which results may be influenced by an element of monopoly. But, in abstract reasoning, the long-period equilibrium analysis is based on a 'broader' set of assumptions.

The position then is this: we are investigating the equilibrium of normal demand and normal supply *in their most general form*; we are neglecting those features which are special to particular parts of economic science, and are *confining our attention to those broad relations which are common to nearly the whole of it*. Thus we assume that the forces of demand and supply have free play; that there is no close combination among dealers on either side, but each acts for himself, and there is much free competition; that is, buyers generally compete freely with buyers, and sellers compete freely with sellers.[219]

Normal profits and long-period equilibrium

The proposition that normal profit is a constituent element in supply prices can be traced to Adam Smith.[220] With the emergence of explicitly static models and the clear definition of 'opportunity cost' in the period under consideration, one would suppose that the opportunity cost of finance would be the phrase used to express the profit element in any firm's supply price.

This is the implication of Walras' model of production and exchange. For this model, the existence of equilibrium requires that there be exchange equilibrium (effective offer = effective demand, and a stationary current price) in the markets for products and productive services; but there is the extra condition that the selling prices of products must equal the costs of the productive services that enter into them for every firm.[221]

Thus, in a state of equilibrium in production, entrepreneurs make neither profit nor loss. They make their living not as entrepreneurs, but as land-owners, labourers or capitalists in their own or other businesses. In my opinion, rational bookkeeping requires that an entrepreneur who owns the land which he works or occupies, who participates in the management of his firm and who has his own funds invested in the business, ought to charge to business expense and credit to his own account [the corresponding] rent, wages and interest charges calculated according to the going market prices of productive services. In this way he earns his living without necessarily making any profits or suffering any losses as an entrepreneur. Surely, it must be evident that, if he gets a higher or lower price for his productive services in his own business than he can get elsewhere, then the difference represents a profit or a loss.[222]

To the chagrin of Davenport,[223] Marshall refused to adopt this neat model. Marshall's concept of normal profits differs from the ideas of Walras for three important reasons.

In the first place, Marshall includes both the earnings of management and interest payments under profit.[224] When making long-period plans, businessmen will only undertake a project if revenue is expected to ' . . . yield a normal rate of interest (or if earnings of management are counted in, of profit) on the free capital, represented by a definite sum of money that was invested in producing it.'[225]

Secondly, Marshall's characteristically empirical emphasis on differences among firms causes him to reject any model in which equilibrium for the industry requires that every firm earns a normal rate of return on capital. Pigou quotes Taussig approvingly: 'Every one knows that fortunes are made in industries strictly competitive, and are to be ascribed to unusual business capacity.'[226]

The profitability of firms in a freely competitive industry differs not only because of age, but also because of managerial rents which are recorded as profits. This consideration led Marshall to state his condition for long-period equilibrium as requiring that the representative firm be earning normal profits.[227] So Marshall's long-period equilibrium condition, that industry supply price equals industry demand price, has its micro counterpart only in terms of the representative firm.

The third reason for the uniqueness of Marshall's 'normal profit' analysis is his concern for distinguishing *ex post* from *ex ante* considerations; and, in particular, his insistence that the expectations of businessmen (which determine behaviour) do not necessarily coincide with the outcome of that behaviour. So the proposition that industry equilibrium requires that the representative firm be earning a normal rate of profit means that the expectations by businessmen of the profitability of production are such that total industry output will not change.

Like Marshall's long-period supply curve and the representative firm, normal profits can only be recognised *ex post*. The tools do not enable a precise *ex ante* prediction of equilibrium output for the industry. But, if industry output is constant for given demand and supply conditions, then one is able to discover a point on the supply curve as well as the sort of profitability picture which Marshall would choose to call normal. The only 'condition' for the existence of Marshallian long-period equilibrium is that industry output is constant.

Long-period stability

In the above discussion of market-period stability it was shown that, while Marshall did not consider instability in the market period, both he and Walras shared the same stability conditions, although the mechanism by which the price moved differed as between the two writers.

In this section, stability in production will be discussed assuming exchange equilibrium, that is, for every quantity that is produced in each market period, the price will be such that the quantity demanded equals the quantity supplied. This is the assumption upon which the discussions in Marshall and Walras proceed. The stability conditions and the process by which production equilibrium is achieved are the same for Walras as they are for Marshall. However, this time, the form of Marshall's functions causes him to consider the possibility of instability – a possibility which is not considered by Walras.[228]

In discussing equilibrium of production, Walras always assumes that production coefficients are constant. Depending on whether the prices of productive services are assumed to be constant or assumed to be positively related to the demand for the final product (Walras uses both assumptions), supply schedules will either be horizontal or forward rising. In either case, given a forward-falling demand curve, production will always adjust to equilibrium.[229] The stabilisation mechanism is the following:

> In fact, under free competition, if the selling price of a product exceeds the cost of the productive services for certain firms and a *profit* results, entrepreneurs will flow towards this branch of production or expand their output, so that the quantity of the product [on the market] will increase, its price will fall, and the difference between price and cost will be reduced; and, if [on the contrary], the cost of the productive

services exceeds the selling price for certain firms, so that a *loss* results, entrepreneurs will leave this branch of production or curtail their output, so that the quantity of the product [on the market] will decrease, its price will rise and the difference between price and cost will again be reduced.[230]

The production stabilisation mechanism of Walras differs from that of Marshall in only two respects. In the first place, Marshall does not talk as if an excess of industry demand price over industry supply price implies that every firm is earning excess profits. Secondly, Marshall's supply price is rather more complicated than a mere record of unit costs which are constant among firms.

The major difference in *analysis* between the two is that Marshall considers the possibility of instability deriving from the likelihood (for

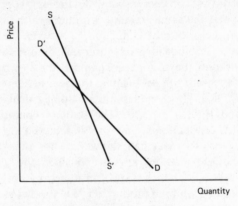

Long-Period Instability

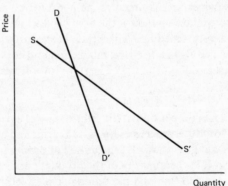

Long-Period Stability

manufacturing industries at least) that the long-period supply curve will be forward falling. This possibility raises two alternatives as illustrated. The conditions for stability are that ' . . . the demand price is greater than the supply price for amounts just less than the equilibrium amount, and *vice versa.*'[231] If this were not the case (the unstable case) then a quantity less than equilibrium would cause the supply price to exceed the demand price. Marshall's representative firm would reduce production because, given a long-period planning horizon, it would expect its rate of profit to be less than normal. Given the possibility of a forward-falling unit cost schedule, a parallel story could be told which would be perfectly sound Walrasian economics.

7. MONOPOLY

The study of monopoly in the second half of the nineteenth century was largely stimulated by debate over public policy. In France, discussion of the pricing and construction of roads, bridges and railways in the 1840s and 1850s produced valuable work on price discrimination (Dupuit) and on the relationship between prices and costs and the extent of the market (Lardner). In the United States, the controversy over the determinants of railway rates lasted well into the present century while the trust movement stimulated much work on the conditions needed to protect monopoly prices. Writers in Germany and in Britain further explored the themes of railroad pricing and combinations.

That railway companies provoked fruitful speculation was probably due to a number of factors. The revolutionary effects they had on the lives of large numbers of people, the need for newly established firms constantly to make major policy decisions rather than to follow established patterns of behaviour, and the vigorous (and sometimes spectacularly profitable) entrepreneurship of the railway promoters may account for much public interest. However, theory largely benefited by the multi-product nature of these companies and the adjustments this necessitated to models of single product firms if the relationship between prices and costs was to be explained.

American professional (and public) interest in trusts was boosted dramatically by the activities of the Standard Oil Trust, formed in 1882.[232] Writings on trusts helped to define both the concept of competition and the conditions needed to earn monopoly profits, as well as yielding valuable industry studies. [233] Significant writings on trusts did not come from Britain until the first decade of the present century.

The normative interest in monopoly had yielded positive analysis for centuries,[234] and this normative motivation was naturally evident during our present period.

Marshall's exposition of monopoly is based on a statement of Cournot's model. This statement is then overlain with qualifications as to the degree of competition to which the monopolist is subject (a function of time) and the time horizon of the firm. Marshall begins by considering a single firm.

At present we consider only those general causes determining monopoly values, that can be traced with more or less distinctness in every case in which a single person or association of persons has the power of fixing either the amount of a commodity that is offered for sale or the price at which it is offered.[235]

The use of this model is not meant to imply that the number of firms within an industry is of any strategic importance; but rather it is a handy way of isolating the decision of a firm with a very short time horizon which is presently unconstrained by the possibility that other firms may change their rate of sales. He supposes that , ' . . . the owner of a monopoly [fixes] the price of his commodity with exclusive reference to the immediate net revenue which he can derive from it.'[236]

The abstract nature of Cournot's model is made plain in both the *Principles* and in *Industry and Trade*. Indeed, the interpermeation of competition and monopoly is the 'keynote' of Book 3 of *Industry and Trade* where we are reminded over and over of the rarity of absolute monopoly and of the conditional nature of monopoly. Marshall envisages that industries could be ranked according to their degree of monopolistic control.[237] This ranking would depend on two factors:

(i) The extent to which a firm could price above the average long-period costs of extra production undertaken by potential competitors; and

(ii) the period of time for which this differential could be sustained.[238]

In language anticipating the 'barrier to entry' of Bain,[239] Marshall writes of obstacles to the establishment of effective competition[240] which are the sources of a firm's monopolistic control.

He refers, at that place, only to two such obstacles. The first of these is the initial cost of establishing a business – the capital, risk and effort involved. Secondly, he refers to inertia among entrepreneurs who, being opposed to change, do not invade the market of the monopolist.

However, at other points, particularly in *Industry and Trade*,

Marshall discusses other obstacles to free competition. In the case of retailing, he claims that the practice of branding goods lowered the obstacles to free competition, for customers were able to trust a product by knowing the brand name rather than being forced to rely on the judgment of a trusted retailer. In this way the branding of goods assisted the invasion of retailing markets by the co-operatives.[241]

When discussing trusts and cartels,[242] Marshall refers to many ways in which the behaviour of businesses may be directed towards the erection of obstacles to effective competition: these are practices by which potential competitors may be prevented from entering or by which existing competitors may be prevented from expanding their output. Such behaviour is *destructive* competition. 'One runner may outdo his rivals by greater energy as much as he can: but, if he puts his hand on another's shoulder to pull him back, while pulling himself forward, that is the unfair competition against which the Anti-trust Act[243] is directed.'[244] The behaviour to which Marshall refers includes predatory price-cutting, price discrimination, exclusive dealing, tying contracts, and aggregated rebates.[245]

That positions of monopoly rest on a business's ability to compete is set out beautifully in Macgregor's book on *Industrial Combination*[246] — the first half of which analyses the various 'factors of competing strength'. As with the distinction between profits and rents to institutional advantage, so the distinction between competitive and monopolistic conduct relies on normative rather than positive criteria.

Marshall maintains that, for any but a short-run view, concentration is secondary to the obstacles to free competition as a determinant of monopoly power.[247] Once such obstacles exist, concentration and the existence of factors which facilitate collusion may be significant.[248]

In this analysis of monopoly, Marshall is firmly in the tradition of the English classical school — wherein monopoly is generally considered to mean the limitation of the free flow of resources that permits a differential between market price and natural price to persist.

While many of Marshall's contemporaries shared his definition of monopoly,[249] the increasing vogue for deterministic models towards the close of the nineteenth century favoured the simpler classification of markets according to the number of sellers which is the Cournot — Walras — Edgeworth — Chamberlin tradition.

Cournot's equilibrium model

Cournot's model is of simple (that is, non-discriminatory) monopoly;

the seller quotes a price common to all buyers and the buyers adjust their purchases to the price.

Using notation similar to that of Marshall,[250]
x = quantity produced and sold in the period,
demand price = $f_1(x)$,
average cost = $f_2(x)$.
The monopolist's profit from selling output will be $x f_1(x) - x f_2(x)$. This is maximised when $x f_1'(x) + f_1(x) = xf_2'(x) + f_2(x)$.

Following Joan Robinson, the left hand side may be termed marginal revenue and the right hand side, marginal cost. Edgeworth shows that, by changing the signs and reinterpreting the symbols, Cournot's formulation may be extended to a 'monopolist consumer' – a unilateral monopsonist.[251]

Marshall warns against simple statements that the Cournot monopoly solution results in a lower rate of output than does free competition. For various reasons, costs are likely to be lower under monopoly than under free competition.[252]

Stability under monopoly

While Cournot devotes much space to the comparative statics of monopoly,[253] neither he nor Marshall explores the process of adjustment towards equilibrium.

In 1935, Hicks established the static stability conditions for monopoly in his 'Survey' article.[254] The second-order conditions imply that the marginal revenue curve cuts the marginal cost curve from above. Reder explores the modifications which the consideration of interactions between markets imposes.[255] It was left to Lange to generalise the Samuelson stability analysis to include adjustments under monopoly.[256] Lange coins the terms 'monopolistic underrestriction' and 'overrestriction' of supply. (One can also talk of monopsonistic underrestriction and overrestriction of demand.) These monopolistic over and underrestrictions perform the roles of excess demand and excess supply in the Walras–Hicks–Samuelson model.

Arrow claims that the only reason for not supposing instantaneous adjustment by the monopolist is that he may not know his entire demand curve. Uncertainty is a crucial consideration. As the monopolist gains knowledge, he converges to Cournot's equilibrium, earning higher profits in each successive time period.[257]

Qualifications by Marshall

Marshall's restriction of the application of Cournot's model to the myopic monopolist is at variance with the Arrow-Lange view of the monopolist's process of convergence – unless that convergence is a remarkably rapid process. For Marshall, the time horizon of the monopolist differs among firms depending on various factors.[258] Consideration of the future may influence a firm's pricing policy in two ways. A firm may be careful to set the price below that which will encourage entry: 'That is to say, it adjusts its price rather closely to the cost of production *including profits*, on which a new-comer in an ordinary competitive market would base his calculations. But it adds to this something for the insurance against extra risk which a new-comer into its market would expect to face.'[259]

Secondly, the monopolist may adjust his present prices after reflecting, ' . . . that the demand for a thing depends in a great measure on people's familiarity with it; and that if he can increase his sales by taking a price a little below that which would afford him the maximum net revenue, the increased use of his commodity will before long recoup him for his present loss.' . . . 'This sacrifice by a monopolist of part of his present gains in order to develop future business, differs in extent—rather than kind—from the sacrifices which a young firm commonly makes in order to establish a connection.'[260]

Woven into Marshall's discussions of monopoly is a recurring emphasis on the influence of the personalities and judgment of business leaders on the policies their firms pursue. The age of the business leaders, their sensitivity to public opinion and their taste for the Hicksian 'quiet life' may be important determinants of the competitive vigour of an industry. *Industry and Trade* demonstrates that Marshall found the literature of 'scientific management' an important source of information of the internal organisation of businesses.[261] As J. S. Mill had learned much from Babbage, so Marshall could learn from contemporary writers in the field of management.

Discriminating monopoly

The study of railway rates played an important catalytic role in the development of the theory of the firm during the century following the introduction of the railway. The interest in this applied issue led to generalisations and clarifications of such matters as the differences between pricing under monopoly and pricing under competition, the influence of indivisibilities on long-period value, the conditions needed for price discrimination, and the difficulties of applying the concept of costs. In the period under consideration, Dupuit, Lardner and Ellet made early contributions; while later contributions from Edgeworth, Taussig and Pigou provided much combative interest.[262] As was his wont, Marshall's pronouncements were those of a disinterested spectator of the debate. Also characteristic of Marshall was his omnivorous digestion of the empirical literature and the strong reliance on inductive generalisation of his own contribution.

Towards the end of our period the Pigou-Taussig debate served to highlight one of the key issues in empirical studies of price discrimination: the criteria by which one distinguishes price discrimination (which, it is usually assumed, can only exist if the firm has some monopoly power) from the competitive pricing of joint products. Hicks hints that these influences can be separated in theoretical discussions by discussing discrimination in the absence of jointness, that is, on the assumption that the firm is selling a single product, the singleness of which, ' . . . consists solely in its various units being perfect substitutes on the supply side.'[263] We will first consider the case of perfect substitutes in production, then the case of perfect complements, and, finally, the case of a degree of substitutability between zero and perfect.

Perfect substitutability

The two outstanding early expositors of price discrimination were trained as engineers. Both Ellet[264] and Dupuit[265] set out to show how the net revenue (statically conceived) from certain works could be maximised. Both acknowledged that cost could influence profit-maximising prices; but each paid relatively little attention to the specification of which costs are relevant.

It is not surprising that neither Ellet nor Dupuit tried to disentangle the discriminatory element in the pricing of railway services from the joint cost element: both wrote prior to the publication of Mill's *Principles* which first showed that competitive joint-product pricing could account for differences between prices. Besides, unlike Edgeworth, Pigou and Taussig, Ellet and Dupuit were not concerned to explain the pricing policies of private railway companies. Rather, they attempted to advise the relevant authorities how, given that discrimination was possible, they should set prices so as to maximise their net revenue.

Dupuit's model of a bridge whose crossing involves zero cost may be interpreted as a model of the pricing of goods which are perfect substitutes in production. In discussing examples of bridge crossings and railway journeys, Edgeworth hints that it is 'admissible, if indeed it is not essential', to suppose that very low prices do not create such demand that a capacity constraint becomes operative.[266]

Pigou classifies the discriminating power of the monopolistic firm into three degrees.

1. 'A first degree would involve the charge of a different price against all the different units of commodity, in such wise that the price exacted for each was equal to the demand price for it, and no consumers' surplus was left to the buyers.'

2. 'A second degree would obtain if a monopolist were able to make n separate prices, in such wise that all units with a demand price greater than x were sold at a price x, all with a demand price less than x and greater than y at a price y, and so on.'

3. 'A third degree would obtain if the monopolist were able to distinguish among his customers n different groups, separated from one another more or less by some practicable mark, and could charge a separate monopoly price to the members of each group.'[267]

In real life, discrimination of the third degree is the most common; and it is this which ocupies the attention of Ellet and Dupuit. Both acknowledge that a usable classification into Pigovian groups may be made either, (i) by means of the products being transported (higher value products will generally be able to bear a higher price, *cet. par.*), or (ii) by means of the wealth of the passengers.

Ellet considers how price will vary within categories of consumers or products as the cost (distance) of transportation varies. This exposition may be interpreted as explaining price differentials among products which are perfect substitutes on the supply side by focussing on his discussion of the price differentials among the categories rather than the discussion of the price differentials within the categories.

In *An Essay on the Laws of Trade* Ellet outlines a model using the first means of classification. In his later article, Ellet outlines the analogous principle of discrimination among classes of passengers.

For each grade of passengers, the following terms may be defined:

$¢$ = gross charge per mile of railroad,
δ = expense per passenger mile on the railroad,
c = toll (or charge in excess of costs) per passenger mile on railroad,
h = distance from assumed origin to tributary,
T = number of passengers on the railroad when price is zero.

Assume that for every lc increase in the charge, the number of passengers decreases by t.

$$\zeta \equiv \delta + c \qquad \dots (1)$$

Gross charge between the two places $= \zeta h$
Number of passengers $= T - \zeta ht$
Net Revenue $= (T - \zeta ht)ch \qquad \dots (2)$

Maximise (2) by differentiating with respect to c and equating to zero. Net revenue will be a maximum when the charge in excess of expenses is

$$ch = \tfrac{1}{2}\left(\frac{T}{t} - \delta h\right) \qquad \dots (3)$$

To obtain the value of gross charge, and expenses,

$$\zeta h = \tfrac{1}{2}\left(\frac{T}{t} + \delta h\right) \qquad \dots (4)$$

From which we conclude that under the circumstances assumed, the gross charge will yield the highest revenue on all the travellers who pass between the two cities, at which they reside, will be obtained by *adding half the actual expenses to a certain constant quantity.*[268]

Passengers may be classified into groups and for each group the constant term, $\tfrac{1}{2}\frac{T}{t}$, will vary; so that distinctions among different grades of passengers will produce a version of equation (4) for each grade.

But, it is probable that such distinctions would be found productive of inconvenience sufficient, in this country [the U.S.], to limit them to two classes – the first consisting of those who regard cheapness as more important than the superior comforts and more select society offered in the best class of cars, and the second, of those who are willing to pay something for these considerations.[269]

Dupuit establishes rules for the maximisation of net revenue given a bell-shaped total revenue curve; but gives more suggestions than does Ellet as to how a firm might be able to classify potential customers.

Dupuit expatiates on the proposition that product differentiation may be a device by which the surplus utility of the wealthy may be captured. So railway companies may need to give third-class passengers uncomfortable carriages so as to encourage the wealthy passengers into more expensive second or first-class seats. Indeed, one problem for the firm is that categories are not always independent: 'Taken in isolation, it may be worth it to provide cover and upholstery [for third-class passengers], but it would interfere with revenue from first class and second class.'[270]

As Pigou later emphasised, a necessary condition for price discrimination is that there exists some imperfection (cost) in the transferability of the product among consumers, or in the transferability of consumers among products.[271]

The substitutability of the products of other producers (both existing and potential) may also influence the pattern of market division. Ellet lays down a qualification to his equation (4): that it '. . . can never be applied at [the extreme limits of the sums designating the elevations of the grades]; since in practice the charges can never descend as low as δh, or the actual expense of conveyance, nor ascend as high as the sum which would justify the establishment of a rival.'[272] He makes it clear that the fraction $\dfrac{T}{t}$ will also depend on the availability of substitutes. Dupuit illustrates that the price elasticity of demand for transporting intermediate goods depends, in part, on the price elasticity of demand for the final product, and, in part on the elasticity of factor substitution.[273]

Monopolistic power and discrimination

The policy advice of Ellet and Dupuit is not arranged in the form of strictly deductive models with explicit premises; and it is only from their choice of illustration and various scattered remarks that one can infer that their prescriptions are meant to apply to firms with a degree of individual monopolistic power. In the quotation above, Ellet refers to the firm pricing with an eye to potential competitors, and Dupuit's articles refer to his discriminating firms as able to earn monopoly profits through being sheltered from competition.

Edgeworth's contract-curve model formally outlines reasons as to why discrimination depends on a limited number of sellers.[274] One may well ask why, in Pigou's discrimination of the first degree, every exchange does not involve bilateral bargains of the type suggested by Edgeworth's model of isolated exchange? To achieve such discrimination, the separability of exchanges must be perfect, so the reason must lie in an assumption of zero bargaining power on the part of the buyer.

The assumption that the single firm sells to a large number of buyers implies that the monopolist derives a negligible proportion of his net revenue from any one buyer; but it does not imply that the seller is indifferent between selling and not selling. Foldes claims that this latter condition is required if the all-or-nothing offer of the seller is not to be subject to bargaining. [275] Alternatively, one could suppose that the seller will always refuse to bargain because the cost of his beginning to bargain with *all* those buyers who would prefer to bargain rather than to lose all consumer surplus, exceeds the extra net revenue the firm will get when some buyers carry out their threat to refuse the all-or-nothing offer.

Both Walras and Marshall record that they have observed price discrimination in more or less competitive situations. Walras' examples of such discrimination involve market segmentation by means of product differentiation and he qualifies his observation by saying that the long-run tendency is for competition to narrow any difference between prices and costs. [276]

However, Marshall is less cautious. Characteristically, he generalises from his intimate knowledge of industry: 'It [the classification of markets on which price discrimination by shipping companies is based] is maintained in great measure even in an eager rate-war for the exclusive or partial occupation of any area of trade: rates may be lowered generally; but a proposal to carry first-class goods at fourth-class rates would be regarded as short-sighted even during the heat of combat.' [277]

8. BILATERAL MONOPOLY

The theory of isolated exchange

In chapter 2 [278] Turgot's classification of markets according to the number of parties to the exchange was mentioned.

In the period relating to the present chapter, many wirters subjected the problem of isolated exchange to reconsideration. Menger's contribution (and its influence on the formulation of Böhm-Bawerk) must be ranked highly among these reconsiderations. Menger supposes that two individuals (A,B) meet to exchange grain for wine. Individual A is indifferent between 100 units of grain and 40 units of wine. B is indifferent between 80 units of grain and 40 units of wine. If the price of grain in terms of wine were not between 100 and 80 then one of the parties would refuse to participate in the exchange. The actual price will depend upon ' . . . their various individualities and upon their greater or smaller knowledge of business life and, in each case, of the situation of the other bargainer.' [279]

Menger proceeds to an empirical generalisation.

In the formulation of general principles, however, there is no reason for assuming that one or the other of the two bargainers will have an overwhelming economic talent, or that other circumstances will operate more in the favor of one than the other. Under the assumption of economically equally capable individuals and equality of other circumstances, therefore, I venture to state, as a general rule, that the efforts of the two bargainers to obtain the maximum possible gain will be mutually paralyzing, and that the price will therefore be equally far from the two extremes between which it can be established.[280]

Edgeworth's model was a a great advance in its simplicity as well as the care with which the model is specified. His model does not permit single-valued demand and supply schedules, so an original specification of equilibrium conditions is required. 'Equilibrium is attained when the existing contracts can neither be varied without recontract with the consent of the existing parties, nor by recontract within the field of competition.'[281]

If there are only two players (individual decision-making units) in the exchange game, then the only economic moves permissible will be those taken with the consent of the other party. So a move will only be made if both parties stand to gain. In these circumstances, one party requires no information from the other (apart from his consent) before making a move. If both players are self-seeking, then disequilibrium will exist if and only if one party can gain and the other will not lose by a move.

The analysis is most easily assimilated by the contemporary reader when it is presented with the aid of the Paretian box diagram.[282]

There are two individuals, Y_1 and X_1. X_1's indifference curves are convex when viewed from OX. Good M is measured on the vertical axes, and good N on the horizontal axes.

Given that point E represents the initial endowments of both X_1 and Y_1,[283] such that IC^{ox} and IC^{oy} represent the indifference curves of X_1 and Y_1 through point E, X_1 will not accept a position closer to OX than IC^{ox}, and Y_1 will not accept a position closer to OY than IC^{oy}. If cc' is the locus of points of tangency of the two sets of indifference curves, then cc' contains the set of equilibrium points.

Edgeworth's contract curve is a solution to the bargaining problem in the sense of von Neumann and Morgenstern.[284] It consists of a set of imputations which do not dominate each other; but for each point off

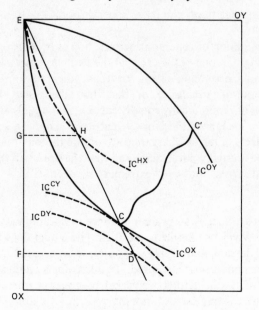

Paretian Contract Curve

the contract curve there exists a point on the contract curve which dominates it. Edgeworth's solution establishes the boundaries to the set of equilibrium points. However, there exist a number of equilibirum points – any further reduction of which would require a more detailed specification of the model.

Wicksell suggests that one such specification might be that the sum of the utility derived by the two participants is a maximum. He notes that such a requirement may lie outside Edgeworth's contract locus implying that one party may need to make a loss to achieve this requirement.[285]

Marshall, in the course of his search for the conditions for the determinacy of stability in the market period, notes that pure exchange between two individuals of two goods will be determinate if one of the commodities has marginal utilities for each of the parties which are constant between transactions.[286] The purpose of Marshall's Appendix on barter was to show that the indeterminacy in the two person/two good model is caused by the varying marginal utilities as transactions occur rather than by the fewness of the parties.

However, Edgeworth suggests that the indeterminacy is due to the fewness of the parties and offers a proof for this proposition by introducing further pairs of X and Y (they happen to be identical to X_1

and Y_1 – but this is not necessary) which narrows the range of the contract locus. Edgeworth claims that with the addition of further parties the system will converge to a single point on the contract curve. The contraction of the contract curve occurs in the following way.[287] Introduce X_2 and Y_2 with preferences identical to those of X_1 and Y_1 respectively.

Allocation c is an equilibrium point in the two-person case. But Y_1 prefers IC^{DY} to IC^{CY}. Y_1 will attempt to get to point D by offering X_1 and X_2 FD of N, in return for EF of M, of which each X will provide $\dfrac{EF}{2}$.

If they accept this offer, X_1 and X_2 will be at point H – at a higher indifference curve than IC^{OX}. But Y_2 will be left with his initial endowment, so he will give a counter-offer to both X_1 and X_2. Because of this rivalrous behaviour, point c will not be an equilibrium possibility when four parties are being considered.

It is important to note that, as a result of the counter-offer by Y_2, *both* Y_1 and Y_2 will be on less preferred indifference curves than if they had both accepted the original point c. So, in making the first offer to X_1 and X_2, Y_1 must be extraordinarily myopic – in that he cannot see that this will encourage Y_2 to make his counter-offer. If this myopia were not present, then there would be no reason to suppose that point c would not be an equilibrium point for quadrilateral exchange. Thus, without the implicit assumption of myopia, the contraction of the contract curve through the addition of traders would not occur.

Complementary monopolies

'Bilateral Monopoly' may be used to refer to two different industrial structures: complementary monopolies which will be considered in this section, and two-stage monopoly which will be considered under the following heading. (Under the latter, the second firm is a monopsonistic buyer of the product from the preceding stage.) Zeuthen points to certain similarities between this successive monopolies case and that of Cournot's complementary monopolies where two inputs (each of them monopolised) are used in fixed proportions by a competitive industry. Zeuthen uses the term 'bilateral monopoly' both for two-stage monopoly and for Cournot's complementary monopolies.[288]

Cournot's model has two inputs, copper (x_1) and zinc (x_2) whose sole use is in the production of brass.[289] Wicksell presents an illustration of Cournot's model by supposing that the demand for each of the inputs may be represented by a linear function: $x_1 = x_2 = 1 - \rho_1 - \rho_2$.[290]

Costs are assumed to be zero. Cournot wants to say that price is the sole decision variable for the producers of x_1 and x_2. The reason for this is presumably that, if producers are assumed to act independently and if quantity were the decision variable, then they may choose to produce quantities which do not satisfy the fixed proportions requirement. Such an outcome would not be an equilibrium decision for that firm which was left with unsold stocks. In such circumstances a realisation of interdependence would be imposed on the producers. However, Cournot wants to construct a model in which each producer reacts in a myopic maximising manner to a given demand function.

If the owner of x_1 decides on a certain price, ρ_1, then the most advantageous price for the owner of x_2 will be that which maximises $\rho_2(1 - \rho_1 - \rho_2)$. Thus ρ_2 is set at $\dfrac{(1 - \rho_1)}{2}$.

When he adopts this price, the owner of x_1 will adjust to $\dfrac{1 - \rho_2}{2} = \dfrac{1}{4} + \dfrac{\rho_1}{4}$, then the owner of x_2 will adjust to $\dfrac{3}{8} - \dfrac{\rho_1}{8}$ etc . . . The second term in these expressions approaches zero, and can therefore be neglected. The first term approaches $\dfrac{1}{3}$ – the price of x_1 and x_2 which will be approached by this stabilisation process. Such prices will represent an equilibrium for they satisfy the simultaneous equations:

$$\rho_2 = \frac{1 - \rho_1}{2},$$

$$\rho_1 = \frac{1 - \rho_2}{2}.$$

With $\rho_1 = \dfrac{1}{3}$ and $\rho_2 = \dfrac{1}{3}$, the total price is $\dfrac{2}{3}$ of that price which would have prevented all sales. The producers will sell one third of the quantity of goods which would have been consumed at a price of zero. This will be less than the outcome of a price and quantity of half a unit which would have resulted from joint profit-maximisation.

Marshall was sceptical of the use of such 'abstract reasonings of a general character' when applied to the conflicts and alliances between monopolistic associations. He maintained that Cournot's model was particularly unrealistic in supposing that the input producers had a precise knowledge of the demand functions for the products they were producing. Besides, the notion of absolute monopolies in long-period equilibrium seems very unlikely to occur.[291]

Two-stage monopoly

By attributing simple, mechanistic decision rules to the firms, one can construct a model for the monopolisation of successive stages of production similar to that of Cournot's model of complementary monopolies. It was on this basis that Zeuthen argues for the similarities between the models.

Ellet had illustrated this similarity ninetyone years earlier in his discussion of two adjoining transport networks. The model, remarkable for its similarities to Wicksell's illustration of Cournot on complementary monopoly,[292] uses the differential calculus to arrive at the following (Cournotesque) conclusion.

If the proprietors of the longer of the two works were to establish their toll without reference to the other, they would appropriate the half of this balance [between unit cost and the maximum price chargeable without excluding the traffic] for their profits, and leave the residue for the encouragement of the trade. If, then, the owners of the shorter line were to establish the tariff for their work, they would levy upon the half of this residue, and leave but one fourth of the original tax in shape of the toll, which the trade would bear, to go to the increase of the tonnage.

But the consequence of this would be, to cause the first company to reduce its toll down to one half the amount not taken by the second company, and thus give opportunity to the second, again to increase its exactions. And the ultimate result would be, if there were much disparity between the lengths of the lines, to cause two-thirds of the whole toll which might be levied without excluding the trade, to be charged upon the two lines, and to leave but one-third for encouragement of the business.[293]

Following the publication of Edgeworth's model of isolated exchange, many writers on both two-stage monopoly and on complementary monopoly opted for a statement that the only correct *general* statement was that the final outcome depends on a number of factors peculiar to any industrial situation. This was the attitude of Pareto, Marshall, and of Marshall's pupil, A. L. Bowley.

In his *Mathematical Groundwork*, Bowley showed, rather tersely, how exchange under two-stage monopoly is indeterminate.[294] Under pressure from Wicksell's review of the book[295] (which supported the determinate, Cournotesque approach to the problem), Bowley outlines his views in an article.[296] He shows that one can achieve various uniquely-determined solutions by assuming that: (i) the buyer dictates the price while the supplier adjusts the quantity; (ii) that the supplier dictates the price while the buyer adjusts the quantity; or (iii) that they agree to maximise joint gains and then divide the spoils. The particular extra assumptions favoured by Ellet and Wicksell have no more to commend them than do any others.

In the field of bilateral monopoly, as in so many other sections of the theory of the firm, the old methodological tensions were to be felt well after Marshall's death. Marshall and his followers were to suffer a temporary eclipse by those who were eager to build simple, deterministic models of the world which, Marshall had taught, is exceedingly complex.

9. DUOPOLY

The importance of behavioural hypotheses

In his *Manual*, Pareto emphasises that 'the problem' of duopoly is not one problem but many. The nature of the problem posed varies according to 'an infinite number' of circumstances.[297] Depending on these circumstances, as to how the two firms choose to use their monopoly power, a variety of solutions can be generated – including collusive monopoly, price leadership, product competition, a fight to the death, etc.

This, Paretian, attitude to criticism of duopoly models became fashionable in the late 1920s and the 1930s when a number of writers spelled out the propositions implicit in the models of Cournot and Edgeworth (et. al.), and the way in which differences in behavioural hypotheses yield different results. But, until Bowley's book[298] (published in 1928), no duopoly model had attempted to incorporate into formal behavioural functions, anticipations of the reactions of the rival to the move being considered.

Cournot

Having expounded his monopoly model in chapters V and VI of *Researches*, Cournot proceeds, in chapter VII, to develop his duopoly model and to use the model to deal with a number of sellers larger than two.

Cournot assumes a homogeneous product so that the total sales of the market are divided equally between the two firms. Thus, any solution other than the (unique) joint-revenue maximising solution of simple monopoly will imply a loss in revenue to each of the firms. This further suggests that any solution other than joint-revenue maximisation (assuming, with Cournot, that costs do not vary with output) conflicts with Cournot's maximisation dictum: ' . . . that each one seeks to derive the greatest possible value from his goods or his labour . . . [and] to deduce the rational consequences of this principle . . .'.[299] But Cournot's firms possess no foresight beyond the time period in which their decision is made: ' . . . for in the moral sphere men cannot be supposed to be free from error and lack of forethought any more than in the physical world bodies can be considered perfectly rigid, or supports perfectly solid, etc. . . .'.[300]

This myopia of each firm permits Cournot to construct, for each firm, a static decision function. But this does not prevent him from exploring certain dynamic properties of the model. In each successive time period the firm is confronted with a set of parameters which forms the basis of its peculiarly myopic decision. The myopia hypothesis and the process of price formation are the two elements of Cournot's model which have borne the brunt of the frequent criticism levelled at the model.

Myopia hypothesis

Cournot's dynamic pattern of stability adjustment is of consecutive time periods. Each time period in the process of adjustment to equilibrium contains a decision by one producer. The producers take decisions alternatively. It is assumed that each producer knows the market demand function and that the adjustment of quantity demanded to changes in price takes place within the time period in which the decision is made. The decision will affect the amount supplied to the market which in turn influences the price and the quantity demanded.

The failure of firm 1, in taking a decision in time period t_1, to consider the likely move of firm 2 in time period t_2,[301] has been roundly condemned. Fisher,[302] H. L. Moore,[303] and Wicksell[304] are among the condemners. Pigou claims that the Cournotesque duopolist is inconsistent, in that he believes that by varying his supply the price will alter, but he also believes that his rival's output will not alter.[305]

Amoroso, a consistent champion of Cournot on duopoly, offers a defence of the myopia hypothesis on the grounds that, while life is naturally more complex than the model, the hypothesis is required in order to obtain a determinate result.

> In the mathematical theory of duopoly it is a question not of what the one or the other monopolist will do in a given circumstance – because this is a matter not only of formulae, but of knowing whether we have to do with a violent man, or shrewd one, or a submissive one – but rather of finding out what action would be to the best advantage of both if both were pure and perfect specimens of *homo oeconomicus*. . . . The true *homo oeconomicus* makes cool and conscious calculations and has no long-term projects. The future is always in the lap of the Gods and is a matter of imagination as much as of cold measured reasoning. Economic Man manoeuvres quietly, with no great ambition or hopes, and tries to better his position little by little.[306]

It seems odd that Amoroso's cooly calculating homo oeconomicus does not look beyond his nose. However, Amoroso is expressing Stigler's concern that to deal in anticipated reactions requires, ' . . . that we deal only with special cases.'[307] Stigler's worry is that the truth-content of a catalogue of special cases may be minimal. However, the falsity-content of the Cournotesque generalisation may be very great.

The process of price formation

Cournot's model envisages that the decision variables for the producers are the quantities they each supply. In each period, quantities are decided and placed on the market. Price is then fixed, by an independent authority, such that the quantity demanded equals the quantity supplied. Equilibrium will occur when neither firm thinks that it can gain by varying the quantity which it places on the market.

It is not clear why Cournot denied to the firms the possibility of varying price directly. Certainly, the time period analysis with full adjustments by consumers in the period of the decision would cause very odd results if firms producing a homogeneous product were to take turns to fix their prices in alternative periods. The producer with the lower price would capture all the sales in a particular period. To introduce a degree of realism into a price-initiator model, it would be necessary to suppose some friction in the adjustment of consumers.[308]

Equilibrium

In his monopoly model, Cournot assumes a linear demand function of the form $\rho = a - bD$. The firm maximises

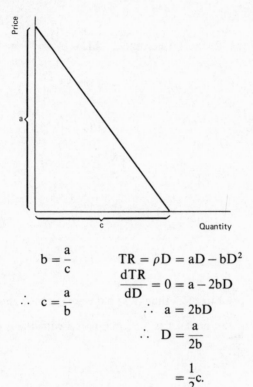

$$b = \frac{a}{c} \qquad TR = \rho D = aD - bD^2$$

$$\qquad \frac{dTR}{dD} = 0 = a - 2bD$$

$$\therefore \quad c = \frac{a}{b} \qquad \therefore \quad a = 2bD$$

$$\therefore \quad D = \frac{a}{2b}$$

$$= \frac{1}{2}c.$$

Cournot has a closely analogous model when he comes to duopoly. D is replaced by $D_1 + D_2$ ... (1) and each firm maximises independently.

For firm 1

$$\rho = a - b(D_1 + D_2)$$
$$TR = \rho D_1 = aD_1 - bD_1{}^2 - bD_1 D_2$$
$$\text{to maximise,} \quad \frac{dTR_1}{dD_1} = 0$$
$$= a - 2bD_1 - bD_2 \qquad \qquad \dots \quad (2)$$

Note that TR_1 is differentiated with respect to D_1. This implies that

D_1 is the only decision variable which firm 1 operates. Similar maximising conditions may be derived for firm 2.

$$a - 2bD_2 - bD_1 = 0 \tag{3}$$

$$D_1 = D_2 \tag{4, from (2) & (3)}$$

$$D_1 = D_2 = \frac{D}{2} \qquad \text{from (1) & (4)}$$

∴ equations (2) and (3) become $a - bD - b\dfrac{D}{2} = 0$

$$\therefore \quad a = bD + b\frac{D}{2}$$

$$\therefore \quad \frac{a}{b} = D + \frac{D}{2}$$

$$\therefore \quad 2\frac{a}{b} = 3D$$

$$\therefore \quad \frac{2}{3}c = D$$

$$\therefore \quad D_1 = D_2 = \frac{1}{3}c.$$

Each firm produces less than it would were it a monopolist; but total production of the product is $\frac{2}{3}c$ – compared with the outcome under monopoly of $\frac{1}{2}c$.

Stability

The producer making a decision in time period t will assume that his rival maintains his output of time period $t-1$. Cournot, by means of words and graph, outlines an adjustment process of the following form. On the assumption that it is trying to maximise revenue in time period t, firm 1 will have a reaction function whose implicit form is the following:

$$f(D_{1t} + D_{2t-1}) + D_{1t}f'(D_{1t} + D_{2t-1}) = 0.$$

A similar function can be constructed for the decision of firm 2 in time period $t+1$.[309]

Such functions (hypothetical examples of which are given in much of the secondary literature[310]) are stable in the sense that the output levels and price converge to the equilibrium, no matter from which point the system commences.

Alternative processes of price formation

It is intriguing to speculate on the causes of the reputations of past economists. Today, Bertrand is often credited with the production of a duopoly model as an alternative to that of Cournot. In fact, all that can be attributed to Bertrand on this score is a singularly confused paragraph in his review of the *Recherches*.[311] In this paragraph he refers to Cournot's duopoly model; but he refers to the Cournotesque duopolist as having power to name the price at which he sells. Given alternative decisions, that myopic duopolist whose turn it is to make a decision will shave the price to capture the whole market. In the following period, the rival will shave the price yet further. The price will fall until it equals average cost (presuming this to be the same for each firm).

The importance of these few sentences by Bertrand lay in the stimulus they provided for Edgeworth. As if the naive boy's explanation that the Emperor had no clothes sparked off a coup d'État which ushered in the reign of Edgeworth. Bertrand can be credited with a confused cry. Certainly it was Edgeworth who reigned supreme in the field of duopoly theory for the next twenty years; the only opposition being provided by the dexterous guerilla action of Amoroso.

Edgeworth

Edgeworth's duopoly model is oddly titled in that the pattern of bahaviour it represents is not contingent on the number of sellers. However, as it was originally presented as a duopoly model, it is convenient to discuss it under this section.[312]

The uniqueness of the model lies in its assumption regarding the cost conditions facing producers. The 1897 version has each firm facing constant costs up to an absolute capacity constraint. The cost functions need not be identical between the firms; but each producer must know the other's cost function. Forthermore, the total capacity constraint of the two producers operates at a level of production less than that which would supply the total market demand at prices equal to the average costs.[313]

The producers take alternative decisions — one decision being taken in each time period. As in the Cournot model, the producers are unredeemably myopic and the possibility of the entry of new firms is not considered. The producers fix the prices to which consumers respond. Producers fix their prices on the assumption that consumers' preferences between the products are so slight as to be overridden by any slight price difference.

Moreover, the response of consumers to changes in price, both in switching between producers and in adjusting their aggregate consumption, occurs within the time period of the decision to change the price. Machlup points to a further hypothesis necessary for the model.[314] This is that all consumers are uniform. If this were not the case, then those consumers who were willing to pay less may be clustered around the producer who is pricing so as to utilise his full capacity; while those consumers who are willing to pay more may be left to the producer charging a higher price. But if this distribution of consumers were reversed, the producer charging the higher price would sell less. In fact, Edgeworth operates his model on the assumption that the market demand function is single-valued.

The outcome of this model is that there is no equilibrium point: there is no pair of prices from which one producer will not wish to move. If one firm sets a Cournotesque monopoly price, there will occur the alternate shaving of price envisaged by Bertrand. This shaving will continue until one producer realises that, rather than a further shave, it would be more profitable to leave his rival with all the customers he can supply and to charge the Cournotesque monopoly price for the rest. But this move will encourage the rival to start the shaving process once again.

Machlup[315] mentions that because two different prices exist during one time period, there is a possibility of arbitrage operations. Such operations are unlikely to cover costs while prices are being shaved by small amounts. They may be significant during the period in which one firm (say 'Secundus') charges a low price capturing sufficient customers to use his full capacity while the other firm ('Primus') decides to charge a monopoly price.

Edgeworth did not claim any precise applicability for his model. The leap of a firm (Secundus) up to the monopoly price may not follow the precise Cournotesque calculation.

Practical considerations may induce him to make a less violent jump. For Primus it will then be a matter of deliberation whether he should cut the price fixed by Secundus, or, jumping to a still higher price, deal separately with the custom left to him by Secundus. We cannot foresee what the jumps will be; theory predicts only that the jumping will go on for ever, as long as the monopolists are uncombined.[316]

It was stated at the commencement of this section that the solution to Edgeworth's 'duopoly' model is not contingent on there being only two firms. If we increase the number of firms in the model towards infinity and maintain all the other assumptions, a similar solution will be obtained. A. J. Nichol constructs a simple Edgeworth-type model and shows that as the number of firms increases, the range within which prices may fluctuate actually increases.[317]

Looking towards the 1930s

Throughout the period we are considering the problem of duopoly was approached in terms of the framework established by Cournot and Edgeworth. But in his 'Pure Theory of Monopoly' paper (1897), Edgeworth had already likened the case of competing monopolists producing complementary articles to that of a game of chess. 'And, as in chess, when only the two kings and one of the inferior pieces remain on each side, may not the two monopolists go on making moves against each other to all eternity?'[318]

Even Edgeworth questioned the myopia hypothesis in this case. Fisher's article on Cournot (1898) applied the game analogy to duopoly,[319] and Kotany,[320] Moore,[321] and Pigou,[322] all acknowledged that some consideration by a firm of decisions to be made in future time periods must be incorporated into duopoly models.

However, these seeds fell on barren ground. The seed which finally germinated was planted by A. L. Bowley. He gave a 'simple example' so as to illustrate a possible approach to the problem of duopoly. Given a market demand function and cost functions for the two firms, each will vay his output (x_1 or x_2) in the Cournotesque manner so as to maximise his own net revenue. One can differentiate firm 1's net revenue equation with respect to x_1 and that of firm 2 with respect to x_2. But, added Bowley: 'To solve these we should need to know x_2 as a function of x_1, and this depends on what each producer thinks the other is likely to do.'[323]

Bowley's book, and its subsequent reviews by Wicksell[324] and Allyn Young[325], clearly influenced many writers whose work was based on the hypothesis of non-zero conjectural variation. The incorporation of this hypothesis into formal models characterises the 'oligopoly' theory of the post-Marshallian age.

5 Marshall and the Post-Marshallians

In his presidential address to Section F (Economic Science and Statistics) of the annual meeting of the British Association for the Advancement of Science of 1861, William Newmarch noted the increasingly empirical foundation of economics since the time of Adam Smith.

> . . . we have learned that in these enquiries the only sound basis on which we can found doctrines, and still more the only safe basis on which we can erect laws, is not hypothetical deduction, however ingenious and subtle, but conclusions and reasoning supported by the largest and most careful investigation of facts. This vital change of method, this substitution of observation and experiment (and for our present purpose the two words mean very much the same thing) for deductions arrived at by geometrical reasoning, seems to me to be the most prominent fact of the last thirty or forty years, as regards the progress of the branches of knowledge which more immediately interest us in this section.[1]

Newmarch proceeded to list those previously dominant doctrines which had been modified as a result of experience and observation;[2] and he urged his audience to continue with empirical work. Sharing J. S. Mill's optimistic opinion of exchange theory, Newmarch considered that empirical work in this field would yield little other than confirmation of received knowledge.

Newmarch's observation of the growing significance of empiricism for the thirty or forty years to 1861 could be applied to the whole period since he spoke – and particularly to the period following the death of Marshall. This empirical work has, despite the predictions of Newmarch, led to significant modifications being made to the theory of exchange, particularly as that theory applies to short-run adjustments. The recording of observations has enabled us to reach some tentative judgments as to the degree of verisimilitude of the theory bequeathed to us by Marshall as compared with its subsequent developments. These judgments form the subject of this penultimate chapter.

1. THE MOTIVATION OF THE FIRM

A recurring issue in the methodological debates among economists is the extent to which an inconsistency between observations and the 'assumptions' of theories is a cause for concern. During the 1940s and the 1950s this issue was focussed in a debate as to whether the assumption that firms maximise their net revenue was either a realistic proposition or a useful assumption. The focus was provided by the report of a survey undertaken by Hall and Hitch of the methods by which a sample of thirty-eight businesses (principally engaged in manufacturing) set their prices.[3] The authors considered that the most striking feature of their survey was that the firms interviewed failed to set prices by equating marginal cost with marginal revenue. While pricing methods varied among the respondents, many seemed to set price at direct cost plus certain percentage additions to cover overheads and profit.

This innocent article (which incidentally provided evidence that those surveyed considered both demand and cost conditions when setting prices) provoked a major debate.[4] However, it was not always clear that the disputants were clear as to which assumption of economic theory was being challenged.[5] Their observations were not inconsistent with Marshall's hypotheses as to motivation. Marshall's firm has no unique maximum which it aims to achieve. Indeed, the increasing size of businesses and the resulting formation of policy by salaried managers imply that firms may not always seek out that policy option which maximises expected net revenue. The degree to which a firm strives to maximise its net revenue, is, for Marshall, dependent on the internal organisation of the firm and the personalities in positions of power.

But if the observations of Hall and Hitch did not contradict Marshall, neither did they contradict the static maximising assumption of Cournot, Walras and Joan Robinson. The timeless maximisation of net revenue in these models (together with the appropriate stability conditions) facilitates a qualitative prediction as to the direction in which change will occur in response to a change in parameters. The stability conditions of such models yield no predictions as to the speed at which change will occur; so the models yield no predictions as to the policies firms will be pursuing at any point in time. It might be that the full-cost pricing observed by Hall and Hitch is quite consistent with movement towards the equilibrium positions predicted by Cournot, Walras and Joan Robinson.

The observations by Hall and Hitch could only have been inconsistent with a maximising assumption which was specific as to the time path of the firm in moving towards equilibrium. Indeed, the reason their article provoked such a reaction was that they were seen to be attacking the assumption of myopic maximisation.

Up to the time of Marshall's death the myopia assumption was of little importance. As seen above,[6] this assumption was used by Cournot, Edgeworth, and Amoroso when constructing models of duopoly; but the assumption was attacked by Fisher, Kotany, H. L. Moore, Wicksell, Pigou, Bowley, Allyn Young, and Chamberlin. By the time of Hall and Hitch the assumption was held to be inapplicable to oligopoly theory.

However, in the 1920s and 1930s the myopia assumption was incorporated, as if by stealth, into a stability analysis for the emerging model of perfect competition. This analysis consisted in elaborating the large-numbers model of Cournot and Walras so as to spell out a time path of movement towards equilibrium along the lines of the Marshallian time-period analysis. Given a parametric change, firms would move over time to a new long-run equilibrium having first traversed a market-period and a short-run equilibrium. Because each of these equilibria were positions of maximisation for each firm in the industry, the analysis implicitly required that the firm be a myopic maximiser but one confronted by constraints which differed according to the lapse in time since the parametric change.[7]

One of Machlup's responses to criticism of the hypothesis of the myopic maximiser is to admit that it is not universally true, but to claim that it is a sufficiently good approximation to the actions of firms under competitive conditions to yield predictions whose degree of verisimilitude is greater than that of contending models. Under competitive conditions, firms are compelled to take advantage of brief opportunities to increase their net revenue because they can never hope to trade lower returns now for returns higher than normal over a long time span.

It was just this latter point which was urged by E. A. G. Robinson in his review of P. W. S. Andrews' *Manufacturing Business*.[8] Robinson questioned Andrews' proposition that the time horizon of firms was such that they would not take advantage of short-lived opportunities to capture quasi-rents in excess of average fixed cost. Andrews claims that such action (to be expected from a myopic maximiser) would lessen the valuable goodwill the firm has striven to establish with its purchasers.

The analysis by Andrews explains the findings of the Hall and Hitch survey in terms of the rational conduct of businessmen who are faced with a market into which entry can be quickly effected and in which customer goodwill largely determines the division of market demand among firms.

Sir John Hicks[9] characterises as 'snatchers' those who weight immediate profits highly compared with future profits and as 'stickers' those who weight future profits highly when compared with immediate returns. Hicks does not meet Andrews and Harrod on their own ground because he does not consider the case in which firms have discretion as to price. If firms adjust quantities in a Walrasian competitive market, they are unlikely to allow the possibility of potential entrants to influence their present policies; but in a market where firms deal directly with their customers such a longer-term outlook may be expected.

As to whether firms are snatchers or stickers and to what extent they are, is an empirical question. It appears that the businessmen interviewed by Hall and Hitch and by Andrews were solidly sticking. But other behaviour has been observed. If we only desire a theory which will yield the type of comparative static predictions expected by Machlup, then this empirical question is not particularly important; but if we desire to predict the rate at which variables move towards equilibrium values then this empirical question becomes important.

Despite the spirited defences by Machlup, the work of Andrews, and of other Oxford economists, has not been the only development facilitating some consistency between motivational assumptions and survey findings. In the last few decades increasing evidence of the influence of imperfect information and of uncertainty on business decisions has encouraged further qualifications to be placed on the assumption of profit maximisation.

Investment, uncertainty and knowledge

While there exist differing conjectures as to the time horizon of firms in making pricing decisions (as is seen by the debate between Andrews and E. A. G. Robinson mentioned above), there are few such differences when it comes to investment decisions. A firm making an investment decision is unlikely to be a myopic maximiser; rather, it will adopt a Marshallian long-period horizon.

That a firm is faced with uncertain future demand and future cost functions is not a proposition new to economics. A return for the bearing of risk is acknowledged in the distribution theory of the eighteenth century; and Galiani's equilibrium and stability analysis incorporates the hypothesis that the expectations guiding new investment may be confounded.[10] The distinction between insurable and uninsurable risks is to be found in the German literature of the first half of the nineteenth century.[11]

The complication to the assumption of the maximisation of net revenue caused by the need to specify a firm's willingness to bear risk and to embrace uncertainty is a more recent development. These recent developments follow Marshall's lead in seeking to explain and to predict the determinants of market structure. Marshall's time-period analysis, together with the concept of quasi-rent, formalised the way in which the time horizon of a firm changes as the variables subject to decision change. The more distant the time horizon the more uncertainty the decision involves. Consequently, Marshall refuses to predict the direction in which the investment policy of any particular firm will lead.

The need to make decisions relating to an unknowable future suggests that actuarial principles may be employed. Irving Fisher devotes a carefully-written chapter and Appendix in his *Nature of Capital and Income*[12] to an outline of the subjectivity of all probability estimates and the way in which such estimates may be used to discount future returns.

G. L. S. Shackle's *Uncertainty in Economics* proposes that actuarial principles cannot be applied to many market decisions (for example, to investment decisions) because, in the first place, their uniqueness means that no large number of sufficiently similar events can be found for the estimate of a probability; and, secondly, the firm usually will not be offered the opportunity of repeated trials if it fails at first. Shackle proposes that in such circumstances a firm's decision will be based not on a distribution of subjective probabilities but on a pair of particularly significant possible outcomes chosen both for the gain or loss they would occasion and for the degree of surprise they would cause.[13]

Alchian is quite explicit as to the incompatibility of decisions made under uncertainty with the hypothesis of profit maximisation.

> Under uncertainty, by definition, each action that may be chosen is identified with a *distribution* of potential outcomes, not with a unique outcome. . . . Essentially, the task is converted into making a decision (selecting an action) whose potential outcome *distribution* is preferable, that is, choosing the action with the *optimum distribution*, since there is no such thing as a *maximising distribution*.[14]

Alchian proceeds to argue that while it is meaningless to operate with the hypothesis that firms seek to maximise an objective function, firms will, in some long run, only survive if they do realise positive profits. So, for long-run, aggregative predictions it is safe to say that only profitable firms will survive. For the purpose of the qualitative, aggregative predictions yielded by the comparative static analysis under conditions of heavy competition, the qualifications to the profit-maximiser hypothesis are of little importance. If the theory is used to predict merely the directions of adjustments to prices or quantities traded then the theory will predict well providing firms are aware of changes in the demand or cost parameters. But if theory is to yield predictions as to the speed of adjustment and as to changes in industry structure, then the hypothesis as to the motivation of firms may be crucial.

Alternative motivational hypotheses

If the maximising hypothesis becomes meaningless when applied to long-period decisions relating to an uncertain environment, is there any class of decisions to which it can be applied? Pricing decisions, or market-period decisions as to output, are the obvious contenders. If the time horizon of a firm making these decisions is a matter of weeks rather than months, uncertainty might be negligible and the hypothesis may have some meaning – even if it be incorrect.

Very few economists are prepared to accept the myopic-maximiser hypothesis except in circumstances of 'heavy competition'.[15] But the use of the myopic-maximiser hypothesis for the market-period decisions of firms under heavy competition entails a rejection of the evidence offered by Andrews and Harrod as to the harmful effects of short-sighted maximisation on long-run returns in those industries in which firms deal directly with their customers. Perhaps the hypothesis is applicable to market-period decisions undertaken by firms which do not deal directly with customers, but rather deliver their output to a central selling agent.[16]

The increasing disenchantment with the maximising hypothesis since the death of Marshall has been facilitated by documentation of the process by which control over the goals of firms has been moving from holders of equity to management. Adam Smith had observed that joint-stock companies allowed investors little control over policy.[17] Following the removal in 1825 of restrictions on the free formation of joint-stock companies, this form of company organisation grew in importance. J. S. Mill and Alfred Marshall considered this growth to be significant for the goals businesses would pursue.[18] The study by Adolf

Berle and Gardiner Means of the 200 largest non-financial corporations in the United States documented this process of the separation of ownership from control.[19]

The hegemony of the manager and frequent observation of the preoccupation of managers with sales rather than with current profits led Baumol to propose that firms with market power tend to maximise sales subject to the condition that profits do not fall below some specified minimum value.[20] In his second edition Baumol proposes that managers seek to maximise the rate of growth of sales while trying to generate funds for investment which will yield growth in the future. The pricing policy predicted by the models is closer to the long-run competitive level than is that predicted under the assumption of the myopic maximisation of net revenue.

That it is possible to gain insight into the motivation and policies of firms by reading the literature on business management is not a recent suggestion. Marshall clearly benefited from his reading of books on 'Scientific Management'.[21] In the 1930s and 1940s the London School of Economics (as a product of the interfaces at that School between economics, accounting and management studies) yielded both much work on the application of the concept of opportunity cost to decision-making within firms, and Thirlby's attack on the economist's firm as controlled by an omniscient decision-maker.[22]

In the 1950s and 1960s the interface between management studies and economics was most fruitful on the other side of the Atlantic. At the Carnegie Institute of Technology, the work of Herbert A. Simon, and its more formal statement by Richard W. Cyert and James G. March[23] developed a more truth-like model of the process by which the firm generates decisions. The firm is pictured as a coalition of individuals. The goals of the firms will change over time in response to the changing power of the various members of the coalition. The significance of such changes for the policies of the firms would not seem to be great. For the purpose of comparisons of market or short-period decisions, changes in the power structure would not be significant; and for long-period policy the constraints of the capital market would ensure that the firm must pursue profits. (This latter point does not imply a maximising goal.)

The significant advance in the Cyert and March model is the statement of the determinants of the type of information which is sought and the degree to which it is pursued. Empirical studies undertaken by members of the Carnegie Institute suggest that firms faced with an uncertain environment which they cannot regulate immediately (by, for example, understandings between firms) will avoid long-period plans by using short-period decision rules reacting to short-period feedback from present policies. By use of a computer simulation model, Cyert and March concluded that such a firm operating in a duopoly will have its (market-period) behaviour influenced by parameters internal to the firm.

The prohibitive search and computational costs which would be entailed in seeking some ideal maximum leads Simon to his hypothesis that firms may be content with some satisfactory standard of profit performance.[24] The improvements in the period since the second world war in the techniques of operations research have increased the ability of firms to make decisions with limited information and computational abilities. The application of linear programming methods is justified, not on the grounds of the existence of linear production functions, but on the grounds that working with this approximation is less costly than the alternative of discovering the true production function and applying more complex techniques. Baumol and Quandt suggest that firms may be considered to maximise the net revenue yielded by the gathering of information and the refining of calculations.[25]

Empirical studies of the ways in which firms make long-period decisions given limited knowledge (bounded rationality in the jargon) of an uncertain future have recently been used to yield important, testable propositions as to the structure of industries. Much of this work uses a profit-seeking hypothesis rather than a profit-maximising hypothesis. A brief mention will be made of its results in the following section.

2. COST FUNCTIONS AND SUPPLY FUNCTIONS

During the 1920s and 1930s, many articles and books were devoted to the determinants of the firm's costs and to the determinants of total industry supply. Much of this writing on costs and almost all of that on supply functions was presented within the context of the model of perfect competition. This model, which is an elaboration of Cournot's static, large-numbers, quantity-adaptor model, was married to Marshall's time-period analysis after the death of Marshall. Cournot's static model with its timeless cost functions was adapted for the short-period normal and for the long-period normal.

This elaboration on Cournot's static model caused an alteration to his hypothesis of the maximisation of profits. The static maximisation hypothesis became the proposition of myopic maximisation.[26] At each point in time the myopic maximiser, confronted by a revenue function and by a cost function, will choose that quantity which would be an equilibrium quantity for the firm. For each point in time there exists a unique equilibrium price/quantity-supplied relationship for the firm.[27] As price is uniform among firms in the industry at any point in time, there will always exist a unique price/quantity relationship for the industry.

The emergence of the quantity-adaptor, perfect competition model, led to a preoccupation by professional economists with the nature of the function expressing average cost and marginal cost as a function of the output of the firm. Cournot and Marshall had spoken ambiguously of average cost and marginal cost;[28] but Edgeworth demanded clarity on this point.[29] Edgeworth's call for precision may have derived, at least in part, from the demands placed on his reasoning by the debate as to the determinants of railway rates. It was this policy concern which had attracted J. M. Clark to the subject of overhead costs; and Clark served greatly to clarify the distinction between returns to the variable factor and economies of scale.[30]

Marshall spoke of the tendency to diminishing returns in terms of product and was aware that *ex post* estimates of scale economies must confront the problem of variable rates of capacity utilisation[31]; so he cannot be convicted of gross error on this score. However, J. M. Clark remains throughout his book clear on this distinction. He states that *decreasing* returns to the variable factor (decreasing average product) may be associated with *falling* average costs when the rate of fall with respect to output of average fixed costs is more rapid than the rate of increase of average variable costs.[32]

These distinctions, together with their application to the quantity-adapting firm in a perfectly competitive environment, were incorporated into Viner's article of 1931[33] – a model of expositional clarity. Viner shows how cost/output graphs for the short run and for the long run may be used to derive, for any given price, both unique equilibrium outputs for the firms as well as a unique rate of production for the industry.

Short-period cost functions

During the 1920s and 1930s it came to be accepted that the firm's short-run marginal costs were positively related to its rate of output. This belief was held to be the general result of the application of extra units of a variable factor to a given quantity of fixed factor (in a two-input model).[34] As with the statements of this principle by J. B. Clark and Wicksteed[35], the proof of this deduction was rather careless. It was not clear just which assumptions were necessary to reach the conclusion; nor was it clear how the deduction proceeded.

In two articles in the *Zeitschrift für Nationalökonomie* (1936), K. Menger demolished the 'axiomatic' acceptance of the forward-rising short-run marginal cost curve. Menger shows that the 'deductions' by earlier economists are simply invalid. It is not possible to deduce a diminishing marginal product from a diminishing average product; and the strongest principle that can be deduced from the subhomogeneity of a production function (that is, a function for which equi-proportional increases in both inputs will not increase output more than pro-portionately) is that the *average* product of the variable input will diminish. Menger proceeds to urge that ' . . . the crucial issue for economics [is] as follows: Are the return laws true or false, that is, are they or are they not empirically confirmed? Whether they do or do not follow from certain other propositions is only a secondary issue.'[36]

Unfortunately, both Menger's reasoning and his methodological prescription are still being largely ignored. Empirical evidence on the form of short-period supply functions is notably scarce. Marshall's empirical generalisation as to the rising nature of the short-period supply price is given without detailed supporting evidence.[37] His arguments that firms will need to pay overtime rates to labourers and to have recourse to inferior quality inputs to increase supply in the short-period are disputed by Andrews.[38] Andrews (who was, unfortunately, unable to present his raw data) argues that businesses plan to run with excess capacity so that, (i) they do not lose (possibly irretrievable) customers in times of high demand; (ii) they have the capacity to cover contingencies for breakdowns and of machines being idle for repairs; and (iii) they can take advantage of any opportunities for the capture of growing markets.

> In general, average direct costs per unit of product will be expected to remain constant over large ranges of output, so long as the business continues to employ the same methods of production, and the total of such costs will vary with total output. The specification of the product will call for so much of each material to be embodied in the finished product, and the quantity of the materials so used must necessarily be constant per unit of product.[39]

These conclusions, based on the study of a number of manufactur-ing firms, have been confirmed by a number of studies of the regulated public utilities of the United States.[40]

Long-period cost functions

To a large extent, the verbal explanations of the shape of long-period cost functions has remained unaltered since the writing of J. S. Mill. Following the death of Marshall the indivisibilities of capital equipment has been mentioned as an explanation of technical scale economies[41] and more attention has been paid to the influence of scale on the cost of sales effort and the gaining of knowledge.[42] However, most economists would agree with Marshall that technological real economies of scale generally are limited; and that if diseconomies of scale are to occur they will probably be caused either by transport costs or by managerial factors.[43]

If technical diseconomies of scale are possible, they can be avoided by the planning of a multi-plant firm. One question of debate since Marshall's death is whether managerial diseconomies of scale may similarly be overcome by decentralisation. Given a static model of a perfectly competitive market, increasing long-period marginal costs must be the explanation why firms do not plan an indefinite expansion and thereby alter the structure of the market. Applying the implications of such a model to the real world, Amoroso argues that because the size of firms does not expand indefinitely, the long-period marginal cost curve must be forward rising.[44]

J. M. Clark argues that organising power is the chief limit to firm size, but the best-known formulation of this proposition comes from the first edition of E. A. G. Robinson's, *Structure of Competitive Industry*. Robinson argued that the problem of co-ordination limits the size of firms. Florence bases his criticism of this position on evidence from the literature of business management. Florence distinguishes the logic of internal organisation from that which occurs in practice. The logic of organisation consists in latest knowledge, skillfully applied: 'Apart from economists, however, those who have made a special study of organisation come to the conclusion that no limit is set to the size of the organisation if correct principles are adopted to enable the single leader to delegate control.'[45]

Despite the testimony of many of those who study internal organisation, and the apparent ability of even the largest firm in the world to escape scale diseconomies by means of a divisional organisation[46], many theorists continue to draw U-shaped long-run average cost curves. Such U-shaped long-run average cost curves were used prior to the death of Marshall,[47] but they became widespread in the late 1920s and the early 1930s. Pigou adopted them for his equilibrium firm in

1928;[48] and in 1931 Harrod showed the relationship between this curve and the short-run average cost curves in the now-familiar envelope construction.[49]

Even as an inference from the postualtes that technical economies of scale are limited and that problems of co-ordination eventually impose diseconomies, the U-shaped long-run average cost curve is not acceptable. Given these postulates, there is no reason why the curve should not have a lengthy horizontal section. The U-shape was not derived from the postulates, but was drawn so that the size of the firm could be uniquely determined in the long-run equilibrium of the omniscient, quantity-adjusting firm.

It is little wonder that observations provide little support for the U-shape. E. A. G. Robinson, whose name is usually invoked in its defence, notes that there is much practical and theoretical evidence to suggest that long-run average cost curves first decline and then have a large horizontal section before finally rising.[50] Those who have undertaken empirical studies, and there have been quite a few in the last twenty years, have discovered either L-shaped curves or curves which rise after a long horizontal section.[51]

3. COMPETITION AND THE SIZE OF FIRMS

Given a Cournotesque large-numbers model with the motivational hypothesis adjusted to that of myopic maximisation, equilibrium for the firm in the short period requires that short-run marginal cost be equal to price with marginal cost increasing at the equilibrium quantity. Given a change in price the existing firms will adjust their outputs such that short-run marginal cost (on the forward-rising segment of the marginal cost curve) equals price.[52]

If, at this new equilibrium, each firm were not to earn the normal rate of return on capital in the long run, then either entry or exit will occur so that long-run rates of return are adjusted to normal. This long-run stabilisation process is similar to that of Marshall and Walras.[53] Indeed, the long-run competitive output as that at which returns are normal is a version of Adam Smith's model in *The Wealth of Nations*. This model of the natural price has never been discarded. It has been invested with increased empirical content (not always corroborated) by elaborations to more immediate time horizons and allowances for more complex motivational hypotheses; but the basic structure of the model remains to this day.

One feature of the model of perfect competition is that (unlike the models of Marshall and Walras) the output of each firm is uniquely determined in the long run.[54] The output will be that at which long-run average cost will be at a minimum. (See the figure.) This uniquely-determined output is contingent on the postulate that the long-run average cost curve is U-shaped.

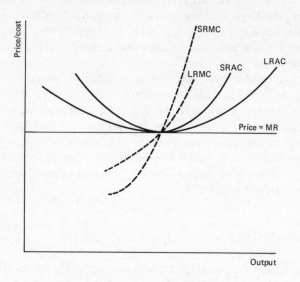

Long-Run Equilibrium for the Firm

AR = average revenue
MR = marginal revenue
LRAC = long-run average cost
LRMC = long-run marginal cost

The long-run industry supply curve

Marshall's long-period supply schedules do not show the quantities which will be supplied by the industry at any given price. Marshall does not offer a set of conditions which would enable us to judge whether an industry has reached the 'normal' position at which it would be located on its long-period supply schedule.[55]

However, in the model of perfect competition each firm is always in, at least a temporary, equilibrium. In the long-period normal each firm will be at an equilibrium as pictured in the figure above. For each price the (unique) equilibrium outputs may be summed to yield a point on the long-period supply schedule. Changes in output will be occasioned by the entry or exit of firms. If each firm is at long-period equilibrium then some of Marshall's explanations of a changing long-period supply price are eliminated. It is no longer possible to rely on increasing access to technical economies (internal or external) as the industry expands.[56] If the long-run supply price is to change with changing output, the reason must be found in pecuniary economies or diseconomies which are external to the firm. As Joan Robinson argues,[57] if the resources absorbed by one industry are to increase in a time of full employment, then the extra resources must be transferred from other industries. It is possible that the expanding industry will require factors in a mix different from those activities which are shrinking. So, depending on the degree of idiosyncracy of the expanding industry, and the possibilities for input substitution in the expanding industry, external pecuniary diseconomies (rising factor prices) will be the cause of any forward-rising gradient discovered in long-run supply curves.

The size of firms under competition

At least since the publication of *The Wealth of Nations* economists have acknowledged that the size of the firm may be limited by the extent of the market. This theorem became important in the monopolistic competition literature of the 1930s and 1940s. Even for standardised commodities, Marshall stressed that when the firm deals directly with the customer, goodwill will influence the allocation of output among firms.[58] These factors could not be used for the theory of perfect competition in which standardised products were dumped on a market to be sold by some Walrasian tâtonnement process. In such a market direct contact between buyer and seller is impossible.

The U-shaped long-run average cost curve was adopted to explain the size of firms under perfect competition; but the shape of the curve is inconsistent with observations. As Hicks explains: 'The elements which limit the size of firms in practice are very largely dynamic elements; it is therefore not surprising that static theory has had so much trouble over the matter.'[59]

In 1934, Kaldor objected, on *a priori* grounds, to the explanation of the forward-rising section of the LRAC curve in terms of co-ordination problems. His objection is that co-ordination is only required when the firm needs to change. No co-ordination is needed when every function is to be replicated from the previous period.

> For the function which lends uniqueness and determinateness to the firm – the ability to adjust, to co-ordinate – is an *essentially dynamic function*; it is only required so long as adjustments are required; and the extent to which it is required (which, as its supply is 'fixed', governs the amount of other factors which can be most advantageously combined with it) depends on the frequency and the magnitude of the adjustments to be undertaken. . . . There is thus no determinate ideal or 'equilibrium' position which a firm is continuously tending to approach, because every approximation to that situation also changes the ideal position to which it tends to approximate.[60]

In the revised edition of his *Structure of Competitive Industry*, Robinson admits this point.[61]

Kaldor's hypothesis that firm size is limited by management's inability to handle the co-ordination problems raised by rapid clange, is a basic idea behind Edith Penrose' *Theory of the Growth of the Firm*.[62] This book points to the teamwork needed for management. The management team cannot be expanded rapidly or else this cohesion is threatened. New members of the team take a while to gain confidence in and knowledge of other team members and of the work needed for planning.

Kalecki[63] proposes that, rather than lack of knowledge of the internal environment, it is lack of knowledge of future market conditions which limits the growth of firms. Kalecki claims that an entrepreneur (or creditor) will limit his investment in a particular venture at any point in time because larger investments incur increasing marginal risk. The larger the investment the more one's wealth position is threatened by failure; and the larger the investment the greater is the danger of personal illiquidity caused by owning assets (like capital) which are illiquid. There seems to be some evidence that the more uncertain the market environment, the smaller do firms tend to be.[64]

The effects on industry structure of the uncertainty caused by lack of knowledge is a topic the implications of which have been increasingly explored in recent years. Williamson proposes that the size of firms can be explained by efforts to gain knowledge or by efforts to cope with a world where knowledge is limited. His basic proposition in *Markets and Hierarchies* is that the organisation of productive units is determined by transactional factors rather than by technology. By intra-firm co-ordination (as opposed to co-ordination by means of the market) administrators use long-term contracts with resources to adapt to uncertainty in a sequential fashion. Long-term contracts for the products of resources are much less flexible. Information sought through resources internal to the firm is less likely deliberately to be made misleading than is information purchased in the market place. Although this book suffers from the identification of monopoly power with the number of sellers, it is a fertile source of hypotheses which, using a little ingenuity, could be tested.

Observations of business motivation have yielded a far more complex picture than that of the myopic maximiser postulated in the model of perfect competition. Models are being built on the foundation that businesses grope in an uncertain environment to gain knowledge of profitable opportunities, and form their internal structure and behaviour so as to assist this search and to allow flexibility to respond to a constantly changing picture of the market. This view of firms iterating decisions in the face of an uncertain environment is the basis of the Marshallian reservations concerning the static maximising view of Cournot and Walras. Marshall's interest in the determinants of business size has been re-kindled in new minds following the clear inadequacy of the U-shaped long-run average cost curve explanation. The new hypotheses may be more difficult to test than those incorporated in the model of perfect competition (their variables are rarely found in government statistics); but they are testable in principle.

4. EQUILIBRIUM AND STABILITY UNDER MONOPOLY

Marshall's analysis of monopoly is planted firmly in the tradition of Adam Smith and J. S. Mill. The extent to which an industry is monopolised is the extent to which the free flow of resources is impeded. Given this definition it is possible to rank industries according to their degree of monopolistic control. Such ranking depends on: (i) the extent to which a firm can price above the long-period unit costs of potential competitors; and (ii) the period of time for which this differential can be sustained.[65]

This model has never been completely discarded, although the theorists of imperfect competition, Joan Robinson, and Chamberlin, did their best to achieve this end. At the death of Marshall, the model needed important work. In particular, the key parameters representing the impediments to the free flow of resources needed to be identified and estimated. This work has been furthered by those, such as Bain, who would claim to be following the perfect competition/Chamberlinian tradition.

Bain's *Barriers to New Competition* attempts to quantify the barriers to the entry of new firms (compared with resources) into an industry. Bain succeeded in promoting the Marshallian idea that a firm's awareness of potential competition limits the extent to which it is prepared to exercise monopoly power. Bain defines the 'condition of entry' as ' . . . the advantages of established sellers in an industry over potential entrant sellers, these advantages being reflected in the extent to which established sellers can persistently raise their prices above a competitive level without attracting new firms to enter the industry.'[66] By careful argument and empirical investigation, Bain establishes a strong case for the significance of such conditions of entry on the pricing policy of firms.

Others have developed this theme of the influence of barriers to entry on pricing policy. Sylos-Labini's model of limit pricing[67] is constructed for a homogeneous product for which the cost function is identical for all firms. The barrier to entry is economies of scale, so there are no problems of imperfect knowledge (all firms have the same cost function). Accordingly, while Sylos is exploring the effects of barriers to entry, his assumptions preclude any consideration of many of the issues of expectations, degree of monopoly, time horizon, etc. suggested by the Marshallian analysis. The lack of congruence between Sylos and Marshall is explained by the hegemony of market classification in the 1930s and 1940s.

Classification

The continuum from absolute monopoly to free competition in the models of the English classical economists may be contrasted with the approach to monopoly taken by Cournot. Cournot classifies markets according to the number of sellers and draws conclusions as to the pricing policies which will emerge. Because a study of the long-run implications of policy must include the possibility of the entry and exit of firms (and thus the destruction of the system of taxonomy) the models explored must envisage a short time horizon. The exception to this rule is the case of large numbers for which entry and exit can be considered without considering the possibility of a change in market structure.[68]

These comments apply not only to Cournot, but to all those who follow the method of classification. This method was widely accepted following the publication of Joan Robinson's *Economics of Imperfect Competition* and Chamberlin's *Theory of Monopolistic Competition*. Joan Robinson developed the Cournot-Edgeworth static theory of monopoly – developing theorems of comparative statics, the difference between the outcomes of monopoly and perfect competition, and the literature of monopolistic discrimination among markets. Chamberlin proposed a two-fold classificatory system: that markets be classified both according to the number of sellers and according to the existence or non-existence of product differentiation. Chamberlin is largely responsible for the elevation of oligopoly to a subject of widespread interest. His development of additional market categories stems from a study of the Pigou-Taussig controversy[69] as to railway prices and discrimination; and the impossibility of deciding the question as to whether monopoly or competition with joint costs explains the formation of the prices.[70]

Chamberlin's problem in dealing with the Pigou-Taussig debate serves to illustrate the poverty of empirical content caused by the method of classification. The problem derives from the difficulty in deciding which model to apply. If the rules for application are not made explicit, the models become difficult to test. It is for this reason that Friedman pleas for the articulation of the rules for application. 'But, [he proceeds] no matter how successful we may be in this attempt, there inevitably will remain room for judgment in applying the rules. Each occurrence has some features peculiarly its own, not covered by the explicit rules.'[71]

Chamberlin's 'solution' to his problem raised in the Pigou-Taussig debate is also interesting. Given an inapplicable range of alternative models he added to the range so as to increase the 'realistic' possibilities available. Following his lead, Bain further added to the range by including barriers to entry as a criterion of market classification. Bain, always keeping an eye on empirical content, warns against the proliferation of structural models. However, the proliferation has continued such that the price theorist is now confronted with a bewildering plethora of models from which he may choose the one to apply. This development may be seen as a classic conventionalist methodological strategem. 'If this model doesn't fit, restrict its range of applicability and add a new model to fill the gap.' In this way, models can always avoid the test of verisimilitude.

Conventionalist methodology uses strategems to explain the lack of congruence between the theory's consequences and experiential propositions. Any congruence is hailed as a triumph. 'The conventionalist ethic is: use the theory where it is applicable. Different theories may be required for different problem situations within the same problem area. The question of their truth or falsity, or even truthlikeness, does not arise. Theories are tools for predictions.'[72]

This taxonomic trend exposes the writing of Chamberlin as leading 'towards an expanding range of theories' rather than 'towards a general theory of value'. In an essay by this latter title,[73] Chamberlin explains his quest.

> I must begin by making clear that I am using the term monopolistic competition in its broad sense to include all situations where elements of both monopoly and competition are present – both product heterogeneity and oligopoly, and of course all combinations of the two. In this general schema, pure competition and pure monopoly appear as limiting cases where one or the other of the ingredients is zero. The purpose of the theory is to do a better job of explanation by presenting a continuum between two extremes rather than two sharply distinguished and mutually exclusive categories.[74]

Shortly after Chamberlin's book had been published, Machlup outlined his classificatory system.[75] Mason's 'Price and Production Policies of Large-Scale Enterprises',[76] proposed that from the various elements of industry structure, the behaviour of the industry can be explained. Many industry studies have since utilised this organisational schema – an early landmark being Wallace's study of the aluminium industry.[77]

One outcome of this taxonomy of markets according to seller concentration, product differentiation and barriers to entry has been a refinement of the concept of the industry. One cannot measure a concentration statistic unless one knows where the industry starts and finishes. Triffin's suggestion that the degree of interdependence between firms could be measured by cross elasticities of demand[78] produced a debate in the early 1950s as to whether and how an industry could be defined using statistical measures.[79]

Monopoly, monopolistic competiton, and oligopoly

The static theory of monopoly pricing was developed in the 1930s, the contributions of Joan Robinson and von Stackelberg being pre-eminent. Joan Robinson's, *Economics of Imperfect Competition* represents a determined effort to extract theorems of comparative statics from Cournotesque monopoly theory. Von Stackelberg tackles the problem of equilibrium for a monopolist producing joint products.[80] These two writers are also the most fertile in the field of price discrimination. Joan Robinson develops the Dupit-Edgeworth-Pigou analysis of a monopolist discriminating between separate markets. Von Stackelberg opens the analysis to Pigou's discrimination of the second degree, where the monopolist is able to segment a market vertically.[81]

Again, it was theorems of comparative statics which dominated the early discussions of Chamberlin's model of large numbers with product differentiation. Chamberlin's models are essentially timeless; and his famous prediction of excess capacity derives from the tangency of the average revenue curve with the average cost curve at an output at less than that of minimum efficient scale. Harrod argues that misleading structural and motivational hypotheses in Chamberlin's model are responsible for this prediction. Chamberlin's assumption that all firms are located at a point (the symmetry assumption) side-steps the issues raised by product differentiation. If the symmetry assumption is discarded then individual firms will discourage others from encroaching on their markets by pricing at the minimum of long-run average costs. The only circumstance in which this would not occur would be if the firms were myopic. In this case they may attempt to extract 'monopoly profits', thereby attracting entrants who would reduce the size of the market and thus the original (myopic) firm will be left with capacity which it is unable to utilise.[82]

This dynamic explanation of excess capacity is reached via a route very different from that of Chamberlin. For Harrod, the consideration of time raises the issue of the firm's time horizon and of its knowledge. Further, the structure of the relevant 'market' may alter through the entry of new firms, so it is impossible for static theorems of behaviour to be deduced from hypotheses as to market structure.

Following the death of Marshall, the literature on oligopoly pursued Bowley's suggestion[83] that firms will consider the likely reaction of a rival before making a move. This hint was developed by Frisch,[84] Zeuthen,[85] Chamberlin,[86] and von Stackelberg.[87] Naturally, by varying one's hypotheses as to anticipated reactions a whole series of variant models can be produced. The growth of available models between which to choose followed the path to be expected from the taxonomic procedure advocated by Cournot and Chamberlin.

Chamberlin's justification for treating oligopoly as a set of market structures bounded by pure monopoly on one side and the case of large numbers on the other is that only when numbers are few do firms recognise their interdependence with other firms. In a misleading extrapolation from the model of pure competition, where large numbers *coupled* with the proposition of the firm being a quantity-adaptor (which excludes the possibility of contact with purchasers), Chamberlin claims that the existence of large numbers causes any one firm to be oblivious to considerations as to the likely reactions of competitors. As the number of sellers increases there comes a point where such anticipations are excluded.

Evidence

The discontinuities in market behaviour between different market structures as predicted by Chamberlin and Cournot may contain some empirical content so long as observed markets can be unambiguously classified. This requirement entails that industries can be unambiguously defined and that structural characteristics recognised. These tasks are not easy to accomplish.

In fact, most of the empirical work in recent years directed to the testing of alternative hypotheses in the theory of the firm has been to determine the significance of various variables in explaining differences in rates of return among industries.[88] Such cross-sectional studies yield little by way of evidence to decide between the taxonomic approach and that of Marshall. Both of these approaches would lead one to expect that both concentration and certain proxies for entry barriers would be significant variables in explaining differences in rates of return among industries, although Marshall would lead one to expect that concentration is not a major influence.[89] The models of the English classical school imply that markets differing in numbers of sellers do not exhibit behaviour differing in *kind*. They do not deny that fewness in numbers will facilitate collusion.[90]

A major barrier to deciding on this quantitative issue is the high degree of collinearity between concentration and technical barriers to entry.[91] George found that the inclusion of concentration as a separate variable added nothing to the degree of explanation of inter-industry rates of profit and concluded that differences in concentration exert a significant effect on profitability only within the very high barriers to entry class of industries.[92]

Marshall's model moves us towards predictions as to where certain industry variables will be at particular points in time. For the evaluation of this model, cross-sectional data is of little help. Neither is cross-sectional data very useful in assessing the type of qualitative predictions which Machlup would expect a theory of the firm to yield. While the taxonomic approach has led to a multitude of models to which it is very difficult to apply any tests at all, it is clear that these models demand a type of test which has rarely been conducted.

In their present forms, both the models of the taxonomists and those of the Marshallians yield merely qualitative predictions. However, the potential degree of verisimilitude of the Marshallian approach is greater than that of the taxonomic approach for two reasons.

In the first place, the taxonomic approach easily eludes any assessment of verisimilitude. It is elusive because, if an implication of the theory is contradicted by observations, then a person wishing to conserve the theory can claim that the theory is inapplicable because the structural assumptions of the theory do not correspond to the structural characteristics of the observed market.

The second reason why the potential degree of verisimilitude of the Marshallian approach exceeds that of classification is that Marshall spells out in far greater detail than market category models the time paths by which various variables will approach a new equilibrium. If these stability conditions were to be quantified (that is, if their parameters were to be estimated) they would yield predictions as to the value of variables at specific points in time.

In his address 'The Old Generation of Economists and the New',[93] Marshall stressed that economists must search for a small number of basic principles to explain the complexity of social phenomena. He considered that many of these principles had been discovered, and pleaded for an effort to quantify the parameters. If Marshall's performance is to be assessed fairly, then his disciples must put their minds to the empirical programme which he outlined.

6 Some Reflections

The period from 1776 to the death of Marshall witnessed successive elaborations on the equilibrium and stability model presented in *The Wealth of Nations*. The model proposes an equilibrium in which price would equal unit costs plus the opportunity cost of capital. At such an equilibrium all firms would be earning similar rates of return on capital after allowance is made for differences in riskiness and agreeability. Impediments to the achievement of this equilibrium are labelled as monopolistic restrictions.

The preceding chapters have considered this model of equilibrium and stability: the way in which it has been modified over time and the alternatives which have been offered as a challenge. The theme of equilibrium and stability may seem rather *passé* to certain economists of the present day. However, the empirical importance of analysis of equilibrium and stability lies in the analysis of stability.

Statements postulating equilibrium positions have a zero truth-content. They use language (for example, the long run) which does not correspond to an observable reality; so their degree of verisimilitude cannot be assessed. Efforts by Adam Smith and J. S. Mill to say that natural (long-run normal) values correspond to an average of observable (market) values are misleading, if not wrong. But this is not to say that equilibrium models are without value.

The assessable propositions yielded by such models derive from the stability analysis. This analysis yields propositions as to the direction in which variables are changing and, less frequently, the rate of change of such variables. It is these propositions which can be compared with observations so as to assess verisimilitude. This is true both of models in the English classical tradition as well as of those in the Cournot-Chamberlin-Mason tradition of the classification of market structures.

Models convey the greatest degree of verisimilitude if they yield the most correct predictions as to the direction in which, and the rate at which, variables are changing. If both of these dimensions are known, then prediction of variables at a point in the future is possible. For this reason, Machlup's well-known defence of marginalism is unsatisfactory. It is unsatisfactory because it is complacent: it expects too little of economics.

Machlup's defence of marginalism is that it fulfils the requirements of a theory of the firm: it predicts the direction of changes in prices and outputs of particular products resulting from some other change. While this qualitative comparative statics[1] is the best that is yielded by much economic theory, it should only be accepted as an intermediate stage in our approach to the truth. '*In the absence of complete quantitative information*, it is hoped to be able to formulate qualitative restrictions on slopes, curvatures, etc., of our equilibrium equations so as to be able to derive definite qualitative restrictions upon the responses of our system to changes in certain parameters.'[2] To increase the truth-content of predictions, we must estimate the parameters of the stability conditions.

The acceptance of Popper's standard of verisimilitude implies that one will value 'conjectures' as to the time path a firm or market travels towards equilibrium. Marshall's distinction between prime and supplementary cost, his concept of quasi-rent, and his time-period analysis were all efforts towards an articulation of this time path.

The importance of observations

Popper's standard of verisimilitude defines the degree to which a theory approaches the truth. He defines the truth-content (falsity-content) of a theory t_1 as the class of the true (false) logical consequences of t_2.

Assuming that the truth-content and falsity content of two theories t_1 and t_2 are comparable, we can say that t_2 is more closely similar to the truth, or corresponds better to the facts, than t_1, if and only if either
  (a) the truth-content but not the falsity content of t_2 exceeds that of t_1, [or]
  (b) the falsity-content of t_1, but not its truth-content, exceeds that of t_2.[3]

In seeking to approach the truth, it is important that scientists record their observations so that others may check the validity of their judgments. The modifications to Adam Smith's basic model to be found in the work of Mill and Marshall were effected largely as a result of the conflict between the inherited theory and observations. But despite Marshall's constant visits to factories and discussions with managers there is no record of the resulting raw observations which caused him to modify received hypotheses.

Compared with Marshall (and Senior, McCulloch and William Thornton among the classical economists) Mill seems to have derived less stimulus from the conflict between received theory and observation. Mill seems to have become aware of such conflict more through the writings of his contemporaries than through personal observation.

Both Marshall and Mill (as he grew older) were hesitant publicly to dismiss a theory when it conflicted with observations. Rather, their willingness to record the many facets of the truth caused them to modify inadequate theories. But to modify a theory is to replace it. All changes in theory (no matter how 'significant' or 'insignificant') must be assessed by the same standard. The conciliatory style of Marshall and the mature Mill should not conceal the real changes they effected in the theory. Their style of writing and their failure precisely to record their observations should not lead us to believe that they proceeded other than by alternating conjectures with refutations.

In this process of conjecture and refutation it is frequently impossible to distinguish the alterations to a theory occasioned by conflict between received theory and observations from the process of induction. The conflict between received theory and observations causes the theory to be altered so as to fit the facts more closely. When Popper denies the possibility of induction he is, of course, not denying the occurrence of this process. Rather, he is denying that theories arise from un-prejudiced observations. One must have some prejudice; for it is this which guides one's selection of observations.

The rejection of verisimilitude

If the way to greater verisimilitude is through the analysis of stability, then the 1920s and 1930s signalled a rejection of verisimilitude. In these two decades it became increasingly popular to classify markets, primarily according to the number of sellers, and to derive equilibrium patterns of conduct for each category. This is the basis of Archibald's criticism of Chamberlin.[4]

While the bulk of the work with each category has been directed towards the specification of assumptions and to the derivation of equilibrium conditions, the models have yielded certain predictions as to the directions in which change will occur given certain parametrical changes. It is these propositions which should be comparable with observations.

However, the ambiguity of the classification of markets permits the proponents of the models always to escape such assessment. Because it is impossible unambiguously to place an observed market within a particular theoretical category, the proponents of a particular category can always avoid a comparison with observations by claiming that the observed market structure does not fit the particular category. The propositions derived from such models as those of pure competition, single-firm monopoly, large-numbers monopolistic competition, Cournotesque oligopoly etc., cannot be compared with observations because no market corresponds precisely to the structural characteristics of any of the models.

This work on the classification of markets according to structural elements not only robbed price theory of empirical content, but it also diverted the profession's interest away from work on the determinants of the size of firms and of the size distribution of firms within the industry. This work, to which Mill and Marshall had made significant contributions, did not fit easily into a classificatory schema based on the hypothesis that elements of industry structure determine the behaviour patterns to be observed. If the models were to acknowledge behaviour which modifies the structure, the schema of classification would be rendered ambiguous.

The re-acceptance of verisimilitude

The strategy of classification became quite ubiquitous following the death of Marshall. The proponents of the strategy, when confronted with awkward observations, had recourse to the conventions expounded by Machlup. In the last two decades the Machlupian conventions as to the scope of economics and as to the characteristics of good economic theory increasingly have been discarded in favour of a more ambitious approach. The determinants of organisational structure and of motivation are being revived as subjects to be explained. For this expanded range of theory a wider range of observations is necessary.

While some of these observations have been more or less direct — through interviews or through questionnaires — many have been indirect — through reference to those who study the internal organisation and the management of companies. This managerial literature has suggested that the process by which firms make decisions is largely determined by the availability of knowledge. This proposition has been incorporated in the resumed study of the determinants of firm size and the pattern of firm growth.[5]

Furthermore, studies of decision-making within particular firms recently have suggested many hypotheses as to the time-paths by which firms move towards equilibria. While some of the work based on this suggestion is presented within the framework of market classification,[6] it does attempt to produce far more precise propositions so that contradiction by observations is more easily accomplished than would be possible under the conventions proposed by Machlup.

The best work leading to the emergence of the theory of the firm has arisen largely from a careful procedure of alternate conjecture and refutation. The foregoing study has illustrated the need for discipline by the facts. If we are to approach the truth, each step on our way must be checked lest we stray from our chosen path.

Notes

The following abbreviations are used:
W.N., for A. Smith, *An Inquiry into the Nature and Causes of the Wealth of Nations*, Edited by E. Cannan (New York: Modern Library, 1937);
Mill, *P.*, for J. S. Mill, *Principles of Political Economy*, Edited by W. J. Ashley (London: Longmans, 1909);
Marshall, *I. and T.*, for A. Marshall, *Industry and Trade*, 3rd ed. (London: Macmillan, 1920);
Marshall, *P.*, for A. Marshall, *Principles of Economics*, Variorum Edition (London: Macmillan, For the Royal Economic Society, 1961).

NOTES TO CHAPTER 1

1. R. H. Coase, in G. J. Stigler and K. E. Boulding (eds.), *Readings in Price Theory* (London: Allen and Unwin, for the American Economic Association, 1953).
2. D. H. Robertson, *The Control of Industry*, 2nd ed. (London: Nisbet, 1928) 85.
3. Notably E. Cannan, *A History of the Theories of Production and Distribution in English Political Economy from 1776 to 1848*, 3rd ed. (London: Staples, 1917); and G. J. Stigler, *Production and Distribution Theories* (New York: Macmillan, 1946).
4. F. A. von Hayek, 'Scientism and the Study of Society', Part I, *Economica*, New Series, IX (1942) 267–91. Part II, X (1943) 34–63.
5. See M. Blaug in S. J. Latsis (ed.), *Method and Appraisal in Economics* (Cambridge: Cambridge University Press, 1976) 412.
6. D. Patinkin, *Money, Interest, and Prices*, 2nd ed. (New York: Harper and Row, 1965), was particularly significant in this respect.
7. I. Lakatos, in I. Lakatos and A. Musgrave (eds.), *Criticism and the Growth of Knowledge* (Cambridge: Cambridge University Press, 1970) 135.
8. Lakatos notes that externally directed problem choice does not occur, but claims that external history is secondary to internal history because the 'most important problems of external history are defined by internal history'. This may not be true of the social sciences where politicians may perceive 'problems' with which the scientist must then cope. See I. Lakatos, in R. C. Buck and R. S. Cohen (eds.), *Boston Studies in the Philosophy of Science*, vol. VIII (Dordrecht: Reidel, 1971) 102–5.
9. F. A. von Hayek, 'The Trend of Economic Thinking', *Economica*, XIII (1933) 121–37.
10. Popper contrasts the technical approach to knowledge (learning so as to aid

172 *The Emergence of the Theory of the Firm*

the improvement of existing social relationships) with the historicist approach (attempts to divine the broad sweep of history). K. R. Popper, *The Poverty of Historicism*, 2nd ed. (London: Routledge and Kegan Paul, 1960).

11. I. Lakatos, in R. C. Buck and R. S. Cohen (eds.), *Boston Studies in the Philosophy of Science*, vol. VIII, 107, his emphasis.

12. *Ibid.*, 107.

13. On this point, see G. C. Archibald, 'Refutation or Comparison?', *British Journal for the Philosophy of Science*, 17 (1966) 279–96.

14. K. R. Popper, *The Logic of Scientific Discovery*, first German ed. 1934, translated by the author (London: Hutchison, 1959) 82–3.

15. I. Lakatos, in I. Lakatos and A. Musgrave (eds.), *Criticism and the Growth of Knowledge*, 182.

16. *Ibid.*, 118.

17. Lakatos admits that this is a 'sort of simplicity requirement'. See *Ibid.*, 131–2.

18. *Ibid.*, 137.

19. Latsis, defending the Lakatosian programme, seems to realise that the demarcation criterion is of little value unless the positive heuristic is stable; because he requires that the positive heuristic be 'as hard as the hard core'. S. J. Latsis in S. J. Latsis (ed.), *op. cit.*, 16.

20. See S. J. Latsis, in S. J. Latsis (ed.), *op. cit.*; S. J. Latsis, *Situational Determinism in Economics* (PhD thesis presented to the University of London, 1974); and S. J. Latsis, 'Situational Determinism in Economics', *British Journal for the Philosophy of Science*, 23 (1972) 207–45.

21. S. J. Latsis, in S. J. Latsis (ed.), *op. cit.*, 22, his emphasis.

22. See chapters 2 and 3.

23. See chapter 5.

24. K. R. Popper, *Conjectures and Refutations*, 3rd ed. (London: Routledge and Kegan Paul, 1969) 233.

25. F. A. von Hayek, *op. cit.*

26. Letwin dates scientific economics from 1660, but he means by a scientific approach the attempt to explain and predict using a limited number of variables. See W. Letwin, *The Origins of Scientific Economics* (London: Methuen, 1963).

27. See R. L. Meek, *The Economics of Physiocracy. Essays and Translations* (London: Allen and Unwin, 1962) 374.

28. J. A. Schumpeter, *History of Economic Analysis* (London: Allen and Unwin, 1954) 52.

NOTES TO CHAPTER 2

1. See p. 8.

2. This is discussed widely in the literature. See J. J. Spengler, 'Adam Smith's Theory of Economic Growth', Part I, *Southern Economic Journal*, XXV (1959) 397–415. Part II, XXVI (1959) 1–12; and R. Kroebner, 'Adam Smith and the Industrial Revolution', *Economic History Review*, Second Series, XI (1959) 381–91.

3. See W. H. B. Court, *A Concise Economic History of Britain from 1750 to*

Recent Times (Cambridge: Cambridge University Press, 1954) 84; and E. F. Heckscher, *Mercantilism*, Translated by M. Shapiro, 2nd ed. (London: Allen and Unwin, 1955) vol. I, 415.

4. *W.N.*, 700. Smith also charged that joint-stock companies were highly inflexible. For this reason, they could only withstand free competition in those trades the operations of which are reducible to strict rule and method (for example, banking, insurance, the maintenance and insurance of navigable cuts and canals, and water supply). But in these trades the joint-stock organisation is merely viable. For it to be desirable, the trades also should be of abnormal general utility and require a greater capital than can easily be collected into a private copartnery. In the four examples given, 'both these circumstances concur'. See *W.N.*, 713–15.

5. See N. Rosenberg, 'Some Institutional Aspects of the *Wealth of Nations*', *Journal of Political Economy*, LXVIII (1960) 557–70.

6. *W.N.*, 700.

7. Compare with the claim of J. A. Schumpeter, *History of Economic Analysis* (London: Allen and Unwin, 1954) 555.

8. For a clear account of the history of the concept of the entrepreneur see B. F. Hoselitz in J. J. Spengler and W. R. Allen (eds.), *Essays in Economic Thought: Aristotle to Marshall* (Chicago: Rand McNally, 1960).

9. See R. L. Meek, *The Economics of Physiocracy. Essays and Translations* (London: Allen and Unwin, 1962) 387.

10. These words are used interchangeably. See P. D. Groenewegen, 'A Reinterpretation of Turgot's Theory of Capital and Interest', *Economic Journal*, 81 (1971) 155.

11. But von Mangoldt had made the observation in 1855. See H. K. E. von Mangoldt in F. M. Taylor (ed.), *Some Readings in Economics* (Ann Arbor: George Wahr, 1907) 39. Von Mangoldt claims that the ownership of capital is not a necessary condition for entrepreneurship, ' . . . if his personal characteristics have given him credit enough to place at his disposal the necessary funds of other persons.'

12. F.A. Walker, *The Wages Question*, Ch. XIV. Quoted in Marshall, *I. and T.*, 169.

13. *W.N.*, 52–3.

14. *Ibid.*, 48.

15. *Ibid.*, 96.

16. *Ibid.*, 97.

17. Encountered in *Ibid.*, 52 and 97.

18. *Ibid.*, 48.

19. *Ibid.*, 87.

20. See J. F. Weston, 'The Profit Concept and Theory: A Restatement', *Journal of Political Economy*, LXII (1954) 152–70.

21. F. H. Knight, *Risk Uncertainty and Profit*, 1st ed. 1921 (London: L. S. E. Reprint, 1933) 308–9.

22. R. Cantillon, *Essai Sur La Nature Du Commerce En Général*, Translated from the French ed. of 1775 by H. Higgs (London: Macmillan, For the Royal Economic Society, 1931) 49.

23. *Ibid.*, 55.

24. *Ibid.*, 53.

25. See H. J. Bitterman, 'Adam Smith's Empiricism and the Law of Nature', Part I, *Journal of Political Economy*, XLVIII (1940) 487–520; Part II, XLVIII (1940) 703–34; and R. H. Coase, 'Adam Smith's View of Man', *Journal of Law and Economics*, XIX (1976) 529–46; and A. Onken, 'The Consistency of Adam Smith', *Economic Journal*, XII (1897) 443–50.

26. The writers discussed in this chapter did not envisage the policy decisions of the firm as being taken with respect to a complete map of possibilities. Thus the word 'maximisation' is used loosely when used to refer to pre-Cournot economics. See Chapter 5.

27. Aquinus in A. E. Munroe (ed.), *Early Economic Thought* (Camridge, Mass.: Harvard University Press, 1924) 54.

28. Aquinus in *Ibid.*, 56.

29. J. Hales (attributed), *A Discourse of the Common Weal of this Realm of England*, 1st ed. 1581, edited by E. Lamond (Cambridge: Cambridge University Press, 1929) 43.

30. 'A Discourse of Corporations' in R. H. Tawney and Eileen Power (eds.), *Tudor Economic Documents* (London: Longmans, Green and Co., 1924) Vol. III, 268.

31. N. Barbon, *A Discourse of Trade* (London: 1690). For detailed references to the pamphlet literature on profit-maximisation see J. Viner, *Studies in the Theory of International Trade* (London: Allen and Unwin, 1937) 91 ff.

32. J. Steuart, *An Inquiry into the Principles of Political Economy*, Edition of 1767, edited by A. S. Skinner (Edinburgh and London: Oliver and Boyd for the Scottish Economic Society, 1966) 142.

33. *Ibid.*, 168.

34. See pp. 12–13.

35. *W.N.*, 355.

36. *Ibid.*, 365.

37. *Ibid.*, 111.

38. This may be contrasted with Galiani (see p. 28) who allows for the possibility of dynamic instability – the 'overshooting' of equilibrium in a similar model.

39. This is the title to Book 1, Chapter 3, *W.N.*, 17.

40. A. A. Young, 'Increasing Returns and Economic Progress', *Economic Journal*, XXXVIII (1928) 529.

41. J. A. Schumpeter, *op. cit.*, 214.

42. The passage to which Schumpeter is referring (regarding the extent of the market) is presumably W. Petty, *The Economic Writings*, edited by C. H. Hull (Cambridge: Cambridge University Press, 1899) 260.

43. C. Bücher, *Industrial Evolution*, Translated from 3rd German ed. by S. M. Wickett (New York: Henry Holt, 1912) 286–7.

44. T. S. Ashton, *An Economic History of England: The Eighteenth Century* (London: Methuen, 1955) 103.

45. *W.N.*,4.

46. *W.N*., 706.

47. On Cournot and Marshall, see pp. 93ff.

48. While this Smithian underpinning is not fully explicit in *Letter from Sydney*, it is quite clear in the analytically superior *A View of the Art of Colonization* (1849) which was written after the author had been occupied

in editing *The Wealth of Nations*, 1835–9.
49. G. J. Stigler, 'The Division of Labor is Limited by the Extent of the Market', *The Organization of Industry* (Homewood, Illinois: Irwin, 1968) 129–41.
50. *Ibid.*, 133.
51. H. Spencer, *The Principles of Sociology* (London: Williams and Norgate, 1894) vol. III, 345–403.
52. B. Webb. *My Apprenticeship*, 1st ed. 1926. (Harmondsworth: Penguin, 1971) 48.
53. A. B. Laffer in B. S. Yamey (ed.), *Economics of Industrial Structure* (Harmondsworth: Penguin, 1973). For less developed economies the process of vertical disintegration is also not apparent. Ashton claims: 'The elimination of middlemen in the sale of manufactured goods was, indeed, one of the outstanding features of the rise of large scale industry.' See Ashton, *op. cit.*, 68. P. T. Bauer and B. S. Yamey, 'Economic Progress and Occupational Distribution', *Economic Journal*, LXI (1951) 741–55, show how the high cost of capital and the absence of social overhead capital in less-developed British West Africa produced highly-disintegrated, labour-intensive productive units.
54. See quotation on p. 21. See also *W.N.*, 86.
55. A. A. Young, *op. cit.*.
56. For a review of the early developments in this theory, see H. W. Arndt, 'External Economies in Economic Growth', *Economic Record*, XXXI (1955) 192–214.
57. See M. Blaug, 'Welfare Indices in the Wealth of Nations', *Southern Economic Journal*, XXVI (1959) 150–3.
58. N. Barbon, *op. cit.*.
59. For a review of the work of Boisguilbert see H. Van D. Roberts, *Boisguilbert, Economist of the Reign of Louis XIV* (New York: Columbia University Press, 1935).
60. See Steuart, *op. cit.*.
61. For a further explanation of these concepts see P. A. Samuelson, *Foundations of Economic Analysis* (Cambridge, Mass.: Harvard University Press, 1947).
62. *Ibid.*, 261. In the analysis of general equilibrium it is important to distinguish Samuelson's perfect stability of the first kind from stability of the first kind in the small. The latter exists if for sufficiently small displacements the equilibrium is stable. Our study will be concerned primarily with analysis within particular markets and so will not maintain this distinction.
63. *W.N.*, 55.
64. A. R. J. Turgot, *Turgot on Progress, Sociology and Economics*, translations by R. L. Meek (Cambridge: Cambridge University Press, 1973) 152.
65. R. L. Meek, *op. cit.*, 297.
66. For detailed citations of the role of utility and demand in *The Wealth of Nations* see S. Hollander in A. S. Skinner and T. Wilson (eds.), *Essays on Adam Smith* (Oxford: Clarendon, 1975).
67. A. E. Munroe, *op. cit.*, 298.
68. J. Harris, *An Essay upon Money and Coins* (London: 1757) 9, his emphasis.

69. *W.N.*, 56.
70. Mill, *P.*, 448.
71. See p. 59.
72. *W.N.*, 101.
73. *Ibid.*, 110–11.
74. Given his definition of monopoly, Smith's remarks that the price of land is a monopoly price becomes perfectly clear. For the classic explanation of Smith on rent see D. H. Buchanan, 'The Historical Approach to Rent and Price Theory', *Economica*, ix (1929) 123–55.
75. *W.N.*, 126.
76. Smith uses this word in *Ibid.*, 66.
77. *Ibid.*, Book 1, Chapter 10, Part ii.
78. *Ibid.*, 394.
79. Quoted in G. S. L. Tucker, *Progress and Profits in British Economic Thought 1650–1850* (Cambridge: Cambridge University Press, 1960) 69.
80. See chapter 5.
81. See T. S. Ashton, *op. cit.*, 97–8.
82. *W.N.*, 60.
83. See T. S. Papola, 'A "Primitive" Equilibrium System: A Neglected Aspect of Smith's Economics', *Indian Economic Journal*, xvii (1969) 93–100; and G. J. Stigler, 'Perfect Competition, Historically Contemplated', *Journal of Political Economy*, lxv (1957) 1–17.
84. J. A. Schumpeter, *op. cit.*, 220.
85. R. Cantillon, *op. cit.*, 119.
86. J. R. Hicks, *Value and Capital*, 2nd ed. (Oxford: Clarendon, 1946) 62.
87. Marshall, *P.*, 758.
88. J. A. Schumpeter, *op. cit.*, 309.
89. R. de Roover, 'Monopoly Theory Prior to Adam Smith', *Quarterly Journal of Economics*, lxv (1951) 492–524.
90. E. Cannan, *A Review of Economic Theory* (London: King, 1929) 225.
91. See p. 27.
92. Book I, s. 11.
93. Book V, s. 5.
94. For references to the scholastic literature see J. A. Schumpeter, *op. cit.*, and R. de Roover, *op. cit.*.
95. E. F. Heckscher, *op. cit.*, vol. i, 273.
96. 'Instructions Touching the Bill for Free Trade', reprinted from Journals of the House of Commons, vol. i (1604), in A. E. Bland, P. A. Brown and R. H. Tawney (eds.), *English Economic History. Select Documents* (London: Bell, 1914) 446.
97. For a detailed exposition of Becher see E. F. Heckscher, *op. cit.*, vol. i, 271.
98. Steuart, *op. cit.*, 247, his emphasis.
99. *Ibid.*, 173.
100. A. R. J. Turgot, 'Valeurs et Monnaies', in E. Daire (ed.), *Oeuvres de Turgot*, Tome Premier (Paris: Guillaumin, 1844) 82.
101. *Ibid.*, 86 and 87.
102. See p. 131.
103. For that of a leading scholar of Turgot see P. D. Groenewegen, 'A Reappraisal of Turgot's Theory of Value, Exchange, and Price De-

termination', *History of Political Economy*, 2 (1970) 177–96.
104. A. R. J. Turgot, *Turgot on Progress, Sociology and Economics*, 136, his emphasis.

NOTES TO CHAPTER 3

1. G. J. Stigler, *Five Lectures on Economic Problems* (London: Longmans, Green, 1949) 26.
2. 'Report of the Commissioners for inquiring into the Condition of the Unemployed Hand-Loom Weavers in the United Kingdom', *Parliamentary Papers*, x (1841) 273–420.
3. R. Torrens, *On Wages and Combination*, 2nd ed. (London: Longman, Orme, Brown, Green, and Longman, 1838).
4. William Thornton was a close friend of J. S. Mill, with whom he worked in the India Office. William Thornton was not a close relation of Henry Thornton – famous for his writing on money. See M. St. J. Packe, *The Life of John Stuart Mill* (London: Secker and Warburg, 1954). See also entries in *Dictionary of National Biography*.
5. J. -B. Say, *A Treatise on Political Economy*, 1st French ed. 1803, translated from 4th ed. by C. R. Prinsep (New York: Kelley, 1964) 329n.
6. See G. S. L. Tucker, *Progress and Profits in British Economic Thought 1650–1850* (Cambridge: Cambridge University Press, 1960) 13.
7. J. -B. Say, *op. cit.*, 330n. Exactly the same point is illustrated by means of a numerical example at 345n.
8. F. H. Knight, *Risk, Uncertainty and Profit*, 1st ed. 1921 (London: L. S. E. Reprint, 1933) 25.
9. Hoselitz in J. J. Spengler and W. R. Allen (eds.), *Essays in Economic Thought: Aristotle to Marshall* (Chicago: Rand McNally, 1960) 248–9.
10. Mill, *P.*, 411.
11. See D. Ricardo, *Des Principes de L'Économie Politique, et de l'impôt*, traduit de l'anglais par F. S. Constancio, avec des notes explicatives et critiques par Jean-Baptiste Say (Paris: J. P. Ailland, 1819) 7 and 158.
12. Say did not deny that all the components of gross profits accrued to the capitalist class. In fact he acknowledged that: 'It very seldom happens, that the party engaged in the management of any undertaking, is not at the same time in the receipt of interest upon some capital of his own.' J. -B. Say, *op. cit.*, 330.
13. See *An Essay on the Political Economy of Nations* (London: Longman, Hurst, Rees, Orme, and Brown, 1821); and T. Hopkins, *Economical Enquiries Relative to The Laws which Regulate Rent, Profit, Wages, and the Value of Money* (London: Hatchard, 1822).
14. W. Ellis, 'Effect of the Employment of Machinery &c. upon the Happiness of the Working Classes', *Westminster Review*, ix (1826) 101–30.
15. T. Tooke, *Considerations on the State of the Currency*, 2nd ed. (London: Murray, 1826) 16.
16. S. Read, *Political Economy* (Edinburgh: 1829) 244.
17. J. S. Mill, *Essays on Some Unsettled Questions of Political Economy*, 1st ed. 1844 (London: L. S. E. Reprint, 1948) 111.

18. G. Ramsay, *An Essay on the Distribution of Wealth* (Edinburgh: Black, 1836) 210.
19. Mill, *P.*, 406.
20. G. P. Scrope, *Principles of Political Economy* (London: Longman, Rees, Orme, Brown, Green and Longman, 1833) 159.
21. See G. S. L. Tucker, *op. cit.*, 82.
22. J. A. Schumpeter, *History of Economic Analysis* (London: Allen and Unwin, 1954) 556 and 556n.
23. See J.-B. Say, *op. cit.*, 316–18. Both Say and Mill mention the possibility of certain cooperative ventures in which labour might be the first to bear the result of the failure of the firm to make profits.
24. J.-B. Say, *Catechism of Political Economy*, Translated by J. Richter (London: Sherwood, Neely and Jones, 1816) 28.
25. S. Read, *op. cit.*, 271.
26. Translation of the *Isolated State*, Part II, in B. W. Dempsey, *The Frontier Wage* (Chicago: Loyola University Press, 1960) 246–7.
27. See preface to Mill, *P.*
28. J.-B. Say, *A Treatise on Political Economy*, 330–2.
29. See p. 43.
30. Mill, *P.*, 476.
31. Marshall, *P.*, 432n.
32. Von Mangoldt, *Gundriss*, Book IV, Chapter 3, Section 4.
33. H. Storch, *Cours D'Economie Politique*, Avec Des Notes Explicatives et Critique par J.-B. Say, 1st ed. 1815 (Paris: 1823), Tome Premier, liv. III, Chapter 5.
34. See J. Craig, *Elements of Political Science* (Edinburgh: Blackwood, 1821) vol. II, 82ff.
35. *Ibid.*, vol. II, 86.
36. See also J. Craig, *Remarks on Some Fundamental Doctrines in Political Economy* (Edinburgh: Constable, 1821) 137–8.
37. Mill, *P.*, 444.
38. J. Maitland, 8th Earl of Lauderdale, *An Inquiry into the Nature and Origin of Public Wealth*, 1st ed. 1804 (New York: Kelley, 1962) 167–8.
39. D. Ricardo, *The Works and Correspondence of David Ricardo*, Edited by P. Sraffa with the collaboration of M. H. Dobb (Cambridge: Cambridge University Press, 1951); vol. I, *On the Principles of Political Economy and Taxation*, Ch. XXXI.
40. Mill, *P.*, 94 ff.
41. J. H. von Thünen, *Von Thünen's Isolated State*, Translated by C. M. Wartenberg, Edited by P. Hall (Oxford: Pergamon, 1966).
42. J. H. von Thünen, English translation of *Isolated State* in B. W. Dempsey, *op. cit.*, 297.
43. See pp. 47–8.
44. Mill, *P.*, 475–7.
45. *Ibid.*, 473.
46. A. Cournot, *Researches into the Mathematical Principles of the Theory of Wealth*, 1st French ed. 1838, Translated by N. Bacon (New York: Macmillan, 1929) 60.
47. J. H. von Thünen, *op. cit.*, 14.

48. See, for example, D. Lardner, *Railway Economy* (New York: Harper, 1855) 194.
49. N. W. Senior, *Letters on the Factory Act* (London: Fellowes, 1837) 13, his emphasis.
50. 'Report of the Commissioners for inquiring into the Condition of the Unemployed Hand-Loom Weavers in the United Kingdom', *Parliamentary Papers*, x (1841) 50.
51. N. W. Senior, *Industrial Efficiency and Social Economy*, Edited by S. L. Levy (New York: Holt, 1928) Part iv, 15.
52. R. Torrens, *op. cit.*, 63–4.
53. G. J. Stigler, 'The Nature and Role of Originality in Scientific Progress', *Economica*, New Series, xxii (1955) 298. C. Babbage, *On the Economy of Machinery and Manufactures* (London: Knight, 1832) has a chapter, Chapter xxi, 'On the Causes and Consequences of Large Factories'.
54. In particular, see A. Smith, *The Wealth of Nations*, Edited by E. G. Wakefield (London: Knight, 1843) for comments by Wakefield; J. Rae, *The Statement of Some New Principles on the Subject of Political Economy* (Boston: Hilliard, 1834); and C. Babbage, *op. cit.*.
55. Mill, *P.*, 134.
56. C. Babbage, *op. cit.*, 214 ff. While claiming subjective originality on this point, Babbage acknowledges a prior version by Gioja, *Nuovo Prospetto della Scienze Economiche* (Milano: 1815) tom i, capo iv.
57. J. Rae, *op. cit.*, 164.
5⁰. C. Babbage, *op. cit.*, 173 ff.
59. From the Report of the House of Commons Committee on the Woollen Trade 1806. Quoted in *Ibid.*, 185.
60. See p. 44.
61. Mill, *P.*, 136.
62. *Ibid.*, 136.
63. *Ibid.*, 134.
64. A. Cournot, *op. cit.*, 59, his emphasis. The statement indicates a notable lack of care in discriminating between marginal and average costs.
65. Mill, *P.*, 145.
66. *Ibid.*, 134.
67. G. J. Stigler, *The Organization of Industry* (Homewood, Illinois: Irwin, 1968) 71–94.
68. Mill, *P.*, 444–8. Mill's ordering does not correspond to that above.
69. S. Bailey, *A Critical Dissertation on the Nature, Measures, and Causes of Value*, 1st ed. 1825 (London: L. S. E. reprint, 1931) 185.
70. W. T. Thornton, *On Labour*, 2nd ed. (London: Macmillan, 1870) 52.
71. C. Babbage, *op. cit.*, 109.
72. W. T. Thornton, *op. cit.*, 52–75, gives many examples of discontinuous functions in which the results expected from the demand and supply analysis of Mill, *P.* do not eventuate. However, Thornton does not state that these examples illustrate the general point that continuity is necessary. Cournot explicitly assumes continuous functions. He concedes that the assumption of $D = F(\rho)$ being continuous may not be realised, ' . . . if the number of consumers were very limited. . . . But the wider the market extends, and the more the combinations of needs, of fortunes, or even of

caprices, are varied among consumers, the closer the function F(ρ) will come to varying with price in a continuous manner.' See A. Cournot, *op. cit.*, 50.

73. C. Babbage, *op. cit.*, 110–11.
74. J. E. Cairnes, *Some Leading Principles of Political Economy Newly Expounded* (London: Macmillan, 1888) 100.
75. Mill, *P.*, 246.
76. Great Britain, *Parliamentary Papers, op. cit.*, 24–5.
77. C. Babbage, *op. cit.*, 164.
78. Mill, *P.*, 242.
79. *Ibid.*, 242–3.
80. *Ibid.*, 247.
81. J. -B. Say, *A Treatise on Political Economy*, 185.
82. *Ibid.*, 225n.
83. T. R. Malthus, *Principles of Political Economy*, 2nd ed. 1836 (Clifton: Kelley, 1974) 71 and 75.
84. D. Ricardo, *op. cit.*, vol. i, *On the Principles of Political Economy and Taxation*, 344.
85. D. Ricardo, *op. cit.*, vol. ii, *Notes on Malthus*, 48–9.
86. D.Ricardo, *op. cit.*, vol. ix, *Letters*, Letter Dated 5 3 1822, 172.
87. L. Robbins (Lord Robbins) Introduction to Book iv, J. S. Mill, *Collected Works of John Stuart Mill* (Toronto: University of Toronto Press, 1965–), Book iv, viii.
88. J. S. Mill (Attributed), 'Review of Art. 1 of the Quarterly Review No. lx', *Westminster Review*, 111 (1825) 221, his emphasis.
89. These private jottings were published in *Economica*, New Series, xii (1945) 134–9, as 'Notes on N. W. Senior's *Political Economy*'; and Mill writes: 'I do not think limitation of supply is essential to the value of labour.' This not only seems to contradict Mill's usual position, but also contradicts his position in Mill, *P.*, that: 'Finally, there are commodities of which, though capable of being increased or diminished to a great, and even an unlimited extent, the value never depends upon anything but demand and supply. This is the case, in particular, with the commodity Labour; . . .'. Mill, *P.*, 450.
90. G. P. Scrope, *op. cit.*, 44 ff.
91. M. Longfield, *Lectures on Political Economy delivered in Trinity and Michaelmas Terms 1833*, 1st ed. 1834 (London: L. S. E. Reprint, 1931) 110.
92. G. Ramsay, *op. cit.*, 60.
93. N. W. Senior, *An Outline of the Science of Political Economy*, 1st ed. 1836 (London: Allen and Unwin, 1938) 24.
94. J. Steuart, *op. cit.*, 176–7.
95. Mill, *P.*, 569–70.
96. T. Cooper, *Lectures on the Elements of Political Economy*, 2nd ed. (Columbia, S.C.: Morris and Wilson, 1830) 82.
97. A. Cournot, *op. cit.*, 90–2.
98. Mill, *P.*, 569–70.
99. R. Hamilton, *Introduction to Merchandize*, 3rd ed. (Edinburgh: 1797) 414. See also 411 note H, and 493–4.
100. Mill, *P.*, 570.
101. See p. 26.

102. D. Ricardo, *op. cit.*, vol. I, *On the Principles of Political Economy and Taxation*, 250. Marshall, *P.*, 814, claims that, in a model incorporating all goods, the Ricardian assumption of constant costs is as good as any other.
103. Mill, *P.*, 442–3.
104. *Ibid.*, 453.
105. J. E. Cairnes, *op. cit.*, 43.
106. See p. 57.
107. Mill, *P.*, 468.
108. See D. Ricardo, *op. cit.*, vol. I, *On the Principles of Political Economy and Taxation*, 73, 363, and 364. See also M. Blaug, *Ricardian Economics* (New Haven: Yale University Press, 1958) 14.
109. This will be discussed in chapter 4.
110. N. W. Senior, *An Outline of the Science of Political Economy*, 119.
111. *Ibid.*, 120.
112. D. Ricardo, *op. cit.*, vol. I, *On the Principles of Political Economy and Taxation*, 12.
113. N. W. Senior, *An Outline of the Science of Political Economy*, 101.
114. *Ibid.*, 97.
115. *Ibid.*, 102.
116. R. D. Ely, 'Senior's Theory of Monopoly', in, *Papers and Proceedings of the Twelfth Annual meeting of the American Economic Association* (New York: Macmillan, for the American Economic Association, 1900).
117. See particularly M. Bowley, *Studies in the History of Economic Thought before 1870* (London: Macmillan, 1973) study no. III.
118. J. Steuart, *op. cit.*, 127–32.
119. S. Bailey, *op. cit.*, 193–4.
120. N. W. Senior, *An Outline of the Science of Political Economy*, 115.
121. Mill, *P.*, 471–7.
122. See Mill, *P.*, 471–3. Mill's position is very close to that of Ricardo. See D. Ricardo, *op. cit.*, vol. I, *On the Principles of Political Economy and Taxation*, 250–1. Ricardo refuses to call Case II a monopoly on the grounds that entry is free and, therefore, price is regulated by cost.
123. Mill, *P.*, 444.
124. See S. Bailey, *op. cit.*, 227–32.
125. See N. W. Senior, *An Outline of the Science of Political Economy*, 103.
126. See the translation of a letter by Tooke, in M. Blaug, *op. cit.*, 57.
127. S. Bailey, *op. cit.*, 229.
128. See p. 35.
129. Mill, *P.*, 449.
130. D. Ricardo, *op. cit.*, vol. I, *On the Principles of Political Economy and Taxation*, 250–1.
131. D. P. O'Brien, *J. R. McCulloch* (London: Allen and Unwin, 1970) 366–70.
132. J. E. Cairnes, *op. cit.*, 233.
133. R. Torrens, *op. cit.*, 57 ff.
134. S. Bailey, *op. cit.*, 187.
135. In his Lectures of 1850–1 Senior adds a fifth type. This is the case of a creative mind (for example, Sir Walter Scott) who, if he tries to increase his output, will eventually reach a point where the extra efforts yield, 'a less and less valuable return' – a diminution of quality. Senior provides no new

laws to govern price in this case. See N. W. Senior, *Industrial Efficiency and Social Economy*, Edited by S. L. Levy (New York: Holt, 1928) Part VI, 15–20.

136. N. W.Senior, *An Outline of the Science of Political Economy*, 103.
137. *Ibid.*, 104.
138. *Ibid.*, 105.
139. W. T. Thornton, *op. cit.*.
140. J. S. Mill, *Collected Works of John Stuart Mill* (Toronto: University of Toronto Press, 1965–) vol. v, 633–68.
141. See p. 59.
142. W. T. Thornton, *op. cit.*, 52.
143. *Ibid.*, 53.
144. *Ibid.*, 76.
145. *Ibid.*, 78.
146. *Ibid.*, 80.

NOTES TO CHAPTER 4

1. J. A. Schumpeter, *History of Economic Analysis* (London: Allen and Unwin, 1954) 834, his emphasis.
2. See T. S. Kuhn, *The Structure of Scientific Revolutions*, 2nd ed. (Chicago: The University of Chicago Press, 1970).
3. See Marshall's letter to J. B. Clark, in A. C. Pigou (ed.), *Memorials of Alfred Marshall* (London: Macmillan, 1925) 412–13.
4. L. Walras, *Elements of Pure Economics*, 1st ed. 1874, Translated from the 1926 ed. by W. Jaffé (London: Allen and Unwin for the American Economic Association and The Royal Economic Society, 1954) 37.
5. R. René, 'L'Oeuvre Économique d'Augustin Cournot', *Econometrica*, 7 (1939) 143.
6. W. S. Jevons, *The Theory of Political Economy*, 4th ed. (London: Macmillan, 1911) xviii.
7. Marshall, *I. and T.*, 449.
8. J. R. Hicks, 'Leon Walras', *Econometrica*, II (1934) 339n–40n.
9. Julien, 'Du prix des transports sur les chemins de fer', *Annales Des Ponts et Chaussées*, 2ᵉ série (1844) 1–59.
10. R. B. Ekelund, 'Economic Empiricism in the Writing of Early Railway Engineers', *Explorations in Economic History*, 9 (1971–2) 188n.
11. D. L. Hooks, 'Monopoly Price Discrimination in 1850: Dionysius Lardner', *History of Political Economy*, 3 (1971) 217.
12. The notable exception to this generalisation is his stability analysis for duopoly. See p. 137.
13. A. C. Pigou (ed.), *op. cit.*, 100, my emphasis.
14. A. Marshall, *The Early Writings of Alfred Marshall*, Edited by J. K. Whitaker (London: Macmillan, For the Royal Economic Society, 1975) vol. 2, 249.
15. Marshall, *P.*, vol. II, 232–3.
16. A. C. Pigou (ed.), *op. cit.*, 359–60.
17. All firms within the industry will be charging identical prices.

18. P. A. Samuelson, *Foundations of Economic Analysis* (Cambridge, Mass.: Harvard University Press, 1947) 8.

19. A. Cournot, *Researchers into the Mathematical Principles of the Theory of Wealth*, 1st ed. 1838, Translated by N. Bacon (New York: Macmillan, 1929) 1.

20. For example, *Ibid.*, 51–2 where he notes that if the quantity demanded is measured over a year, some average annual price will need to be calculated.

21. L. Walras, *op. cit.*, 307–8. For Marshall's statement of the negligibility of indirect effects, see Marshall, *I. and T.*, 677–8.

22. L. Walras, *Correspondence of Leon Walras and Related Papers*, Edited by W. Jaffé (Amsterdam: North-Holland, 1965) vol. I, Letter 253, 365.

23. In A. C. Pigou (ed.), *op. cit.*.

24. *Ibid.*, 153.

25. *Ibid.*, 155.

26. See p. 14.

27. See L. Walras, *Elements of Pure Economics*. Walras defines 'capital' (212) as all durable goods, ' . . . which are not used up at all or are used up only after a lapse of time' i.e., outlast their first use. 'Capital proper', however, is defined (215) as all capital assets which are neither land nor persons.

28. *Ibid.*, 222.

29. *Ibid.*, 225.

30. F. Y. Edgeworth, 'The Mathematical Theory of Political Economy', *Nature*, 40 (1889) 435.

31. F. Y. Edgeworth, *Papers Relating to Political Economy* (London: Macmillan for The Royal Economic Society, 1925) Vol. I, 26 and 311.

32. J. B. Clark, *The Distribution of Wealth* (New York: Macmillan, 1899) 70 and 369–70.

33. See p. 46.

34. Although Carver, Fetter, Flux, Seager, Holt, Seligman, Hawley, or Frank Knight would be equally suitable. This point regarding the influence of J. B. Clark (at least as to the issues which pre-occupied later American writers) is not necessarily contradicted by Schumpeter's hesitation to speak of 'the Clark school': 'The circle of "allies and sympathizers" was extremely large, and there certainly was a "foreign sphere of influence". But the precise extent of his influence is difficult to determine because, so far as his theory of distribution goes, this influence is inextricably mixed with the influences of all the other builders of similar systems. . . . More important, there is no clearly discernible "core" in the sense in which there was a nucleus consisting of sworn disciples such as Ricardo or Marshall had. Strictly Clarkian treatises are as rare as treatises displaying Clarkian influence are numerous.' J. A. Schumpeter, *op. cit.*, 869.

35. H. J. Davenport, *Value and Distribution* (Chicago: The University of Chicago Press, 1908) 98.

36. J. A. Schumpeter, *The Theory of Economic Development*, 1st German ed. 1911, Translated by R. Opie (Cambridge, Mass.: Harvard University Press, 1934) 74.

37. F. B. Hawley, *Enterprise and the Productive Process* (New York: Putnam's 1907) 107.

38. J. F. Weston, 'The Profit Concept and Theory: A Restatement', *Journal of*

Political Economy, LXII (1954) 152–70.
39. See P. H. Wicksteed, *The Common Sense of Political Economy* (London: Macmillan, 1910) 248 and 370.
40. Marshall, *P.*, 574.
41. *Ibid.*, 627.
42. F. H. Knight in W. Fellner and B. F. Haley (eds.), *Readings in the Theory of Income Distribution* (Philadelphia: Blackiston, 1946) 536–8.
43. F. H. Knight, *Risk Uncertainty and Profit*, 1st ed. 1921 (London: L. S. E. Reprint, 1933) 297, his emphasis.
44. For example, Marshall, *P.*, 302.
45. For example, Marshall, *I. and T.*, 265–6 and 314.
46. *Ibid.*, 314.
47. A. Marshall, *The Early Writings of Alfred Marshall*, 48–9.
48. Marx noted the tendency for the size of businesses to grow under market capitalism as early as 1867: 'The battle of competition is fought by cheapening of commodities. The cheapness of commodities depends, *caeteris paribus*, on the productiveness of labour, and this again on the scale of production. Therefore, the larger capitals beat the smaller.' Marx proceeded to observe that the expanding credit system assists this process. See K. Marx, *Capital*, vol. I, 1st German ed. 1867, translated from the 3rd German ed. by S. Moore and E. Aveling (London: Allen and Unwin, 1946) 640. This proposition seems to have been derived from observations by Engels of the growth of English firms during the eighteenth and nineteenth centuries. See F. Engels, *The Condition of the Working Class in England*, 1st German ed. 1845, translated and edited by W. O. Henderson and W. H. Chaloner (Oxford: Blackwell, 1958) 24 and 88.
49. See Marshall, *I. and T.*, 323–8. Marshall's reliance on 'the influence of motives other than the desire for pecuniary gain' to mitigate the ossification of business leadership does not encompass Wicksteed's (and later Frank Knight's) point of 'playing the game'. P. H. Wicksteed, *op. cit.*, 180, says that the businessman rarely considers motivation: 'He wants to make a good bargain or do a good piece of business, and he is directly thinking of nothing else.' Wicksteed considers that this attitude is similar to that of chess-players and cricketers who, when playing, think only of winning. Their motivation – as to why they play at all – is a separate question.
50. Marshall, *I. and T.*, 327.
51. A. C. Pigou (ed.), *op. cit.*, 307.
52. In defending Mill against criticisms by Cairnes, Marshall explains that the classical economists used 'costs' to mean *both* real efforts and sacrifices, and money expenses forgone by the producer. However, when Mill speaks of 'ratios of costs', he refers to money outlays; for the comparison of diverse efforts and sacrifices necessitates a numeraire such as money. See A. C. Pigou (ed.), *op. cit.*, 126–7.
53. Marshall, *P.*, 350.
54. See p. 51.
55. Marshall, *P.*, 625–6, his emphasis.
56. See L. Robbins, Lord Robbins, *The Evolution of Modern Economic Theory* (London: Macmillan, 1970) 18.

57. See D. I. Green, 'Pain-Cost and Opportunity-Cost', *Quarterly Journal of Economics*, VIII (1894) 218–29. Davenport claims that: 'Without acknowledgment of this contribution, and, indeed, in entire ignorance of it, an article covering very much the same ground was, by the present writer [Davenport], published in the September (1894) number of the *Journal of Political Economy*, under the title of 'The Formula of Sacrifice; . . .'. See H. J. Davenport, *op. cit.*, 93. Davenport did much to promote the notion of opportunity cost. See H. J. Davenport, *Economics of Enterprise* (New York: Macmillan, 1929) 61–5 and 190–1.

58. J. R. Hicks, *op. cit.*, 344.

59. Marshall, *P.*, 378.

60. G. F. Shove, 'The Place of Marshall's *Principles* in the Development of Economic Theory', *Economic Journal*, LII (1942) 312.

61. P. Newman, 'The Erosion of Marshall's Theory of Value', *Quarterly Journal of Economics*, LXXIV (1960) 587–601, promised to write, together with J. N. Wolf, an *Essay on the Theory of Value*, which would give a formal outline of Marshall's time-period analysis; but I can find no evidence of it. It was to contain a Marshallian model of iterative decision-making using Markhov chains.

62. See p. 51.

63. Keynes' memoir of Marshall seems erroneously to attribute to Marshall the introduction of the distinction to the economics profession. See A. C. Pigou (ed.), *op. cit.*, 43.

64. Marshall, *P.*, 360–1.

65. See *Ibid.*, 360.

66. Guillebaud, stating what he considers Marshall would have preferred, does offer a definition: '[Prime costs includes] . . . all those costs (salaries, rates, etc.) which have to be met and paid out, if the business as a whole is to keep running for any considerable length of time. These are in effect the costs that would be saved if the business closed down.' C. W. Guillebaud, 'Marshall's Principles of Economics in the Light of Contemporary Economic Thought', *Economica*, New Series, XIX (1952) 126.

67. Marshall, *P.*, 361.

68. *Ibid.*, 372–3. On page 420, Marshall adds: 'That is to say, some costs which would have been classed as prime costs in relation to contracts, or other affairs, which lasted over a long period, would be classed as supplementary costs in relation to a particular affair which would last but a short time, and which came under consideration when business was slack.'

69. See p. 47.

70. Marshall, *P.*, 432n.

71. See A. C. Pigou (ed.), *op. cit.*, 413–14.

72. A. Marshall, *The Early Writings of Alfred Marshall*, vol. 2, 225.

73. A. Marshall and M. P. Marshall, *The Economics of Industry*, 3rd ed. (London: Macmillan, 1885) 166–7.

74. Marshall, *P.*, vol. II, 495, his emphasis.

75. By 'enter' he means 'determine'.

76. *Ibid.*, vol. II, 498–9.

77. *Ibid.*, vol. I, 424n.

78. W. T. Thornton, *On Labour*, 2nd ed. (London: Macmillan, 1870).

79. C. Ellet, 'Cost of Transportation on Railroads', *Journal of the Franklin Institute*, 3rd Series, beginning IV (1842) 146–7, continuing in subsequent issues.
80. Some notable exceptions will be mentioned later.
81. See A. Marshall, *The Early Writings of Alfred Marshall*, 52–7.
82. The term comes from R. Frisch, 'Monopole – Polypole – La notion de force dans l'économie', *Nationalekonomisk Tidsskrift* (1933), Translated into English under title 'Monopoly – Polypoly – The Concept of Force in the Economy', *International Economic Papers*, 1 (1951) 23–36.
83. In fact, he indicates that, for certain classes of activity, they are likely to be multi-valued.
84. See D. H. Robertson, *Economic Commentaries* (London: Staples, 1956) 20.
85. Marshall, *P.*, 373.
86. On this see G. J. Stigler, *Production and Distribution Theories* (New York: Macmillan, 1946) 66–7.
87. A. C. Pigou, *The Economics of Welfare*, 4th ed. (London: Macmillan, 1946). 216.
88. Marshall, *P.*, 168, my emphasis.
89. Later, Edgeworth was to drive the importance of this point home. See F. Y. Edgeworth, *Papers Relating to Political Economy*, Vol. I, 66–99.
90. See J. B. Clark, *op. cit.*, 47–51 and 183–205.
91. See *Ibid.*, 163–4.
92. P. H. Wicksteed, *op. cit.*, 529.
93. See chapter 5.
94. R. Auspitz et R. Lieben, *Recherches sur la Théorie du Prix*, 1st German ed. 1888, Traduit le L'Allemand par Louis Suret (Paris: Giard et Briere, 1914) 3–10. Cournot had performed the same manipulation using algebra in 1838. See A. Cournot, *op. cit.*, 91.
95. Marshall, *P.*, 370, his emphasis.
96. *Ibid.*, 370.
97. P. A. Samuelson, *op. cit.*, 27.
98. See p. 74.
99. Marshall, *I. and T.*, 272–3. In more recent times Friedman has raised further doubts as to the usefulness of *ex post* measures of long-run costs. See M. Friedman, *Price Theory*, 2nd ed. (Chicago: Aldine, 1976) 145–51.
100. Marshall, *P.*, 344.
101. *Ibid.*, 313.
102. See *Ibid.*, 290. Cournot makes a similar distinction when dealing with monopoly.

The function $\phi'(D)$ [marginal cost] is capable of increasing or decreasing as D increases, according to the nature of the producing forces and of the articles produced.

For what are properly called *manufactured articles*, it is generally the case that the cost becomes proportionally less as production increases, or, in other words, when D increases $\phi'(D)$ is a decreasing function. . . . It may happen, however, even in exploiting products of this nature, that when the exploitation is carried beyond certain limits, it induces higher prices for raw materials and labour, to the point where $\phi'(D)$ again begins to increase with D.

Whenever it is a question of working agricultural lands, or mines, or of quarries, that is, of what is essentially real estate, the function $\phi'(D)$ increases with D, . . . A. Cournot, *op. cit.*, 59–60.

103. Marshall, *I. and T.*, 846.

104. The best theoretical discussion of the relationship between multi-plant economies and the growth of trusts is D. H. Macgregor, *Industrial Combination*, 1st ed. 1906 (London, L. S. E. Reprint, 1935) 19 ff. Van Hise's empirical study acknowledges the difficulty of getting hard data on multi-plant economies. See C. R. Van Hise, *Concentration and Control* (New York: Macmillan, 1912) 35.

105. If Marshall's words are not adequate proof of his opinion (and the misrepresentations seem to indicate that they are not), see D. H. Robertson, *op. cit.*, 16–20.

106. See pp. 52–4.

107. See K. Wicksell, *Lectures on Political Economy*, Translated from the Swedish by E. Classen, Edited by L. Robbins (London: Routledge, 1934) 126–31. J. R. Hicks, *Theory of Wages*, 2nd ed. (London: Macmillan, 1963) 233–9, argues that Walras had seen, even if through a glass darkly, Wicksell's point. The evidence is Walras', 'Note sur la refutation de la Théorie anglaise du fermage de M. Wicksteed.'

108. V. Pareto, *Manual of Political Economy*, Translated from the French ed. of 1927 by A. S. Schwier (London: Macmillan, 1971) 243 and 258.

109. S. J. Chapman and T. S. Ashton, 'The Sizes of Businesses, Mainly in the Textile Industries', *Journal of the Royal Statistical Society*, LXXVII (1914) 515, my emphasis.

110. Marshall, *I. and T.*, 249.

111. See pp. 52–4. Marshall sets out these reasons in A. Marshall and M. P. Marshall, *op. cit.*, 53 ff; and in Marshall, *P.*, Book IV, Chapters IX, X, and XI.

112. See A. Marshall and M. P. Marshall, *op. cit.*, 53 and above, 80. However, risk may cause diseconomies of scale if the firm's expansion were concentrated in a limited product range. See notes on Kalecki's principle of increasing risk, chapter 5.

113. See p. 53.

114. Marshall, *P.*, 282.

115. Marshall, *I. and T.*, 249. This, later, opinion is at variance with that in Marshall, *P.*, 286–7.

116. *Ibid.*, 282.

117. *Ibid.*, 287.

118. *Ibid.*, 284.

119. See note 102 to chapter 4.

120. The latter situation, as represented by the diagram, is consistent with both the first-order and the second-order conditions for profit maximisation. However, it is not consistent with Cournot's model of unlimited competition. See overleaf.

121. A. Cournot, *op. cit.*, 91–2, my emphasis.

122. A. C. Pigou (ed.), *op. cit.*, 406–7.

123. A. Marshall, *The Early Writings of Alfred Marshall*, Edited by J. K. Whitaker (London: Macmillan, For the Royal Economic Society, 1975)

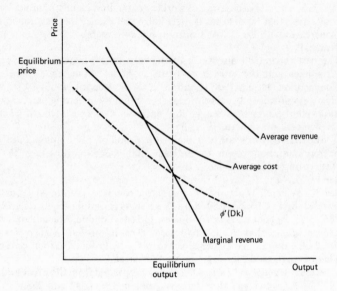

Equilibrium with Decreasing Costs

51n.
124. Marshall, *P.*, 459n, my emphasis.
125. Marshall, *I. and T.*, 182.
126. *Ibid.*, 182.
127. *Ibid.*, 182.
128. See also D. H. Macgregor, *Economic Thought and Policy* (London: Oxford University Press, 1949) 39.
129. Marshall, *I. and T.*, 220; and Marshall, *P.*, 286.
130. *Ibid.*, 287.
131. *Ibid.*, 458.
132. See *Ibid.*, Vol. II, 523–9.
133. A. C. Pigou (ed.), *op. cit.*, 406–7, his emphasis.
134. Marshall, *P.*, 459n.
135. See p. 76.
136. For example, the credit available to a firm largely depends on its past growth and profitability records. See *Ibid.*, 315.
137. *Ibid.*, 316.
138. *Ibid.*, 287.
139. See *Ibid.*, 316; and Marshall, *P.*, Vol. II, 343 ff.
140. Marshall, *I. and T.*, 315.
141. See Marshall, *P.*, 811.
142. See p. 88.
143. Marshall's statement that the allocation of variables between independent and dependent is a matter of convention (*Ibid.*, 457n) is true enough; but

the exposition is awkward if one presents the supply schedule simultaneously with the analysis of equilibrium. It is possible to separate the supply schedule from considerations of demand. This is the path adopted in this chapter; and it is this method of exposition which dictates the verbal interpretation of the supply function.

144. Marshall, *P.*, 266. In his fascinating contribution to the Representative Firm Symposium, Shove claims that Marshall's definition of internal economies fudges the distinction between (i) the costs of a firm's expansion as a part of an expansion of industry output; and (ii) the costs of an expansion of a firm's output while that of the industry remains unchanged.

Now (ii) is likely to be greater than (i) because of the costs both of transporting goods into the markets of competitors and of overcoming buyers' preferences through advertising. If (ii) yields increasing costs but (i) decreasing costs, then the expansion of industry output may yield a lower supply price because of the capturing of further internal economies even though at the original output no firm could find expansion profitable. See G. F. Shove, in D. H. Robertson, Piero Sraffa and G. F. Shove, 'Increasing Returns and the Representative Firm. A Symposium', *Economic Journal*, xl (1930) 103.

145. See D. H. Macgregor,*Industrial Combination*, 27.

146. It is the existence of the externalities (which enable changes in industry output to raise or lower a firm's unit costs) which caused Marshall to stress that his particular expenses curve (see pp. 97–8) is drawn with respect to a particular point in time and to a particular industry output existing at that point in time. If industry output were higher and net external economies prevailed, then the particular expenses curve would be lower than otherwise. See Marshall, *P.*, 810n.

147. See *Ibid.*, 808n. and 809n. For a comment, see A. Marshall, *The Early Writings of Alfred Marshall*, Vol. 2, 184–5.

148. J. A. Schumpeter, 'The Instability of Capitalism', *Economic Journal*, xxxviii (1928) 361–86.

149. D. H. Robertson, *op. cit.*, 19.

150. R. Frisch, 'Alfred Marshall's Theory of Value', *Quarterly Journal of Economics*, lxix (1950) 495–524.

151. See the following section.

152. Marshall, *P.*, 344n; and *I. and T.*, 185.

153. See L. Robbins, Lord Robbins, 'The Representative Firm', *Economic Journal*, xxxviii (1928) 387. Robbin's comment that the concept does not appear in the first edition of the *Principles* is correct as regards the words 'representative firm', but is incorrect as regards the idea. See Marshall, *P.*, vol. ii, 346.

154. L. Robbins, *op. cit.*, 399.

155. D. H. Macgregor, *Economic Thought and Policy* (London: Oxford University Press, 1949). The diagram in the text is a simplified version of that presented by Macgregor on page 44.

156. Marshall, *P.*, 424n.

157. See *Ibid.*, 344.

158. *Ibid.*, 315 ff.

159. A. Marshall, *The Early Writings of Alfred Marshall*, Vol. 2, 3–4.

160. See *Ibid.*, Vol. 2, 119.
161. See Marshall, *I. and T.*, 395–6.
162. As late as the first edition of the *Principles*, Marshall was talking of a 'perfect' market. See G. J. Stigler, 'Marshall's *Principles* after Guillebaud', *Journal of Political Economy*, LXX (1962) 282–6.
163. On Smith, see above, 48 ff. On Mill's Case 1, see above, 92 ff.
164. A. Marshall and M. P. Marshall, *op. cit.*, vi, his emphasis.
165. See pp. 56–7.
166. D. H. Macgregor, *Industrial Combination*, 69.
167. On these points, see Marshall, *I. and T.*, 398.
168. See pp. 97 ff.
169. Marshall, *I. and T.*, 397–8.
170. W. S. Jevons, *op. cit.*, 91.
171. For a few of the earlier statements, see pp. 55–6.
172. F. Y. Edgeworth, *Mathematical Psychics*, 1st ed. 1881 (London: L. S. E. Reprint, 1932) 18.
173. Marshall, *P.*, 341.
174. A. Cournot, *op. cit.*, 90, his emphasis.
175. Such confusion is not uncommon. Machlup's definition of polypoly is a state of mind (independence) frequently *due* to the presence of large numbers. See F. Machlup, *The Economics of Sellers' Competition* (Baltimore: Johns Hopkins, 1952) 136–7.
176. For example, see L. Amoroso, 'La curva statica di offerta', *Giornale degli Economisti* (1930), translated into English under title, 'The Static Supply Curve', *International Economic Papers*, 4 (1954) 39–65.
177. For a review of the evidence relating to the United States, see F. M. Scherer, *Industrial Market Structure and Economic Performance* (Chicago, Rand McNally, 1970) 61–3.
178. It also makes more plausible the use of differentiable functions. Regarding Cournot, see chapter 3, note 72. See also Marshall, *P.*, 407n and 409n.
179. V. Pareto, *Cours D'Économie Politique* (Lausanne: Rouge, 1896) 20 and 20n. For a similar distinction, see V. Pareto, *Manual of Political Economy*, 114–17.
180. Walras' definition of competition is not clear. When outlining his assumptions (see L. Walras, *Elements of Pure Economics* 40–2) he fails to mention the Cournotesque large-numbers assumption. It is only when discussing Cournot's method of exposition (*Ibid.*, 440) that Walras suggests that his competitive case is equivalent to that of Cournot.
181. Jaffé notes (*Ibid.*, Translator's note [13]) that the London silver market had its prices fixed along these lines at the start of each day's trading by the four established firms. See H. M. Bratter, 'Silver – Some Fundamentals', *Journal of Political Economy*, XXXIX (1931) 362 ff.
182. Marshall, *P.*, 517n. and 849–50.
183. This will be discussed in the following section. In *I. and T.*, 401, Marshall refers to ' . . . those who produce things for sale in a large open market in such small quantities, that current prices will not be appreciably affected by anything which they may do or abstain from doing; . . .'.
184. See M. W. Reder, *Studies in the Theory of Welfare Economics* (New York: Columbia University Press, 1947) 148 ff.

185. See K. J. Arrow, 'Toward a Theory of Price Adjustment', in *The Allocation of Economic Resources. Essays in Honor of Bernard Francis Haley* (Stanford, California: Stanford University Press, 1959).
186. See pp. 67 ff.
187. A. C. Pigou (Ed.), *op. cit.*, 130–1.
188. See P. H. Wicksteed, *op. cit.*, 506 ff.
189. A. Marshall, *The Early Writings of Alfred Marshall*, Vol. 2, 187.
190. He refuses to draw such curves on the, rather patronising, grounds that:
    (i) market values are either 'absolutely abstract or terribly concrete'; and
    (ii) the horizontal axis of a demand and supply diagram for market values measures a stock which may confuse those whom Marshall has persuaded to think in terms of flows. See A. C. Pigou (ed.), *op. cit.*, 435; and Marshall, *P.*, Vol. ii, 65, 364 and 808–11. In fact, Marshall talks of the market period as a period of time; and to draw corresponding demand and supply curves, one must envisage flows.
191. See A. Marshall and M. P. Marshall, *op. cit.*, 161; and Marshall, *P.*, 332.
192. H. Sidgwick, *The Principles of Political Economy*, 3rd ed. (London: Macmillan, 1901) 192–3.
193. See A. Cournot, *op. cit.*, 92. Walras raises the possibility of multiple equilibria in the context of his pure exchange model (L. Walras, *op. cit.*, 108 ff.) whereas Marshall does not raise this issue unless he is dealing with the long run. This difference arises from the differences in their supply functions. Both assume monotonically-decreasing demand functions.
194. Marshall, *P.*, 333–4.
195. P. A. Samuelson, *op. cit.*, 258.
196. A. Marshall, *The Early Writings of Alfred Marshall*, 152n.
197. See *Ibid.*, Vol. 2, 204–5; and Marshall, *P.*, 332 ff.
198. See P. H. Wicksteed, *op. cit.*, 218 ff.
199. L. Walras, *Elements of Pure Economics*, 172.
200. This terminology comes from R. F. Kahn, 'The Elasticity of Substitution and the Relative Share of a Factor', *Review of Economic Studies*, i (1933) 72–8.
201. Letter no. 595, dated 1/11/1883 in L. Walras, *Correspondence of Léon Walras and Related Papers*, vol. i, 794.
202. A. Marshall, *The Early Writings of Alfred Marshall*, Vol. 2, 284–5.
203. See L. Walras, *Elements of Pure Economics*, 110–12.
204. N. Kaldor, 'A Classificatory Note on the Determinateness of Equilibrium', in *Essays on Value and Distribution* (London: Duckworth, 1960).
205. See F. Y. Edgeworth, *Mathematical Psychics*, 18 ff. D. A. Walker, 'Edgeworth's Theory of Recontract', *Economic Journal*, 83 (1973) 138–47, professes to find Edgeworth's expositions of the problem far more complex than this. Walker claims that Edgeworth allows pre-equilibrium trading in *Mathematical Psychics*. This is not the case. However, Edgeworth does talk of hypothetical prices 'remaining' in particular positions, thereby, perhaps, given the false impression that trade is occurring.
206. Edgeworth was quite aware that his account of hypothetical trade is unrealistic. See F. Y. Edgeworth, *Papers Relating to Political Economy*, Vol. ii, 311. F. Jenkin, *The Graphic Representation of the Laws of Supply and*

Demand, and other Essays on Political Economy, 1st ed. 1887 (London: L. S. E. Reprint, 1931) 78–9 seems partly to anticipate the problem of indeterminacy.
207. See W. Jaffé 'Walras' Theory of Tatonnement: A Critique of Recent Interpretations', *Journal of Political Economy*, 75 (1967) 1–19.
208. The references are Marshall, *P.*, 334 ff, 791 ff (The Appendix on Barter), and the important exchanges of letters among Marshall, Arthur Berry and Edgeworth, reprinted in *Ibid.*, vol. 2, 791–8.
209. Hicks restates this condition as requiring negligible income effects. See J. R. Hicks, *Value and Capital*, 2nd ed. (Oxford: Clarendon, 1946) 128. But as there strictly is no income in a pure exchange model, Newman prefers to speak of negligible endowment effects. See P. Newman, *The Theory of Exchange* (Englewood Cliffs, N. J.: Prentice-Hall, 1965) 94.
210. Hicks finds this type of difficulty such that he refuses to apply the Marshallian tripartite abstraction to his general equilibrium model. See J. R. Hicks, *Value and Capital*, 122 ff.
211. See pp. 83–5.
212. See pp. 89–90.
213. See Marshall, *I. and T.*, 271–4. These pages refer to disequilibrium exchanges in a competitive market as if they were bargains between firms in positions of bilateral monopoly.
214. Marshall, *P.*, 374, my emphasis.
215. See D. H. Robertson, *op. cit.*, 15.
216. A. Marshall and M. P. Marshall, *op. cit.*, 66. J. B. Clark, *op. cit.*, 78, proposes a similar definition.
217. See quotation on p. 103.
218. Marshall, *P.*, 347–8. See also 33–6.
219. *Ibid.*, 341, my emphasis.
220. See p. 27.
221. L. Walras, *Elements of Pure Economics*, 224.
222. *Ibid.*, 225–6.
223. See H. J. Davenport, *op. cit.*, 377n.
224. For J. S. Mill's justification of a similar procedure, see p. 44.
225. Marshall, *P.*, 424n.
226. A. C. Pigou, *op. cit.*, 370.
227. See pp. 100–2 and Marshall, *P.*, 343–4.
228. The similarities between the stability conditions of Marshall and those of Walras are rarely mentioned in the secondary literature. The notable exception is P. K. Newman, *op. cit.*, 106–7. The normal approach is to follow J. R. Hicks, *Value and Capital*, 62n, in contrasting the two. The contrast is achieved by confusing exchange stability (price adjustment) and production stability (output adjustment).
229. Walras' discussion, while based on partial assumptions, gives a nod towards market inter-relationships. See L. Walras, *Elements of Pure Economics*, 243–54.
230. *Ibid.*, 224–5, his emphasis, parentheses by W. Jaffé.
231. Marshall, *P.*, 345.
232. See pp. 36–7. See also the famous Sherman Act case, Standard Oil Company of New Jersey v. United States [1910] 221, *U. S. Supreme Court*, Law Ed..

619–63.

233. Perhaps the outstanding example among the early studies is F. Walker, *Monopolistic Combinations in the German Coal Industry* (New York: Macmillan, For the American Economic Association, 1904).

234. See note 104, chapter 4.

235. Marshall, *P.*, 377. Marshall's assumptions are expressed carefully. They exclude bargaining with buyers and competition from other sellers. Dupuit and Lardner, offering advice for particular given circumstances apparently did not feel obliged to offer definitions of the circumstances to which the application of their advice regarding the maximisation of net revenue should be confined.

236. Marshall, *P.*, 486. J. A. Schumpeter, *Capitalism, Socialism and Democracy*, 3rd ed. (London: Allen and Unwin, 1950) 99, expresses views similar to those of Marshall. In a world of differentiated products almost every firm is a single seller. Thus, in using Cournot's model: 'We mean [by single seller] only those single sellers whose markets are not open to the intrusion of would-be producers of the same commodity and of actual producers of similar ones or, speaking slightly more technically, only those single sellers who face a given demand schedule that is severely independent of their own action as well of any reactions to their action by other concerns.'

237. Marshall, *I. and T.*, 178.

238. See *Ibid.*, 395–9. Pigou uses the words 'monopoly power' to convey a similar idea. See A. C. Pigou, *op. cit.*, 359.

239. See J. S. Bain, *Barriers to New Competition* (Cambridge, Mass.: Harvard University Press, 1956).

240. Marshall, *I. and T.*, 398.

241. *Ibid.*, 301.

242. See *Ibid.*, Book. III, Chapters VII–XIII.

243. While Marshall is referring to the Sherman Act, he is clearly recalling the Clayton Act.

244. *Ibid.*, 518.

245. Marshall, when making these judgments of business conduct, acknowledges a debt to J. B. Clark, *The Control of Trusts* (New York: Macmillan, 1901).

246. See D. H. Macgregor, *op. cit.*.

247. See Marshall, *I. and T.*, 523–4. Marshall uses the concept of concentration, but not the word.

248. Marshall discusses the factors which facilitate collusion in *Ibid.*, 485 and 537.

249. For example J. B. Clark, *The Distribution of Wealth* (New York: Macmillan, 1899) 78.

250. See Marshall, *P.*, note XXII of the Mathematical Appendix, 856. For Cournot's notation, see A. Cournot, *op. cit.*, 57.

251. See F. Y. Edgeworth, *Papers Relating to Political Economy*, vol. I, 112.

252. See Marshall, *P.*, 484.

253. A. Cournot, *op. cit.*, 61–78.

254. J. R. Hicks, 'Annual Survey of Economic Theory: The Theory of Monopoly', in G. J. Stigler and K. E. Boulding (eds.), *Readings in Price Theory* (London: Allen and Unwin, 1953).

255. M. W. Reder, 'Monopolistic Competition and the Stability Conditions', *Review of Economic Studies*, viii (1941) 122–5.
256. See O. Lange, *Price Flexibility and Employment* (Bloomington, Indiana: Principia, 1944) 36, and Appendix on 'The Stability of Economic Equilibrium'.
257. K. J. Arrow, 'Toward a Theory of Price Adjustment', in *The Allocation of Economic Resources. Essays in Honor of Bernard Francis Haley* (Stanford, California: Stanford University Press, 1959).
258. See Marshall, *I. and T.*, 407–8.
259. *Ibid.*, 524, his emphasis.
260. Marshall, *P.*, 486. See also Marshall, *I. and T.*, 405–7.
261. Marshall, *I. and T.*, Book ii, Chapters xi and xii, are devoted to a discussion of 'Scientific Management'. For a handy review of this literature see, J. G. March and H. A. Simon, *Organizations* (New York: Wiley, 1958).
262. In a later period, important contributions came from Schneider and Joan Robinson. Chamberlin's initial interest in monopolistic competition was aroused by the Taussig-Pigou controversy. Chamberlin explains this in E. H. Chamberlin, *The Theory of Monopolistic Competition*, 8th ed. (Cambridge, Mass.: Harvard University Press, 1962) 293–6. Hicks argues that 'probably the best', and 'certainly the most ingenious' part of Joan Robinson's, *Economics of Imperfect Competition*, relates to discrimination theory. J. R. Hicks, 'Annual Survey of Economic Theory: The Theory of Monopoly', 368.

    From this understanding, it appears that the increasing returns controversy yielded little in terms of theoretical advance. The best work in the thirties was stimulated either by applied interests, or by the attempt to clarify (as distinct from attack) the work of Marshall and Walras.
263. *Ibid.*, 368.
264. C. Ellet's most important works on price discrimination are *An Essay on the Laws of Trade* (Richmond, Virginia, 1839 – a most ambitious work marred by an immensely confusing exposition: in particular, a failure to define mathematical notation before putting it to use; and 'The Laws of Trade applied to the determination of the most advantageous fare for Passengers on Railroads', *Journal of the Franklin Institute*, New Series, xxvi (1840) 369–79. Ellet's reputation as a pioneer in the field has been, until recently, overshadowed by that of Dupuit. J. Viner, *The Long View and the Short* (Glencoe, Illinois: Free, 1958) 388, was one of the first modern economists to rank Ellet along with Dupuit.
265. J. Dupuit wrote a number of articles on the subject. Two of the most important are published in English translation: 'De la Mesure de l'Utilité des Travaux Publics', *Annales des Ponts et Chaussées* (1844), translated into English under title, 'On the Measurement of the Utility of Public Works', *International Economic Papers*, 2 (1952) 83–110; and 'De l'influence des péages sur l'utilité des voies de communication', fourth part: 'Des péages', *Annales des Ponts et Chaussées* (1849), translated into English under title, 'On Tolls and Transport Charges', *International Economic Papers*, 11 (1962) 7–31.
266. See F. Y. Edgeworth, *Papers Relating to Political Economy*, vol. ii, 406.

267. A. C. Pigou, *op. cit.*, 279.
268. C. Ellet, 'The Laws of Trade applied to the determination of the most advantageous fare for Passengers on Railroads', 374, his emphasis.
269. *Ibid.*, 378–9, his emphasis.
270. J. Dupuit, 'On Tolls and Transport Charges', 23.
271. See A. C. Pigou, *op. cit.*, 275; and A. C. Pigou, 'Monopoly and Consumers' Surplus', *Economic Journal*, xiv (1904) 390.
272. C. Ellet, 'The Laws of Trade applied to the determination of the most advantageous fare for Passengers on Railroads', 374.
273. J. Dupuit, 'On Tolls and Transport Charges', 16.
274. To be discussed in the following section. See F. Y. Edgeworth, *Mathematical Psychics*, 47 ff.
275. L. Foldes, 'Some Comments on the Theory of Monopoly', in M. Peston and B. Corry (eds.), *Essays in Honour of Lord Robbins* (London: Weidenfeld and Nicolson, 1972).
276. L. Walras, *Elements of Pure Economics*, 442.
277. Marshall, *I. and T.*, 436.
278. See pp. 38–9.
279. C. Menger, *Principles of Economics*, 1st German ed. 1871, translated by J. Dingwall and B. F. Hoselitz, with an Introduction by F. H. Knight (Glencoe, Illinois: Free, 1950) 195.
280. *Ibid.*, 195–6. This may be compared with Pantaleoni's model in which equilibrium exists when both parties to the exchange gain an equal amount of utility. See M. Pantaleoni, *Pure Economics*, 1st Italian ed. 1889, translated from Italian by T. B. Bruce (London: Macmillan, 1898) 142.
281. F. Y. Edgeworth, *Mathematical Psychics*, 31.
282. On the origins of the diagram, see V. J. Tarascio, 'A Correction: On the Geneology of the so-called Edgeworth-Bowley Diagram', *Western Economic Journal*, x (1972) 193–7.
283. In fact, Edgeworth's lines of indifference do not represent initial endowments, nor do they represent bundles of goods among which the individual is indifferent as to ownership. Rather they represent bundles among whose trade the individual is indifferent. This should be borne in mind so that the construction in the text (using the indifference curves of Fisher and Pareto) does not mislead. See W. Jaffé, 'Edgeworth's Contract Curve: Part 1. A propaedeutic essay in clarification', *History of Political Economy*, 6 (1974) 346.
284. J. von Neumann and O. Morgenstern, *Theory of Games and Economic Behavior*, 3rd ed. (New York: Wiley, 1967) 37 and 40.
285. See K. Wicksell, *Value Capital and Rent*, 1st German ed. 1893, translated by S. H. Frowein (London: Allen and Unwin, 1954) 62.
286. See pp. 114–15.
287. The exposition of Edgeworth contained in the following paragraph is based on P. Newman, *op. cit.*, 111 ff. See also F. Y. Edgeworth, *Mathematical Psychics*, 35–9.
288. See F. Zeuthen, *Problems of Monopoly and Economic Warfare*, 1st ed. 1930 (London: Routledge and Kegan Paul, 1968) 63 ff.
289. See A. Cournot, *op. cit.*, 99 ff.
290. See K. Wicksell, *Selected Papers on Economic Theory*, Edited by E.

196   *The Emergence of the Theory of the Firm*

Lindahl (London: Allen and Unwin, 1958) 219 ff. Wicksell's representation enables the similarity of Cournot's complementary monopolies and Ellet's two-stage monopoly to be seen plainly.

291. See Marshall, *P.*, 493–5.
292. Cournot's *Researches* was published in 1838 and Ellet's *Essay on the Laws of Trade* in 1839. Ellet had studied at the École des Ponts et Chaussées for two years from 1830.
293. C. Ellet, *An Essay on the Laws of Trade* 78–9. The algebra deriving the equilibrium conditions may be found at 79.
294. A. L. Bowley, *The Mathematical Groundwork of Economics* (Oxford: Clarendon, 1924) 62.
295. Reprinted in K. Wicksell, *Selected Papers on Economic Theory*.
296. A. L. Bowley, 'Bilateral Monopoly', *Economic Journal*, xxxviii (1928) 651–9.
297. V. Pareto, *Manual of Political Economy*, 440.
298. A. L. Bowley, *The Mathematical Groundwork of Economics*.
299. A. Cournot, *op. cit.*, 44.
300. *Ibid.*, 83.
301. In the terminology of Frisch, such an assumption is called zero conjectural variation. See R. Frisch, 'Monopole-Polypole-La notion de force dans l'économie', *Nationalekonomisk Tidsskrift* (1933), translated into English under title 'Monopoly-Polypoly-The Concept of Force in the Economy', *International Economic Papers*, 1 (1951) 23–36.
302. I. Fisher, 'Cournot and the Mathematical Economics', *Quarterly Journal of Economics*, xii (1898) 119–38.
303. H. L. Moore, 'Paradoxes of Competition', *Quarterly Journal of Economics*, xx (1906) 211–30.
304. K. Wicksell, *Selected Papers on Economic Theory*, 220.
305. A. C. Pigou, *The Economics of Stationary States* (London: Macmillan, 1935) 94.
306. L. Amoroso, 'La curva statica di offerta', *Giornale degli Economisti* (1930), translated into English under title, 'The Static Supply Curve', *International Economic Papers*, 4 (1954) 56.
307. G. J. Stigler, 'Notes on the Theory of Oligopoly', *Journal of Political Economy*, xlviii (1940) 525.
308. As does F. Zeuthen, *op. cit.*, 29.
309. See J. W. Friedman, 'Reaction Functions and the Theory of Duopoly', *Review of Economic Studies*, xxxv (1968) 257–72.
310. For example, see F. Machlup, *The Economics of Sellers' Competition* (Baltimore: Johns Hopkins, 1952) 372 ff.
311. See J. Bertrand, 'Théorie mathématique de la richesse sociale', *Journal des Savants* (1883) 503.
312. See F. Y. Edgeworth, *Papers Relating to Political Economy* vol. i, 111–42.
313. F. Y. Edgeworth, in 'The Mathematical Economics of Professor Amoroso', *Economic Journal*, xxxii (1922) 400–7, constructs his model, dispensing with his discontinuous cost functions, on the assumption that each firm faces continuously increasing cost functions. In constructing a model with continuous cost functions, Edgeworth does not claim that this assumption is any more realistic than that of discontinuous functions.

With characteristic modesty, he states that Bertrand has covered the case of constant costs, Marshall that of decreasing costs, and it was left to him to deal with that of increasing costs. See F. Y. Edgeworth, *Papers Relating to Political Economy* vol. I, 117–8.

314. F. Machlup, *op. cit.*, 383.
315. *Ibid.*, 395.
316. F. Y. Edgeworth, 'The Mathematical Economics of Professor Amoroso', 405.
317. See A. J. Nichol, 'Edgeworth's Theory of Duopoly Price', *Economic Journal*, XLV (1935) 51–66.
318. F. Y. Edgeworth, *Papers Relating to Political Economy* vol. I, 137.
319. I. Fisher, *op. cit.*.
320. L. Kotany, 'Suggestions on the Theory of Value', *Quarterly Journal of Economics*, XIX (1905) 573–84.
321. H. L. Moore, *op. cit.*.
322. A. C. Pigou, *The Economics of Welfare*, 4th ed., (London: Macmillan, 1946) 267.
323. A. L. Bowley, *The Mathematical Groundwork of Economics*, 38.
324. K. Wicksell, *Selected Papers on Economic Theory*, 204–26.
325. A. A. Young, 'Review of A. L. Bowley's, The Mathematical Groundwork of Economics', *Journal of the American Statistical Association*, New Series, XX (1925) 133–5.

NOTES TO CHAPTER 5

1. W. Newmarch, 'The Progress of Economic Science during the last Thirty Years', *Journal of the Statistical Society of London*, XXIV (1861) 453.
2. Recent critics have looked more sceptically upon the willingness of the English classical school to so modify their doctrines. See M. Blaug, 'The Empirical Content of Ricardian Economics', *Journal of Political Economy*, LXIV (1956) 41–58.
3. In T. Wilson and P. W. S. Andrews, *Oxford Studies in the Price Mechanism* (Oxford: Clarendon, 1951).
4. For the amazed reaction of an accountant to this controversy, see R. S. Edwards, 'The Pricing of Manufactured Products', *Economica*, New Series, XIX (1952) 298–307.
5. See brief comment in final chapter, above.
6. See pp. 137–8.
7. More will be said of these developments in the next two sections.
8. E. A. G. Robinson, 'The Pricing of Manufactured Products', *Economic Journal*, LV (1950) 771–80; and P. W. S. Andrews, *Manufacturing Business* (London: Macmillan, 1949). Harrod makes similar points to those of Andrews in R. Harrod, 'Theory of Imperfect Competition Revised', in *Economic Essays*, 2nd ed. (London: Macmillan, 1972).
9. J. R. Hicks, 'The Process of Imperfect Competition', *Oxford Economic Papers*, New Series, 6 (1954) 41–54.
10. See p. 28. Galiani's producers are essentially myopic – causing cob-web type reactions.

11. See p. 46.
12. I. Fisher, *The Nature of Capital and Income* (New York: Macmillan, 1906) Ch. xvi, and Appendix to xvi.
13. G. L. S. Shackle, *Expectations in Economics*, 2nd ed. (Cambridge: Cambridge University Press, 1952).
14. A. A. Alchian, 'Uncertainty, Evolution, and Economic Theory', *Journal of Political Economy*, lviii (1950) 212–13, his emphasis.
15. The phrase comes from F. Machlup, 'Theories of the firm: Marginalist, Behavioral, Managerial', *American Economic Review*, lvii (1967) 4.
16. See pp. 106–8, for conditions under which the hypothesis of quantity adaptor is applicable.
17. See p. 12.
18. See Mill, *P.*, 138–9. On Marshall, see pp. 80–1.
19. A. A. Berle and G. Means, *The Modern Corporation and Private Property* (New York: Macmillan, 1932).
20. See W. J. Baumol, *Business Behavior, Value, and Growth*, 1st ed. (New York: Macmillan, 1959).
21. See p. 125.
22. See G. F. Thirlby, 'The Economist's Description of Business Behaviour', *Economica*, New Series, xix (1952) 148–67. On the cross-fertilisation at the L. S. E., see J. R. Gould, 'Opportunity Cost: The London Tradition', in H. Edey and B. S. Yamey (eds.), *Debits, Credits, Finance and Profits* (London: Sweet and Maxwell, 1974).
23. See R. M. Cyert and J. G. March, *A Behavioral Theory of the Firm* (New Jersey: Prentice-Hall, 1963).
24. See H. A. Simon, 'From substantive to procedural rationality', in S. J. Latsis (ed.), *Method and Appraisal in Economics* (Cambridge: Cambridge University Press, 1976).
25. W. J. Baumol and R. E. Quandt, 'Rules of Thumb and Optimally Imperfect Decisions', *American Economic Review*, liv (1964) 23–46.
26. See pp. 145–6.
27. See p. 88.
28. See pp. 94 and 89.
29. See above, note 89, chapter 4.
30. See J. M. Clark, *Studies in the Economics of Overhead Costs* (Chicago: University of Chicago Press, 1923) 52n and 53n.
31. See p. 91.
32. Clark, *op. cit.*, pp. 70–1.
33. J. Viner, 'Cost Curves and Supply Curves', in G. J. Stigler and K. E. Boulding (eds.), *Readings in Price Theory* (London: Allen and Unwin, 1953).
34. See pp. 89–90.
35. For representative statements as to the derivation of the short-run marginal cost curve from the principle of diminishing returns, see *Ibid.*, 203; and N. Kaldor, 'The Equilibrium of the Firm', in *Essays on Value and Distribution* (London: Duckworth, 1960).
36. K. Menger, 'The Logic of the Laws of Return: A Study in Meta-Economics', in O. Morgenstern (ed.), *Economic Activity Analysis* (New York: Wiley, 1954) 422. This article incorporates English translations of

both of the articles mentioned in the text.
37. See p. 90.
38. P. W. S. Andrews, *op. cit.*, 87–109.
39. *Ibid.*,102–3.
40. For·references to the studies, see A. A. Walters, 'Production and Cost Functions: An Econometric Survey', *Econometrica*, 31 (1963) 1–66.
41. See J. M. Clark, *op. cit.*, 113 ff.
42. See *Ibid.*, 119–34; and E. A. G. Robinson, *The Structure of Competitive Industry*, 4th ed. (Cambridge: Cambridge University Press, and Nisbet, Herts., 1958) 64–5.
43. See pp. 92–3.
44. L. Amoroso, 'La curva statica di offerta', *Giornale degli Economisti* (1930), translated into English under title, 'The Static Supply Curve', *International Economic Papers*, 4 (1954) 41.
45. P. S. Florence, *The Logic of Industrial Organization* (London: Kegan Paul, 1933) 116.
46. See P. F. Drucker, *The Concept of the Corporation* (New York: Day, 1946).
47. See pp. 92–3.
48. See A. C. Pigou, 'An Analysis of Supply', *Economic Journal*, xxxviii (1928) 238–57.
49. See R. Harrod, *op. cit.*, 100.
50. E. A. G. Robinson, *op. cit.*, 49.
51. For a summary of the evidence up to 1960, see J. Johnston, *Statistical Cost Analysis* (New York: McGraw-Hill, 1960) 168.
52. J. M. Clark points out that, given the type of production function which the theorists of perfect competition implicitly assume, there are five stages of production possible as successively higher rates of variable input are added to a fixed factor: (i) the marginal product of the fixed factor is negative; (ii) the marginal product of the fixed factor is zero; (iii) the marginal product of the variable factor is positive but declining; (iv) the marginal product of the variable factor is zero; and (v) the marginal product of the variable factor is negative. Stage (iii) will be chosen by a cost-minimising management providing both factors have a positive price. See J. M. Clark, *op. cit.*, 86–7.
53. See pp. 119–21.
54. See A. C. Pigou, *op. cit.*.
55. See p. 98.
56. See F. H. Knight, 'Some Fallacies in the Interpretation of Social Cost', in G. J. Stigler and K. E. Boulding (eds.), *op. cit.*.
57. J. Robinson, 'Rising Supply Price', in G. J. Stigler and K. E. Boulding (eds.), *op. cit.*.
58. See pp. 95–6.
59. J. R. Hicks, *Value and Capital*, 2nd ed. (Oxford: Clarendon, 1946) 200.
60. N. Kaldor, *op. cit.*, 45, his emphasis.
61. E. A. G. Robinson, *op. cit.*, 48.
62. E. T. Penrose, *The Theory of the Growth of the Firm* (Oxford: Blackwell, 1966).
63. M. Kalecki, 'The Principle of Increasing Risk', *Economica*, New Series, IV (1937) 440–47.
64. See D. Schwartzman, 'Uncertainty and the Size of Firm', *Economica*, New

Series, 30 (1963) 287–96. Schwartzman uses the frequency and magnitude of price mark-downs by department stores as a proxy for market uncertainty.

65. See p. 122.

66. J. S. Bain, *Barriers to New Competition* (Cambridge, Mass.: Harvard University Press, 1956) 3.

67. P. Sylos-Labini, *Oligopoly and Technical Progress*, 2nd ed., translated from the Italian (Cambridge, Mass.: Harvard University Press, 1969).

68. See pp. 73–4.

69. See pp. 125–30.

70. E. H. Chamberlin, *The Theory of Monopolistic Competition*, 8th ed. (Cambridge, Mass.: Harvard University Press, 1962) 294–6.

71. M. Friedman, *Essays in Positive Economics* (Chicago: University of Chicago Press, 1953) 25.

72. S. J. Latsis, in S. J. Latsis (ed.), *op. cit.*, 14.

73. E. H. Chamberlin, *Towards a More General Theory of Value* (New York: Oxford University Press, 1957) 3–30.

74. *Ibid.*, 4–5.

75. F. Machlup, 'Monopoly and Competition: A Classification', *American Economic Review*, xxxvii (1937) 445–51.

76. E. S. Mason, 'Price and Production Policies of Large-Scale Enterprises', *American Economic Review*, xxix (1939) 61–74.

77. D. H. Wallace, *Market Control in the Aluminium Industry* (Cambridge, Mass.: Harvard University Press, 1937).

78. R. Triffin, *Monopolistic Competition and General Equilibrium Theory* (Cambridge, Mass.: Harvard University Press, 1960) 97 ff.

79. For references and a summary of the debate, see J. S. Bain, 'Chamberlin's Impact on Microeconomic Theory', in R. E. Kuenne (ed.), *Monopolistic Competition Theory: Studies in Impact, Essays in Honor of Edward H. Chamberlin* (New York: Wiley, 1967) 150–9.

80. See J. R. Hicks, 'Annual Survey of Economic Theory: The Theory of Monopoly', in G. J. Stigler and K. E. Boulding (eds.), *op. cit.*, 366 ff.

81. H. von Stackelberg, 'Preisdiskrimination bei willkürlicher Teilung des Marktes', *Archiv für mathematische Wirtschafts und Sozialforschung* (1939), translated into English under title, 'Price Discrimination in an Arbitrarily Divided Market', *International Economic Papers*, 8 (1958) 65–73.

82. See R. Harrod, 'Theory of Imperfect Competition Revised', in R. Harrod, *op. cit.*.

83. See p. 143.

84. R. Frisch, 'Monopole-Polypole-La notion de force dans l'économie', *Nationalekonomisk Tidsskrift* (1933), translated into English under title 'Monopoly-Polypoly-The Concept of Force in the Economy', *International Economic Papers*, 1 (1951) 23–36.

85. F. Zeuthen, *Problems of Monopoly and Economic Warfare*, 1st ed. 1930 (London: Routledge and Kegan-Paul, 1968).

86. E. H. Chamberlin, *The Theory of Monopolistic Competition*.

87. H. von Stackelberg, *The Theory of the Market Economy*, translated from 1932 German ed. by A. T. Peacock (London: Hodge, 1952).

88. For reviews of the literature, see B. S. Yamey, 'Do Monopoly and Near-

Monopoly Matter? A Survey of Empirical Studies', in M. Peston and
B. Corry (eds.), *Essays in Honour of Lord Robbins* (London: Weidenfeld and
Nicolson, 1972); B. S. Yamey, 'Some Problems of Oligopoly', in *International Conference on International Economy and Competition Policy*
(Tokyo: 1973); and L. Weiss, 'Quantitative Studies in Industrial Organiz-
ation', in M. D. Intriligator (ed.), *Frontiers of Quantitative Economics*
(Amsterdam:North-Holland, 1971).
89. B. S. Yamey, 'Some Problems of Oligopoly', 318.
90. See p. 123.
91. See W. S. Comanor and T. A. Wilson, 'Advertising, Market Structure and
Performance', *Review of Economics and Statistics*, XLIX (1967) 423–40.
92. K. D. George, 'Concentration, Barriers to Entry and Rates of Return',
Review of Economics and Statistics, L (1968) 273–5.
93. In A. C. Pigou (ed.), *Memorials of Alfred Marshall* (London: Macmillan,
1925).

NOTES TO CHAPTER 6

1. The term comes from G. C. Archibald, 'Chamberlin versus Chicago', *Review
of Economic Studies*, XXIX (1961) 10.
2. P. A. Samuelson, *Foundations of Economic Analysis* (Cambridge, Mass.:
Harvard University Press, 1947) 20.
3. K. R. Popper, *Conjectures and Refutations*, 3rd ed. (London: Routledge and
Kegan Paul, 1969) 233.
4. See G. C. Archibald, *op. cit.*
5. See A. A: Alchian and H. Demsetz, 'Production, Information Costs, and
Economic Organization', *American Economic Review*, LXII (1972) 777–95;
and O. E. Williamson, *Markets and Hierarchies* (New York: Free, 1975).
6. See model in R. M. Cyert and J. G. March, *A Behavioral Theory of the Firm*
(New Jersey: Prentice-Hall, 1963) 97 ff.

Index

Alchian, A. A., 148, 198, 201
Allen, W. R., 173
Amoroso, L., 137, 146, 154, 190, 196, 199
Andrews, P. W. S., 146–7, 149, 153, 197, 199
Aquinus, St T., 17, 174
Archibald, G. C., 168, 172, 201
Aristotle, 36
Arndt, H. W., 175
Arrow, K. J., 108, 124–5, 191, 194
Ashton, T. S., 20, 92, 174, 176, 187
Augustine, St, 17
Auspitz, R., and Lieben, R., 87, 90, 106, 186

Babbage, C., 41, 52, 55–6, 93, 125, 179–80
Bailey, S., 48, 55, 57, 62–6, 179, 181
Bain, J. S., 123, 160, 193, 200
Barbon, N., 25, 174–5
Bauer, P. T., 175
Baumol, W. J., 150–1, 198
Becher, J. J., 37, 176
Berle, A. A., and Means, G., 150, 198
Berry, A., 192
Bertrand, J., 141–2, 196–7
Bitterman, H. J., 174
Blaug, M., 171, 175, 181, 197
Böhm-Bawerk, E., 130
Boisguilbert, P., Sieur de, 175
Boulding, K. E., 171
Bowley, A. L., 135–6, 143, 146, 163, 195–7
Bowley, M., 62, 181
Bratter, H. M., 190
Buchanan, D. H., 176
Bücher, C., 20, 174
Buck, R. C., 171–2

Cairnes, J. E., 55, 60–1, 66, 180–1, 184
Cannan, E., 4, 19, 35, 171, 176
Cantillon, R., 15–16, 18, 33, 43, 173, 176
Carver, T. N., 183
Case studies, 41, 87
Chamberlin, E. H., 73, 123, 146, 159–63, 166, 168, 194, 200
Chapman, S. J., 92, 187
Clark, J. B., 77–8, 85, 89, 182–3, 186, 192–3
Clark, J. M., 152, 154, 198–9
Coase, R. H., 1, 171, 174
Cohen, R. S., 171–2
Comanor, W. S., 201
Competition
  contrast with custom, 41, 56–7, 103
  free competition, 21, 30–3, 62, 102–8, 117
  perfect competition (*see also* Market structure, number of sellers), 21, 33–5, 77–8, 103, 105–8, 146, 151, 156–7, 159, 161, 169
Cooper, T., 59, 180
Costs, (*see also* price determination, joint costs)
  diminishing returns, 49, 62–3, 89, 152
  externalities, 98–100, 157
  increasing returns, 61–2
  input substitution, 49–50, 119, 129, 157
  opportunity cost (*see also* Profit, normal, *and* Costs, prime and supplementary), 51, 82–3, 117–18, 150
  prime and supplementary (*see also* Costs, opportunity), 84–6, 167

Costs *(contd.)*
   returns to scale, 21, 41, 52–4, 91–3,
      152, 154–8: diseconomies, 53,
      92–3; division of labour, 12,
      19–24, 52; pecuniary, 53, 93
   short-run functions, 89–90, 152–3
Cournot, A. C., 40, 51, 53, 59, 61, 66,
      70–5, 80, 82, 87–8, 93–4, 96–7,
      105–8, 122–3, 133–43, 145–6,
      151–2, 161, 163, 166, 169, 174,
      178–80, 183, 186–7, 190–1, 193,
      195–6
Court, W. H. B., 172
Craig, J., 48, 178
Cyert, R. M., and March, J. G., 151,
      198, 201

Davenport, H. J., 78, 87, 118, 183, 185,
      192
Demand functions, 28, 38, 95, 109
Dempsey, B. W., 178
Demsetz, H., 201
De Quincey, T., 60
De Roover, R., 35, 176
*Discourse of the Common Weal of this
   Realm of England, A*, 17
Discourse of Corporations, 17, 174
Drucker, P. F., 199
Dupuit, J., 40, 70–1, 121, 126–9, 163,
      193–5

Edgeworth, F. Y., 73–4, 77–8, 105,
      113–14, 123–4, 126–7, 129,
      131–6, 140–3, 146, 152, 161, 163,
      183, 186, 190–6, 197
Edwards, R. S., 197
Ekelund, R. B., 71, 182
Ellet, C., 40, 70, 126–9, 135, 186,
      194–6
Ellis, W., 44, 177
Ely, R. D., 62, 181
Engels, F., 184
Entrepreneur
   personality of firms, 11, 125, 145
   theories, 12–14, 16, 42, 77–81
*Essay on the Political Economy of
   Nations, An*, 177
Expectations, 87, 160

Fetter, F. A., 183
Firm
   concept, 1
   determination of size, 7, 30, 53–4,
      61, 92–8, 145, 154–9, 169
   equilibrium under competition, 7,
      22, 74, 93–8, 155–6
   goals, 140–3: net revenue maximis-
      ation, 17–19, 80–1, 103, 125, 145,
      147–51; sales maximisation, 150;
      satisficing, 151; self intere⁻
      17–19; time horizon, 80–1, 125,
      133, 137–8, 146–9, 155, 159, 160,
      163
   internal organisation, 12, 130–1,
      149–51, 169
   representative firm, *see* Supply
      schedule for industry, long run:
      representative firm
   separation of ownership from con-
      trol, 12, 76–7, 78–81, 145,
      149–50
Fisher, I., 137, 146, 148, 196–8
Florence, P. S., 154, 199
Flux, A. W., 183
Foldes, L., 130, 195
Friedman, J. W., 196
Friedman, M., 161, 186, 200
Frisch, R., 100, 163, 186, 189, 196, 200

Galiani, F., 28, 148, 174, 197
Games theory, 131, 143
General equilibrium, 9, 74–5, 91, 108,
      115, 175
George, K. D., 164, 201
German historical school, 76
Gioja, M., 179
Gould, J. R., 198
Green, D. I., 82, 185
Groenewegen, P. D., 173, 176
Guilebaud, C. W., 185

Hales, J., 174
Hall, R. J., and Hitch, C. J., 145–7
Hamilton, R., 180
Harris, J., 28–9, 175
Harrod, R., 155, 163, 197, 199, 200
Hawley, F. B., 79, 183
Hayek, F. A. v., 2–3, 171–2

Hecksher, E. F., 36, 173, 176
Hermann, F. B. W. v., 46–7, 78, 85
Hicks, J. R., 34, 70, 82, 108, 124, 147, 157, 176, 182, 185, 187, 192–4, 195, 197, 200
Hollander, S., 175
Hooks, D. L., 71, 182
Hopkins, T., 177
Hoselitz, B. F., 42, 173, 177
Hurwicz, L., 108

Jaffé, W., 112, 114, 190, 192, 195
Jenkin, F., 191
Jevons, W. S., 71, 87, 182, 190
law of indifference, 104
Joint-stock companies, 12, 18, 79–80, 97, 149, 173
Julien, 71, 182

Kahn, R. F., 191
Kaldor, N., 157–8, 191, 198–9
Kalecki, M., 158, 199
Keynes, J. M., 2, 185
Knies, K., 76
Knight, F. H., 15–16, 19, 42, 79–80, 105, 173, 177, 183, 199
Kotany, L., 143, 146, 197
Kroebner, R., 172
Kuhn, T. S., 182

Laffer, A. B., 24, 175
Lakatos, I., 2–8, 171–2
Lange, O., 124–5, 194
Lardner, D., 51, 71, 82, 121, 126, 179, 193
Latsis, S. J., 6–7, 171–2, 200
Lessius, L. de, 36
Letwin, W., 172
Longfield, M., 59, 180

McCullogh, J. R., 41, 66, 168
Macgregor, D. H., 98–9, 101, 103, 123, 187–90, 193
Machlup, F., 142, 146–7, 162, 165–6, 169–70, 190, 196–8, 200
McLeod, H. D., 85
Maitland, J. (8th Earl of Lauderdale), 49, 57, 178
Malthus, T. R., 43, 49, 57–9, 61, 180

Mangoldt, H. K. E., v. 42, 47–8, 51, 78, 85, 173, 178
March, J. G., 151, 194, 198, 201
Market definition, 21, 55, 73, 95–6, 104–5, 162
Market structure
  barriers to entry, 22, 32, 37, 55, 103, 122–3, 147, 160–1, 164
  knowledge, 33, 105, 108, 111–15, 118, 124, 131, 137, 150–1, 158–9, 163, 169
  number of sellers, 21, 31–3, 37–9, 55, 73, 103, 105–9, 122–3, 129–33, 143, 151, 155, 160–1, 163–4, 169
  product differentiation, 56, 66, 95–6, 128–9, 157, 161–2
Marshall, A., 1, 3–4, 7, 9–10, 14, 16, 21, 29, 33–4, 47, 70 ff, 149–50, 152–3, 155–6, 159–60, 164–8, 174–201
Marshall, M. P., 103, 185, 187, 190, 192
Marx, K., 184
Mason, E. S., 162, 166, 200
Meek, R. L., 27, 172–3, 175
Menger, C., 2, 38, 130–1, 195
Menger, K., 153, 198
Methodology, 1–10
  internal and external history, 2–3, 40, 121
  Marshall's method, 72–6
  methodology of scientific research programmes (*see also* Lakatos), 2–8
  verisimilitude (*see also* Popper), 8, 11, 14, 34–5, 41, 73, 109, 144, 146, 161, 165–9
Metzler, L. A., 108
Mill, James, 58
Mill, J. S., 3, 7, 29, 40 ff, 73, 79, 85, 87, 92, 103, 109, 125–6, 144, 149, 154, 159, 166–7, 177–201
Monopoly
  bilateral monopoly, 38–9, 68, 108, 129, 130–3, 135–6
  collusion, 31–2, 37, 66, 116, 121, 123
  complementary monopolies, 133–5

Monopoly *(contd.)*
  definition, 30–1, 35, 54, 62–3
  monopsony, 36, 108, 124
  prevalence, 64–6, 106
  price discrimination, 3, 12, 125–30,
    161–3
  Smith's attitude, 3
  sources of monopoly power, 66–7,
    104, 121–2, 160
  theories of pricing, 33, 35–9, 72,
    124–5, 162, 169
  trade unions, 66
Moore, H. L., 137, 143, 146, 196–7
Morgenstern, O., 131, 195
Morishima, M., 108
Munroe, A. E., 174–5
Musgrave, A., 171–2

Negishi, T., 108
Neumann, J. V., 131, 195
Newman, P., 185, 192, 195
Newmarch, W., 144, 197
Nichol, A. J., 143, 197

O'Brien, D. P., 181
Oligopoly (including duopoly), 36,
  116, 136–43, 151, 161–3
Onken, A., 174

Packe, M. St J., 177
Pamphleteers, 11, 17
Pantaleoni, M., 195
Papola, T. S., 176
Pareto, V., 73, 75, 85, 92, 106, 131,
  135, 187, 190, 196
Patinkin, D., 171
Penrose, E., 158, 199
Perfect competition, *see* Competition,
  perfect competition
Petty, W., 19, 174
Pigou, A. C., 7, 89, 118, 126–7, 129,
  137, 143, 146, 154, 161, 186,
  192–7, 199
Plato, 19
Popper, K. R., 4–5, 167–8, 171, 201
Price determination *(see also* Mon-
  opoly)
  competitive equilibrium, 116–17:
    determinateness, 113–15, 131–3;

long period, 25–8, 29–31, 54,
    60–1, 118–19, 166; market
    period, 29, 41, 68–9, 108–11,
    113–15; short period, 115–16;
    time period analysis, 83–5, 115,
    146, 148, 167; under joint costs, 3,
    41, 59–60, 126
  stability: long period, 25, 28–31,
    119–21; market period, 105,
    111–15
  supply and demand, 54, 57, 67–9
Price discrimination, *see* Monopoly,
  price discrimination
Profit *(see also* Rent, quasi-rent), 13
  normal profit *(see also* Costs, op-
    portunity cost), 15, 26–8, 41, 77,
    102, 104, 117–19, 155, 166
  risk and uncertainty, 15–16, 30,
    46–7, 78–80, 125, 148
  theories, 14–16, 41–7

Quandt, R. E., 151, 198
Quesnay, F., 9, 13, 18

Rae, J. (biographer of Adam Smith),
  19
Rae, J. (author of *The Statement of
    Some New Principles on the Sub-
    ject of Political Economy*), 52, 179
Railroads, 121, 125–30 *passim*, 152,
  161
Ramsay, G., 45, 59, 177–8, 180
Read, S., 44, 46, 177–8
Reder, M. W., 124, 190, 194
René, R., 182
Rent, 14, 28, 61
  definitions, 51
  producers' surplus, 86
  and profits, 63–4, 118
  quasi-rent *(see also* Profit), 19, 29,
    47–8, 85–7, 146, 148, 167
Representative firm, *see* Supply sched-
  ule for the industry, long run:
  representative firm
Ricardo, D., 40, 43–5, 49, 50, 55,
  57–64, 76, 177–8, 180–1
Robbins, L. (Lord Robbins), 100, 180,
  184, 189
Roberts, H van D., 175

Robertson, D. H., 1, 100, 171, 186, 192
Robinson, E. A. G., 146–7, 154–5, 158, 197, 199
Robinson, J., 36, 124, 145–6, 157, 159, 161–2, 194, 199
Roscher, W. G. F., 76
Rosenberg, N., 173

Samuelson, P. A., 82, 91, 108, 124, 175, 183, 186, 191, 201
correspondence principle, 111
Sandys, E., 37
Say, J.-B., 41, 42–7, 57–8, 79, 177–8, 180
Scherer, F. M., 190
Schneider, E., 194
Schoolmen, 17, 36–7
Shumpeter, J. A., 19, 35, 45, 78, 80, 99, 172–4, 176, 178, 182–4, 189, 193
classical statements, 9, 40, 70
Schwartzman, D., 199
Scientific management, 125, 150
Scrope, G. P., 44, 59, 178, 180
Seager, H. R., 183
Seligman, E. R. A., 183
Senior, N. W., 3, 41, 45, 47–9, 51, 56, 58–9, 61–6, 82, 85, 179–82
Shackle, G. L. S., 148, 198
Shove, G. F., 83, 185, 189
Sidgwick, H., 102, 110, 191
Simon, H. A., 150–1, 194, 198
Smith, A., 3, 4, 6–7, 9, 11 ff, 40, 43, 46, 52, 55, 59–60, 66, 73, 103, 116–17, 149, 155, 159, 166–7, 173–201
Spencer, H., 24, 175
Spengler, J. J., 172–3
Stability (*see also* Price determination, stability)
definition, 26
stability conditions and empirical content, 34–5, 39, 145, 165–8
Stackleberg, H. v., 162–3, 200
Steuart, J., 18, 37, 59, 62, 174–6, 180–1
Stigler, G. J., 4, 23, 40–1, 52, 112, 137, 171, 175–7, 179, 186, 190, 196
Storch, H., 45, 48, 51, 178
Supply schedule for the industry (*see*

also Price determination, competitive equilibrium, *and* Price determination, supply and demand), 88
long run, 98–102, 156–7: representative firm, 100–2, 118
market period, 109–10
short run, 90
Sylos-Labini, P., 160, 200

Tarascoi, V. J., 195
Taussig, F. W., 118, 126, 161, 194
Taylor, F. M., 173
Thirlby, G. F., 150, 198
Thornton, W. T., 41, 67–9, 87, 109, 168, 177, 179, 182, 185
Thünen, J. H. v., 40, 46, 50–1, 70, 72–3, 78, 82, 178
Tooke, T., 44, 64, 177
Torrens, R., 41, 52, 66, 177, 179, 181
Trade unions, *see* Monopoly, trade unions
Triffin, R., 162, 200
Tucker, G. S. L., 176–7
Turgot, A. R. J., 9, 13, 26, 28–9, 38–40, 130, 175–7

Van Hise, C. R., 187
Viner, J., 19, 20, 87–8, 152, 174, 194, 198

Wakefield, E. G., 22, 179
Walker, D. A., 191
Walker, F. A., 14, 77, 173, 193
Wallace, D. H., 162, 200
Walras, L., 70, 73–5, 77, 80, 82, 91, 105–14, 117–20, 123–4, 130, 145–7, 155–7, 182–3, 187, 190–2, 195
Walters, A. A., 199
Webb, B., 24, 175
Weiss, L., 201
West, E., 49
Weston, J. F., 79, 173, 183
Whitaker, J. K., 94
Wicksell, K., 92, 132, 135, 137, 143, 146, 187, 195–7
Wicksteed, P. H., 87, 90, 109, 112, 152, 184, 186–7, 191

Wieser, F. v., 82
Williamson, O. E., 158–9, 201
Wilson, T. A., 201
Wolf, J. N., 185

Yamey, B. S., 175, 200–1
Young, A. A., 24, 143, 146, 174–5, 197

Zeuthen, F., 133–5, 163, 195–6, 200